Transformation of the African American Intelligentsia, 1880–2012

The W. E. B. Du Bois Lectures

TRANSFORMATION

OF THE

AFRICAN AMERICAN

INTELLIGENTSIA,

1880–2012

Martin Kilson

Harvard University Press

Cambridge, Massachusetts
London, England
2014

LIBRARY OF CONGRESS CATALOGING-IN-PUBLICATION DATA

Kilson, Martin.
Transformation of the African American intelligentsia, 1880–2012 /
Martin Kilson.
pages   cm
Includes bibliographical references and index.
ISBN 978-0-674-28354-1 (alk. paper)
1. African Americans—Intellectual life—19th century.
2. African Americans—Intellectual life—20th century.
3. African American intellectuals.   4. African American leadership.
5. African Americans—Race identity.   6. Elite (Social sciences)—
United States.   I. Title.
E185.89.I56K55 2014
305.896'073—dc23   2013039891

This book is dedicated to my wife, children, grandchildren, and sons-in-law

Marion Dusser de Barenne Kilson

Jennifer Kilson-Page

Peter D. de B. Kilson

Hannah Laws Kilson

Jacob Kilson Page

Rhiana Kilson Page

Maya Kilson Page

Caila Marion Kilson-Kuchtic

Zuri Helen Kilson-Kuchtic

Ciaran Martin Kilson-Kuchtic

John Kuchtic

Phillip Page

CONTENTS

Foreword by Henry Louis Gates Jr.   ix

Prologue: The Origins of the Black Intelligentsia   1
1. The Rise and Fall of Color Elitism among African Americans   9
2. Black Intelligentsia Leadership Patterns   44
3. Ideological Dynamics and the Making of the Intelligentsia   86
4. Black Elite Patterns in the Twenty-First Century   115

Appendix: Class Attributes of Elite Strata   157
Notes   165
Analytical Bibliography   191
Acknowledgments   211
Index   215

FOREWORD

Henry Louis Gates Jr.
The Alphonse Fletcher University Professor
Harvard University

IN 1969, ALMOST SEVENTY-FIVE years after W. E. B. Du Bois became the first African American to earn a Ph.D. from Harvard, Martin Kilson also made history by becoming the first black to be promoted to a tenured professorship and to teach in the Faculty of Arts and Sciences, to many the heart and soul of the university. Now, thanks to Harvard University Press, both men of letters are joined in print with the release of Professor Kilson's seminal Du Bois Lectures, *Transformation of the African American Intelligentsia, 1880–2012,* delivered at Harvard over three days in the spring of 2010 as part of an annual series initially funded by the Ford Foundation and now sustained by the Hutchins Center for African and African American Research.

Like his hero W. E. B. Du Bois, Martin Kilson received his A.M. and Ph.D. degrees from Harvard, in political science in 1958 and 1959, respectively (Du Bois had taken his degrees in history). But, as he recalls in the pages that follow, it was at another institution, Lincoln University in Pennsylvania, one of the nation's outstanding historically black universities, that he and Du Bois first breathed the same air. Kilson, a native of Ambler, Pennsylvania, a small mill town just north of Philadelphia, was a freshman there in 1950 and Du Bois, by then chairman of the Peace Information Center in New York, had come to campus on a mission to inspire the next generation of "The Talented Tenth" to embrace community-minded leadership with an emphasis on mastering the nation's economy and lifting their poorest brothers and sisters into it.

There were other illustrious speakers at the chapel that day, but it was Du Bois who made the greatest—and most lasting—impact on the nineteen-year-old freshman—an impact more profound, perhaps, than that from all of the books he would one day read as a graduate student and instructor at Harvard; for when Kilson arrived in Cambridge as a graduate student in 1953 (in the same department that had awarded Ralph Bunche a Ph.D. in 1934 and had offered him a professorship in 1950), after graduating as class valedictorian at Lincoln, he devoted himself to the "romantic notion . . . that Negroes share a culture" and thus "should care about each other," as he put it in an interview with *The Harvard Crimson* (the college's student newspaper) in March 1964.

For Professor Kilson, this sacred obligation extended far beyond teaching and research, realms where, in those early years, he'd already distinguished himself as an expert on contemporary African politics, having traveled extensively in West Africa on a Ford Foundation Research Fellowship after graduate school. While many of Kilson's colleagues did as much as they could to distance themselves from activist political engagement, he chose to spend his "spare time" as a young faculty member aiding the Harvard-Radcliffe Association of African and Afro-American Students, which he helped found in 1963, just months before the historic March on Washington and the death of Du Bois on the night before it, at age ninety-five in Ghana, where the following year Kilson taught as a visiting professor.

Perhaps Professor Kilson most aptly summarized his own philosophy, an extension of and riff upon the principles he inherited from Du Bois, in the following quotation: "I suppose we're looking for a new Negro identity, a psychological process, which has its roots in a broader Negro community," he told *The Crimson* in that same March 1964 interview. "It's true that Negroes, like anyone else, prize individuality. But the thing the compulsive liberal can't understand is that we also like to swing together. You know, like we did in my good father's church back home."

In those early years at Harvard, there were never more than a scattering of black faces on campus outside of the dining hall kitchens and janitorial staff. Yet shortly after Martin Kilson began teaching as a tenured member of the faculty, the college's incoming freshmen class in

1970 was suddenly approximately 10 percent black. In those heady days of almost daily confrontation and transformation in and around Harvard Yard, he did his best to serve as wise counsel to those students, to integrate the new Afro-American Studies Department into the life of the university, and to organize the W. E. B. Du Bois Institute for African and African American Research (now housed in Harvard's new Hutchins Center for African and African American Research). Even before this time he helped design Social Sciences 5, "The Afro-American Experience," as a course for students to participate in the awakening that was happening on historically white campuses across the nation, including my own beloved Yale, which I entered in 1969.

In 1988, Dr. Kilson was named the Frank G. Thomson Professor of Government, which he still occupies as one of our cherished emeriti professors. This year marks his fiftieth at Harvard, and in all the intervening years he never wavered in offering a hand to those journeying up behind him, including his former student and my dear friend, Cornel West, A.B., 1973, and yours truly when he served as a member of the faculty committee that helped recruit me to Harvard as chair of the Afro-American Studies Department and director of the Du Bois Institute in 1991. A decade later, it was my great honor to award Martin Kilson the W. E. B. Du Bois Medal, Harvard's highest honor for outstanding contributions to African and African American society and culture.

Now, in this concise volume of lectures, we have Professor Kilson in full "swing," to borrow from his *Crimson* interview, and, through him Du Bois, a pair of Harvard men who, together, represent an astonishing 133 years of black intellectual history. As anyone knows who attended those lectures in person in Cambridge, Martin Kilson has given the academy a great gift, not only in offering up the wisdom of ages but in writing a synthetic historical analysis on the indispensable role black intellectuals have played in shaping the African American experience from the emancipation of some four million slaves following the Civil War to the flowering of four million black professionals today, an incredible arc of progress. At the same time, by identifying the various modes of black leadership across time—with Du Bois' black communitarian model being judged the most effective—Professor Kilson challenges all of us, as members of the black intelligentsia today (an expansive definition he uses interchangeably with black professionals), to reclaim the mantle of social and moral leadership and, with renewed energy, to build on the solidarity manifested at the polls in President Obama's twin victories by finding new and ever bolder ways to reverse troubling inequalities and those all-too-familiar facts of black childhood poverty; unemployment; mass incarceration; and underfunded, dangerous, crumbling schools in blighted inner cities.

Sharply disagreeing with all those who say this is not the black intellectual's responsibility, Professor Kilson urges us to look to history as our guide. Without the founding of the NAACP by visionary leaders like Du Bois in 1909, would there have been an NAACP Legal Defense Fund in place to convince the U.S. Supreme Court to end racial segregation in our nation's schools in *Brown v. Board of Education* (1954)? And without their leadership in the Big Six organizations of CORE, SCLC, the National Urban League, the NAACP, SNCC, and the Brotherhood of Sleeping Car Porters, would there have been an effective Civil Rights movement around to put pressure on presidents Kennedy and Johnson and the U.S. Congress to pass the Civil Rights Act of 1964 and the Voting Rights Act of 1965? Would affirmative action have ever been conceived, the same affirmative action that led to the large-scale integration of historically white colleges and universities and that led to our appointments as professors at American research institutions such as Harvard or Yale?

In marshalling his argument, Kilson also points to the pivotal—and more pervasive—contributions of two other pillars of the African American community: our historically black colleges and universities, and the black church with its unique blend of populism and faith often the only thing holding its followers back from the abyss. In touching interjections, Kilson testifies to the power of these institutions firsthand as a graduate of Lincoln University at what he calls "the high noon" of the intellectual dominance of the black colleges and as the descendant of a long line of black ministers, from the Rev. Isaac Lee, a free black man who founded St. Paul A.M.E. Church in Kent County, Maryland, in the late 1840s, to Kilson's late father, Martin Sr., a clergyman in their hometown African Methodist church. From them, Martin Jr. not only learned the empowering small-town black values he brought with him to Harvard (what, elsewhere, he has called his "native skepticism toward American-establishment pretenders") but the Christian social gospel that for so long has been the backbone of the civil rights struggle and a bulwark against racial uplift morphing into xenophobia. As the attendees at the first Niagara

Movement conference, convened by Du Bois in 1905, stated in their goals, "the battle we wage is not for ourselves alone, but for all true Americans."

Those raised in the black church know from experience how essential is tough love—but love nonetheless—to a proper union of uplift and instruction, a lesson Professor Kilson reminds us of in one of my favorite passages from his book, in which he relates an anecdote transcribed by Karen Fields in her grandmother Mamie Garvin Fields' 1983 memoir, *Lemon Swamps and Other Places: A Carolina Memoir.* Recalling a driving tour that Mamie Fields and others conducted to give the visiting W. E. B. Du Bois an appreciation of black life in Charleston, South Carolina, in the 1920s, she tells us:

> We took him, as we thought, for a "grand tour" of our city—the Custom House (from before the Civil War), the old Slave Market, the Provost's Dungeon (from the days before the Revolution), and so forth and so on. I can see now that we weren't thinking very well. Most of those places that we showed off with all our city pride had to do with slavery, which brought our people to South Carolina in the first place. . . . In the car, Dr. Du Bois got restless. After a while, he set us straight. "All you are showing me is what the white people did. I want to see what the colored people of Charleston have built." So then we took him to the Negro "Ys," and what do you think? That didn't satisfy him. He said the "Y" was under national auspices. . . . [A] city like Charleston [and its black folks] ought to be able to do more locally than it was doing. I never forgot that lesson. Oh, Du Bois was hard on us, but it woke us up. He was telling us to take pride in our accomplishments, and he wanted us to strive to do more.

Now, anyone who has ever had the pleasure of working with Martin Kilson is aware of the role tough love plays in his fatherly approach to teaching and in his personal friendships. I know I am, as are many of my friends in the academy, and even when we disagree with Professor Kilson (and he, sometimes blisteringly, with us!), we know we are better for his testing and we love him for it. The greatness of this book is that in it he tests all of us anew.

"Who else but us?" Kilson asks implicitly in arguing for a reinvigoration of the Du Bois model in our time. "Who else, pray tell, but the fledgling Negro Talented Tenth were the children, mothers, fathers, and other post–Civil War era offspring of former slaves supposed to turn to as leaders and spokespersons for advice, guidance, and civil society agencies for constructing viable paths through the rugged terrain of the white-supremacist modern American society? Who?"

As Martin Kilson's intellectual descendants, we will be forever indebted to him for cutting a path to follow as one of the founding fathers of African and African American teaching and research at Harvard University. It was a personal honor for me to host Professor Kilson for his Du Bois lectures, and I am grateful to Harvard University Press and the Hutchins Center for giving every future leader a chance to participate in the conversation going forward. Let me close with the simple advice Professor Kilson shared with NPR shortly after his lectures in Cambridge on April 26, 2010.

"It's much better in the inner scheme of things human, it's much better to outreach to the needs of others than to be obsessed with your own personal circumstances. To give a helping hand to the human condition, if you will, it's much better. I pray that more of us will be able to do that as America penetrates the 21st century."

Sixty-three years after Martin Kilson encountered W. E. B. Du Bois at Lincoln University's Sunday Convocation, let us all say amen to the wisdom that Dr. Du Bois' inimitable intellectual heir has shared with us; for as Kilson quotes Du Bois in *The Souls of Black Folk,* published 110 years ago, "We have no right to sit silently by while the inevitable seeds are sown for a harvest of disaster to our children, black and white."

Transformation of the African American Intelligentsia, 1880–2012

PROLOGUE

The Origins of the Black Intelligentsia

THIS BOOK HAS ITS ORIGIN in a query that has fascinated me ever since I first encountered it during my sophomore year at Lincoln University (1950–1951). In that year, I enrolled in a course titled "The Negro in the Old and New World," taught by Horace Mann Bond, a sociologist and the president of Lincoln University from 1945 to 1957.[1]

The course's main focus was the social history of the American Negro, with introductory reference to the ancient history of African societies south of the Sahara. Bond divided the subject matter of the course into three historical periods: the Reconstruction era (1865–1877), the Emancipation era (1880–1900), and the Leadership Formation era (1890s–1920s). Bond had prepared himself to teach this course while a graduate student at the University of Chicago, where he produced an award-winning doctoral dissertation on education policies for Negroes during the Reconstruction era in Alabama, which was later published in 1939.[2]

Among the core themes in Bond's course was the perplexing query, "How do you fashion modern leadership processes for the formerly enslaved American Negro?" The bulk of the course was a narrative and analytical exposition aimed at answering this perplexing question. For Bond, this question remained prominent in his academic and intellectual career. His first scholarly endeavor at fathoming this question was his pioneering 1934 book *The Education of the Negro in the American Social Order,* which appraised the development of public education systems nationwide for African American youth.[3]

1

Of course, one serious answer to that perplexing query—"How do you fashion modern leadership processes for the formerly enslaved American Negro?"—was to provide adequate modern education for the nearly ten million black Americans counted in the 1910 U.S. Census, some 8.7 million of whom lived in the South, with most of the remaining living in the North. But this was no simple task, given the fact that at the dawn of the twentieth century most black Americans were uneducated and almost totally excluded from the American social contract. As the twentieth century commenced, over 80 percent of black Americans were illiterate. A generation and a half later, the first major study of college-educated African Americans—the 1938 book *The Negro College Graduate* by the Fisk University sociologist Charles S. Johnson—reported eighteen thousand by the 1930s.[4] Overall, the total black population was nearly twelve million by 1930, with 9.3 million blacks living in the South and 2.4 million in the North.

Another answer to Bond's query was to advance opportunities for political participation for African Americans. Such opportunities, and the legal rights underlying them, had been available to black folks for a short period through the federal Reconstruction policy after 1865. But when the federal government under President Rutherford B. Hayes removed federal troops from the South in 1878, the full-fledged betrayal of Reconstruction commenced. The result was a legalized racist oligarchy in the South, and a veritable authoritarian governance vis-à-vis black folks ensued.

Indeed, a 2005 reprint of the original five-hundred-page report on a murderous 1898 anti-Negro riot in Wilmington, North Carolina, relates the merciless white brutality that was used to smash Reconstruction in North Carolina. By 1898, Wilmington was North Carolina's largest city, with 3,478 Negroes, or 49 percent of the city's population. As the December 2005 *New York Times* summary of the report on the 1898 Wilmington riot observed:

> In the period immediately after the Civil War, the Democratic Party–ruled government in Wilmington ... was displaced by a coalition that was largely Republican and included many blacks. The loss of power stirred dissatisfaction among a faction of white civic leaders and business owners.
>
> The tensions came to a head on Election Day, Nov. 9, 1898, when the Democrats regained power ... largely by stuffing ballot boxes and intimidating black voters to keep away from the polls. Not waiting for an orderly

transition of government, a group of white vigilantes demanded that power be handed over immediately. When they were rebuffed, in the words of the [1898] report, "Hell jolted loose."

The mob—which the report said grew to as many as 2,000—forced black leaders out of town, dismantled the printing press of a black-owned newspaper, *The Daily Record,* fired into the homes of blacks and shot down black men in the streets.

Estimates of the number of black deaths are as high as 100, state officials said. . . .

Black women and children fled to the swamps on the city's outskirts made frigid by November's chill. There are accounts of pregnant women giving birth in the swamps, the babies dying soon after.[5]

Thus, it was patently clear that the realization of the second response to Bond's query—expand political participation rights for formerly enslaved black Americans—would prove to be a more arduous process than advancing public education opportunities. There were at least two key reasons for this.

First, the authoritarian governance vis-à-vis black people by white supremacist restoration forces that dominated southern states from 1877 onward, coupled with a quasi-feudalistic socioeconomic hegemony over the lives of black Americans well into the first half of the twentieth century, was terrifying. This frightful admixture of a southern political-economic oligarchy over post–Reconstruction era black Americans was graphically portrayed by the abolitionist Frederick Douglass in his speech on the failure of Reconstruction, "Looking the Republican Party Squarely in the Face," which he delivered in Cincinnati in June 1876: "When the Russian serfs had their chains broken and [were] given their liberty," Douglass said, "the government of Russia gave to those poor emancipated serfs a few acres of land on which they could live and earn their bread. But when you turned us loose," he continued, "you turned us loose to the sky, to the storm, to the whirlwind, and worst of all, you turned us loose to our infuriated masters."[6]

The second reason that advancing viable political participation was so difficult pertained, in part, to ideological and political cleavages that commenced in African American society itself during the late Emancipation era (1880s to 1900) and continued into the first several decades of the twentieth century. One cleavage pattern involved "color-elitism" attitudes among the light- and brown-skinned African American middle-class sector that surfaced initially during the Emancipation period. This color elitism denigrated the vast majority of dark-skinned black folks, thereby restricting sociopolitical cohesion in the fledgling African American society.

A second cleavage pattern involved political and ideological leadership, relating to how to manage an overall African American response to the post-Reconstruction racist oligarchy that white Americans erected against African American society in the South. Booker T. Washington, black educator and head of Tuskegee Institute in Alabama from the 1880s to 1915, was the leader of the conservative black intelligentsia sector that favored a so-called accommodationist black leadership methodology. William Edward Burghardt Du Bois, a history scholar and college teacher who taught at Atlanta University in the 1890s and early 1900s, was the leader of the civil rights activist black leadership methodology.

Accordingly, my overall goal in this book is to delineate and analyze the special ideological, political, and institutional dynamics that influenced how the African American intelligentsia acquired capabilities that eventually enabled it to assist the modern development of African American society. Such assistance, after all, was absolutely essential. Why? Because, for the most part and for the last fifth of the nineteenth century and the first half of the twentieth century, the racist-delineated mainstream processes in American society (for example, colleges and universities, professional organizations, business groups, fraternal organizations, and public offices) were not available to assist the modern development of black folks.

Thus, my analysis in this book intertwines the development trajectories of the African American intelligentsia or professional class, on the one hand, and African American society in general, on the other. A core conceptual proposition that informs my analysis is this: the primary defining attribute of post–Reconstruction era African Americans was that they were pro forma citizens without effective institutional processes for viable modern social development.

In the African American intelligentsia's nascent phase, an intrablack color elitism cleavage pattern, with light- and brown-skinned middle-class African Americans acting superior to dark-skinned African Americans (thereby denigrating the dark-skinned Negro masses), marred the African American intelligentsia's ability to fashion an effective and progressive modern leadership. Fortunately, however, those ideas and practices based on color elitism were effectively challenged by a young generation of intelligentsia through the New Negro Movement starting in the 1920s. That crucial and significant liberal development within the early twentieth-century African American professional stratum eventually vanquished the reactionary aspects of intrablack color elitism. These issues are probed in Chapter 1.

Between the 1890s and the 1920s, two skilled leaders—Booker T. Washington and W. E. B. Du Bois—emerged as the Emancipation era morphed into the twentieth century. They produced two competing leadership methodologies to guide the transformation of twentieth-century African American society: (1) conciliation with America's racist oligarchy, initiated by Washington, and (2) a civil rights activist challenge to America's racist oligarchy, initiated by Du Bois. These issues are discussed in Chapter 2.

From the post–World War I era to the 1940s, the Du Boisian leadership methodology gained prominence, articulated through what might be called a combined leadership ethos of black communitarianism and black ethnic commitment. Although claiming fewer than five thousand college-educated persons at the turn of the twentieth century, the fledgling African American intelligentsia (famously termed the "Talented Tenth" in Du Bois' 1903 book *The Souls of Black Folk*) grew steadily during the period between the two world wars. That important growth, by the way, depended mainly on Negro colleges, as higher education institutions for African Americans were originally called. Among the top tier of those institutions from the 1870s onward were Atlanta University (Georgia), Dillard University (Louisiana), Fisk University (Tennessee), Hampton Institute (Virginia), Howard University (Washington, D.C.), Lincoln University (Pennsylvania), Meharry Medical College (Tennessee), Morgan State College (Maryland), Morehouse College (Georgia), Morris Brown College (Georgia), Spelman College (Georgia), Talladega College (Alabama), Tuskegee Institute (Alabama), Virginia Union University, West Virginia State University, Wilberforce University (Ohio), and Wiley College (Texas). Aspects of these foundational dynamics in the African American intelligentsia or professional class are discussed in Chapter 2.

Operationally, the Du Boisian black leadership methodology functioned quite effectively as a blueprint for African American modern development and social advancement. It did so insofar as the Du Boisian leadership methodology nurtured progressive, not accommodationist, ideological and political patterns for black people's development. This, I argue, contrasted sharply with Washington's black leadership methodology of accommodating the American racist oligarchy. Thus, by the post–World War II period of the 1950s, a nationwide broad-gauged Civil Rights movement evolved among African Americans, and that movement's struggle against the racist system of the South especially—but against the North's as well—spurred federal policies that vanquished legal racist practices and institutional edifices that sustained them. These dynamics are discussed broadly in Chapter 3.

From the 1980s into the first decade of the twenty-first century, the African American middle-class and professional sector expanded, while the black poor sector expanded as well. One important systemic outcome of this somewhat asymmetrical sociological development among African Americans during the post–Civil Rights movement era, from the 1970s onward, was the rending of new class and ideological fissures in African American society. These dynamics are probed in Chapter 4. In discourse terms, I use Chapter 4 to bring a kind of analytical closure to the African American intelligentsia's century-old developmental processes—from its nascent phase commencing in the 1880s to its contemporary, mature phase in the early twenty-first century.

Moreover, I should mention in this prologue that my exposure to two institutions that were crucial to the metamorphosis of the twentieth-century African American intelligentsia predisposed me toward a scholarly interest in that intelligentsia. The first was the African American church that I was raised in. The second was the Negro college, as higher-education institutions for African Americans were called when I enrolled in one of those colleges in 1949.

It was the African Methodist denominations of the African American church that influenced my early understanding of the African American intelligentsia. I have a long ancestral connection with several African Methodist church denominations. My maternal great-grandfather, Jacob Laws—a Civil War veteran of the U.S. 24th Colored Infantry Regiment—organized an African Union Methodist Protestant church in a small Pennsylvania factory town in 1885, and my father, the Reverend Martin Luther Kilson Sr., pastored that church during my youth in the 1930s and 1940s. My paternal great-great-grandfather, the Reverend Isaac Lee, who was born to a Free Negro family in Maryland in 1808, was a boot maker, and he organized an African Methodist Episcopal church—St. Paul A.M.E. Church—before the Civil War in the late 1840s for a Free Negro community in Kent County, Maryland. My great-grandfather, the Reverend Joseph Martin, pastored St. Paul A.M.E Church during the Emancipation era. And in the 1940s–1960s, my uncle, the Reverend Delbert Kilson, pastored a Colored Methodist Episcopal church in the shipbuilding city of Chester, Pennsylvania, near Philadelphia.

The African Methodist Episcopal, African Methodist Episcopal Zion, African Union Methodist, and Colored Methodist Episcopal churches dispensed a theological discourse based on Christian social gospel. That discourse emphasized, among other things, the Christian religion's human rights–enhancing predilections, which enabled branches of African Methodism to participate in America's early nineteenth-century antislavery movement and also in the twentieth-century civil rights activist organizations.[7] I had imbibed some aspects of Christian social gospel discourse by the time I entered college in 1949.

At Lincoln University, I commenced my exposure to the second core institution that had contributed to the character of the twentieth-century African American intelligentsia: the Negro college. Most Negro colleges were organized from the Reconstruction era onward—save Lincoln University and Wilberforce University, which were founded in Pennsylvania and Ohio before the Civil War, in 1854 and 1856, respectively.[8] From the 1870s through the 1950s, Negro colleges educated the vast majority of what Du Bois liked to call "college-bred Negroes." When I entered Lincoln University in 1949, over 90 percent of college-going black youth enrolled in Negro colleges. Today, however, only 12 percent attend black-majority institutions of higher education. Times have changed . . .

At Lincoln University, I interacted for the first time with a sizable number of middle-class African American youth (my factory hometown was mainly a working-class town with a majority white population) and especially with African American scholars. Several of those Lincoln University scholars helped me fashion a rigorous intellectual identity by the time I graduated in 1953. Among these scholars who warrant mention were Horace Mann Bond (sociologist), Henry Cornwell (psychologist), John Aubrey Davis (political scientist), Laurence Foster (anthropologist), and Joseph Newton Hill (English literature). Bond influenced my academic interest in Afro-American studies, and Davis—who was among the first generation of African American political science scholars—inspired my academic interest in political science.[9]

I should mention, finally, that from my perspective, the overall status of today's African American intelligentsia or professional stratum in our American social system is still short of adequate. Nevertheless, that status in the early twenty-first century has advanced significantly beyond what it was in 1903, when W. E. B. Du Bois penned the term "Talented Tenth" to characterize the fledgling African American intelligentsia. As will be discussed in Chapters 3 and 4, today's African American intelligentsia, or professional class, contains millions of individuals with top-level professional skills (the 2006 U.S. Census Bureau reported about six million African Americans with "white-collar occupations"). Furthermore, thousands of African American individuals hold mid-level and top-tier public office. Primary among the latter is, of course, an African American president of the United States, Barack Obama, who was elected to a second term in November 2012.

No doubt times have changed significantly for the African American intelligentsia from those nascent years in the early twentieth century. When viewed in comparative developmental terms, today's twenty-first century African American intelligentsia might be viewed as a template for fulsome modern intelligentsia development among people of African descent elsewhere in today's world. Finally, I argue in this book that an important part of today's advanced status of the African American intelligentsia is intimately connected with the Du Boisian leadership and intellectual legacy.

An 1840s photograph of Frederick Douglass, a leader of the Abolitionist Movement who was also an Emancipation-era African American leader. He died in 1895.

(National Portrait Gallery, Smithsonian Institution)

Alexander Crummell was a theologian, a founder of the American Negro Academy in 1897, and a president of Wilberforce University in Ohio.

(Moorland-Spingarn Research Center, Howard University)

William Sanders Scarborough was the first major classics scholar among African Americans, a founding member of the American Negro Academy, and president of Wilberforce University.

(Rembert E. Stokes Library, Wilberforce University)

John Wesley Cromwell was a member of the first graduating class at Howard University Law School in 1879, a founding member of the American Negro Academy in 1897, and founder of the *People's Advocate*—Washington, D.C.'s first African American weekly newspaper.

(Courtesy of Professor Adelaide Cromwell's private collection)

An 1895 photo of Booker T. Washington (center) at Tuskegee Institute, with U.S. president William Howard Taft (to Washington's right), steel industry magnate Andrew Carnegie (to Washington's left), and financier Robert Ogden (right of President Taft).

An African American sharecropper farm family in Virginia in the 1890s.

(Frances B. Johnson Photography Collection, Prints and Photography Division, Library of Congress)

A World War I–era photograph of W. E. B. Du Bois, who was the first African American to gain a Harvard Ph.D. (1895) and founder-editor of the NAACP's journal *Crisis* (1910–1935).

(Moorland-Spingarn Research Center, Howard University)

James Weldon Johnson in 1910. He was the first African American executive secretary of the NAACP.

(Moorland-Spingarn Research Center, Howard University)

Mary McLeod Bethune was founder-president of the National Council of Negro Women (1935–1949).

(Moorland-Spingarn Research Center, Howard University)

African Methodist Episcopal clergyman Reverdy Ransom and wife in front of
Chicago's African Methodist Episcopal Institutional Church in 1902. He was
a founding member of the 1905 Niagara Movement and an A.M.E. bishop.

(Chicago History Museum)

Ida B. Wells-Barnett was the first major female African American journalist, beginning in the 1880s. She launched the Anti-Lynching Movement in the 1920s.

(Schomburg Research Center, New York City)

A. Phillip Randolph was founder of the Brotherhood of Sleeping Car Porters in the 1920s, a founder of the National Negro Congress in 1935, and a leading figure in the 1960s Civil Rights movement.

(Moorland-Spingarn Research Center, Howard University)

Five prominent black intellectuals in New York City in 1925: Langston Hughes (writer/poet), Charles S. Johnson (sociologist and National Urban League official), E. Franklin Frazier (sociologist), Rudolph Fisher (medical doctor and writer), and Hubert Delaney (civil rights lawyer).

Jessie Fauset (poet), Langston Hughes (writer/poet), and Zora Neale Hurston (novelist) on the Tuskegee Institute campus in the 1930s, in front of a statue of Booker T. Washington.

(Photograph by P. H. Polk; courtesy of the P. H. Polk estate)

Two NAACP officials in 1936: Walter White (executive secretary) and Charles
Hamilton Houston (founder-director of the NAACP Legal Defense Fund).

(NAACP Records, Library of Congress)

Carter G. Woodson was founder
of the *Journal of Negro History*
in 1916 and founder of the
Association for the Study of
Negro Life and History
(1915–1950).

(Moorland-Spingarn Research
Center, Howard University)

A 1940 photograph of Roy Wilkins (assistant director of the NAACP), Walter White (NAACP executive secretary), and Thurgood Marshall (chief legal counsel of the NAACP).

(NAACP Records, Library of Congress)

Horace Mann Bond was dean of faculty at Dillard University in New Orleans in the 1930s and president of Lincoln University (Pennsylvania) from 1945 to 1957.

(Langston Hughes Memorial Library Archives, Lincoln University, PA)

The Reverend Martin Luther King Jr. (center) founded the Southern
Christian Leadership Conference (SCLC) in 1960. To the right of
King is the Reverend Ralph Abernathy, an SCLC official; to the left
of King is Bayard Rustin, an adviser to King. They are in front of
the courthouse in Birmingham, Alabama, in February 1956.

(AP/Wide World Photo)

Ella Baker was a founding
figure in the SCLC and its
director in the 1960s.

(Danny Lyons/Magnum Photos)

1

THE RISE AND FALL OF COLOR ELITISM
AMONG AFRICAN AMERICANS

THE FOUNDATION YEARS of a modern social system for the majority of African Americans began after the Civil War, when the federal government enacted legislation to facilitate the full-fledged incorporation of the formerly enslaved Negro population—some four million souls—into America's democratic processes. The progressive Republican Party legislators in Congress from northern and midwestern states who initiated this legislation in 1867 labeled it "Reconstruction policy"—a federal government policy that supported keeping federal armed forces in the South in order to advance voting rights and human rights for the formerly enslaved Negro population. The federal Reconstruction policy, however, barely survived a decade: by 1876. the tumultuous conflict surrounding the Hayes versus Tilden presidential election—whereby the election results were decided by the House of Representatives—resulted in legislative maneuvering that put Rutherford Hayes in the executive office and removed federal armed forces from the South. Thus, Reconstruction came to an end, and the southern states laid the foundation for a restoration of a racist oligarchy in their social and political system. This, of course, was a betrayal of the formative democracy experience of African Americans during Reconstruction—an experience that is vividly related by John Hope Franklin in his 1961 book *Reconstruction after the Civil War*.[1]

Despite the demise of Reconstruction, however, it was during the last several years of this momentous period in modern American history (1875–1878) that the indispensable instrument for the emergence of a viable intelligentsia or professional class for African American society appeared: the Negro college. Apart from Lincoln University in Pennsylvania and Wilberforce University in Ohio, which were founded before the Civil War by liberal white religious denominations associated with the antislavery movement, the vast majority of higher-education institutions for Negroes were located in the South (see Chapter 2, Table 2.5). It is interesting to note that a sizable segment of the earliest Negro colleges were initiated in the 1870s by the liberal white Methodist Episcopal Church denomination, which mobilized its own resources for an extraordinary college development program for Emancipation-era African Americans.

Instead of resting on its laurels after the founding of Wilberforce University in 1856 (which was transferred to the African Methodist Episcopal Church after the Civil War), the white Methodist Episcopal Church built on the momentum of its initial achievement. At the birth of its higher-education program for recently emancipated Negroes was the establishment of Clark University in Atlanta in 1869 and the launching of Meharry Medical College in Nashville in 1875–1876. These higher education institutions were followed later in the nineteenth century by a dozen additional institutions, including Rust College in Mississippi, Wiley College in Texas, Philander Smith College in Arkansas, Bennett College in North Carolina, Flint-Goodridge Hospital and Nurse Training School in Louisiana, Gammon Theological Seminary in Georgia, and Morgan College in Maryland. As reported in Monroe Work's *The Negro Year Book, 1931–1932*, by the 1930s the higher-education institutions for Negroes established by the Methodist Episcopal Church had enrolled some 2,359 students.[2]

The white Methodist Episcopal Church's contribution to higher education for African Americans in the post-Reconstruction period—along with contributions by African American religious denominations— helped to expand the small number of college-educated Negroes that W. E. B. Du Bois characterized in his renowned 1903 essay as the "Talented Tenth," which recorded a total of 1,996 "college-bred Negroes" graduating in the academic year 1899–1900.[3]

Of course, the African American quest for modern advancement depended overwhelmingly upon the existence of a well-formed black intelligentsia or professional class. This book probes select aspects of the social, cultural, ideological, and political trajectories along which a viable black intelligentsia evolved in tandem with twentieth-century

African American society in general. This book's discourse intertwines core elements of the African American intelligentsia's metamorphosis, on the one hand, and the overall development of African American society in the context of the twentieth-century American racial oligarchy, on the other.

This chapter provides an overview of the development of the black intelligentsia and discusses class and status attributes of the formative-phase black intelligentsia, the dynamics of black elite consolidation during the 1880s–1940s, and social democratization of the black elite during the 1930s–1950s. I examine how skin color and color-caste patterns—which is to say, "color elitism"—initially shaped a conservative social class system within the evolving African American intelligentsia of the early twentieth century. Then I discuss how color-caste patterns were eventually challenged by orientations of black ethnic identity—black-consciousness attitudes. This important development was fostered by the so-called New Negro Movement among black professionals from the 1920s into the 1940s.

By the post–World War II period, the prewar New Negro Movement had facilitated ideological patterns among African American professionals that amounted to what might be called the "social democratization" of the black intelligentsia. Accordingly, by the 1950s a major by-product of this social democratization was a precipitous decline in the color elitism dynamic that was prominent in the ranks of the African American intelligentsia from the 1880s into the 1940s. This in turn facilitated the development of the militant phase of the Civil Rights movement from the 1950s through the 1960s.

Throughout this chapter, I use the terms "black intelligentsia" and "black professionals" interchangeably. Why? Because in the development of the twentieth-century African American social system, the opportunity to occupy what might be called "intelligentsia roles" was not limited to African American individuals with "formal knowledge-producing credentials," as the late social theorist Seymour Martin Lipset put it. It is useful here to refer to Lipset's formulation of the generic attributes of an intelligentsia personality, which appeared in a 1959 special issue of *Daedalus: Journal of the American Academy of Arts and Sciences*. In his famous article, Lipset defined the core or generic function of intelligentsia as follows: "We shall here consider intellectuals to be all those who create, distribute, and apply culture—*the symbolic world of man,* including art, science, and religion." Lipset then elabo-rates the range of generic intelligentsia functions. "Within this group," he observed, "two main levels may be discerned: the hard core, who are creators of culture—scholars, artists, philosophers, authors, some edi-tors, and some journalists; and second, those who distribute what others create—performers in the various arts, most teachers, most reporters. A peripheral group are those who apply culture as part of their jobs—professionals such as physicians and lawyers."[4]

As it happened, weakness in color elitism's patterns facilitated a rela-tive fluidity in the ideological boundaries between black Americans' social classes. This fluidity, in turn, enabled a variety of artisan-class and working-class individuals (such as carpenters, mechanics, bricklayers, farmers, cooks, valets, and chauffeurs) to awake one day and, in the proverbial blink of an eye, recast themselves as "self-identified" intelligentsia-type personalities—insofar as such persons articulated social and political ideas for broader consumption in African American society.

One such prominent figure in the 1920s and 1930s was a working-class immigrant from Jamaica named Marcus Garvey, who in his early adult years was employed as a banana picker in Costa Rica, a common laborer on the Panama Canal, and a trade union activist in Jamaica. After migrating to New York City in 1916, Garvey became a kind of street-corner preacher in Harlem around 1918, and after World War I he founded the Universal Negro Improvement Association (UNIA). From the 1920s through the 1930s, the UNIA propelled Garvey to the top ranks of African American cultural and political leadership.[5]

A similar self-made intelligentsia-type figure between the late 1940s and middle 1950s was Malcolm Little, who, after a career as a street hustler and a period of imprisonment, fashioned for himself a self-styled transfiguration via the Nation of Islam Movement and became Malcolm X. He accordingly evolved into an influential "self-made intelligentsia-type figure" in African American society by the mid-1950s, interacting with a wide circle of professionally educated African American intelligentsia personalities. As Columbia University historian Manning Marable re-lates in his 2011 book *Malcolm X: A Life of Reinvention,* Malcolm X sustained interactions with mainstream African American intelligentsia circles until he was assassinated in the mid-1960s.[6]

Interestingly enough, there were precedents for self-made intelligentsia-type personalities like Malcolm X in the post–World War II era that extend back to the pre–Civil War era—a period that witnessed the rise of anti-slavery black abolitionists. Those early nineteenth-century self-made black abolitionist intelligentsia personalities were, in a basic sense, foundational figures in the life cycle of the modern African American intelligentsia. Among them were stellar African American leadership figures like Frederick Douglass, William Wells Brown, J. W. C. Pennington, John Sella Martin, and William Cooper Nell, to name a prominent few.

The professionally educated modern African American intelligentsia began to emerge in the Emancipation era after the Civil War. Let me first delineate a developmental overview of the black intelligentsia, starting with its *formative phase* from the 1870s to the 1920s. The formative phase was developmentally significant for two reasons. First, it witnessed two important events that shaped the sociological character of the first three generations the black intelligentsia. One significant event was the rise of a group that historian Richard Bardolph, in his trailblazing 1959 book *The Negro Vanguard,* called the "out-of-bondage elite": the first generation of black Americans who acquired middle-class attributes during the South's Reconstruction period, when over 90 percent of black Americans resided in the South. The second significant event was what historian Willard Gatewood dubbed the "colored aristocracy": the skin-color-obsessed segment of the African American professional class from the late nineteenth century into the first three decades of the twentieth century.[7]

The African American intelligentsia's second developmental phase can be called the *elite social democratization phase*, which began in the mid-1920s and was completed by the 1950s. The New Negro Movement of progressive intellectuals (writers, actors, academics, lawyers, schoolteachers, and others) initiated the social democratization phase among the evolving twentieth-century black intelligentsia. During this phase, progressive ideas about black consciousness challenged the colored aristocracy's obsession with color elitism among the formative-phase African American intelligentsia. This black-consciousness challenge eventually produced a genuine social democratization dynamic within the evolving African American society. Above all, *the black-consciousness social democratization elements in the New Negro Movement elevated the ideological and cultural status of "blackness."* Blackness (or "Blackways," as the African American sociologist Hylan Lewis called it in his classic 1955 book *Blackways of Kent*) was now for the first time freed from denigration by the color-elitism-obsessed elements among middle-class African Americans.[8]

The third developmental phase, the *elite maturation phase,* ran from the middle 1960s into the twenty-first century. During this period, an elected black political class emerged alongside a broad-based African American professional class. As of 2010, African Americans had nearly ten thousand elected office holders nationwide, forty-two federal-level legislators in the U.S. Congress, and over twenty thousand federal and state bureaucrats—not to mention an African American president of the United States. It should be noted, finally, that as the twenty-first century progresses, the African American intelligentsia has entered what might be called an *elite normalization phase,* a developmental period during which the mainstream elements in the African American intelligentsia experience a slow but steady systemic incorporation within broad spheres of American life and institutions.

From our vantage point here in the early decades of the twenty-first century, it might be difficult to appreciate the strong influence of skin color and color-caste ideas and patterns in shaping the character of the African American intelligentsia during its formative phase from the 1880s into the first two decades of the twentieth century. I grew up in a small black community in a small eastern Pennsylvania factory town during the 1930s, the son of a lower-middle-class African Methodist clergyman. The black population was about three hundred when I was born in 1931, in a total population of four thousand, about 30 percent of whom were Italian American factory workers. Thanks to my father's penchant for relating tales about African American history, I was familiar with the following Negro folk expression: "If you're light, you're all right; if you're brown, stick around; if you're black [that is, dark-skinned], stay back." This folk expression speaks volumes about the place of skin-color attitudes in delineating status patterns among African Americans during the first half of the twentieth century.

As I entered my freshman year in 1949 at Lincoln University—one of Pennsylvania's two colleges for African Americans—I was one among about six hundred other young black men, half of whom came from middle-class backgrounds and all of whom were seeking entrée into the African American professional class. It was here that I became more aware of the meaning of skin color and color-caste patterns in African

American society. I began to recognize the knowledge I had gained from my father's ancestral tales, many of which involved skin color and color-caste issues in African American life. Some of these tales concerned my Free Negro forebears of the late eighteenth and nineteenth century who lived in Maryland's Eastern Shore counties, some of whom had light skin and brown skin. They were the Lee, Taylor, Emory, Kennard, Brown, Martin, and Kilson clans.

My paternal great-great-grandfather, the Reverend Isaac Lee, was born to a Free Negro family in 1808. He was a literate artisan—a boot maker—who in the late 1840s founded an African Methodist Episcopal church in Kent County, Maryland—the St. Paul A.M.E. Church. My paternal great-grandfather, the Reverend Joseph Martin, who was Isaac Lee's son-in-law, pastored the St. Paul A.M.E. Church after the Civil War during the Emancipation period. My father—a person with light brown skin—told stories in which both his clergymen great-grandfather (Issac Lee) and grandfather (Joseph Martin) chastised light-skinned and brown-skinned families for behavior that my father called "mulatto arrogance." My father said that his two clergy ancestors believed that a main obligation of light-skinned and brown-skinned Free Negro families was to translate the social mobility advantage afforded them by their skin color into outreach to the needs of the dark-skinned Negro masses. For my African Methodist clergy ancestors, skin color and color-caste pretensions—color elitism—were foul and unacceptable.[9]

These family anecdotes illustrate the historical fact that issues related to skin color played a prominent role in shaping the social class dynamics of the emerging African American social system in the late nineteenth century and into the first several decades of the twentieth. From the 1880s onward, skin-color issues translated into reactionary color-caste patterns within the emerging African American social system. In a word, color-elitism patterns were Negrophobic sociocultural practices that light-skinned and brown-skinned families executed against the dark-skinned Negro masses.[10]

Color-elitism patterns were also reactionary in political terms. They added a conservative ideological reinforcement to the accommodationist leadership methodology that the Tuskegee Institute leader Booker T. Washington had designed for black people to follow from the 1880s into the twentieth century. But thanks to a Fisk University–educated African American in the late 1880s named William Edward Burghardt Du Bois, both the color-elitism and the Bookerite accommodationism patterns in the evolving twentieth-century black intelligentsia were effectively challenged by the 1940s.

How did skin color and color-caste patterns secure a social mobility advantage for a broad sector of African American middle-class and professional-class families from the 1880s through the 1930s? This query leads to a discussion of the topic of class and status attributes of the formative-phase black intelligentsia.

Since the 1899 publication of W. E. B. Du Bois' pioneering book *The Philadelphia Negro: A Study,* which probed the sociology of that city's black community, there have been numerous examinations of the social structure of black communities in the evolving twentieth century. I have in mind books by Carter Woodson (on black professionals), St. Clair Drake and Horace Cayton (on blacks in Chicago), James Weldon Johnson (on blacks in New York City), Kenneth Kusmer (on blacks in Cleveland), Robert Warner (on blacks in New Haven, Connecticut), Joe W. Trotter (on blacks in Milwaukee), and Adelaide Cromwell (on blacks in Boston), to mention a prominent few. These and other studies influenced my quest for a broad-gauged understanding of the interplay of class and status patterns, on the one hand, and the character of color-caste patterns, on the other. The analytical question that I posed for myself was: What impact did the interplay of status patterns and skin-color dynamics have on the social system of the African American professional sector from the 1880s into the first several decades of the twentieth century?

As I commenced research on this query two decades ago, none of the aforementioned books provided me with adequate materials on the impact of skin color and color-caste patterns on the evolving twentieth-century African American society in general, or the African American professional sector in particular. Therefore, I turned to two interesting works. One was by the American Studies scholar Richard Bardolph, who mined the biographical data provided in *Who's Who in America* and *Who's Who in Colored America* to produce a book of national scope on the evolution of the African American professional class from the 1880s to the 1950s. Bardolph selected the eighty-seven professionals he discussed in *The Negro Vanguard* based on their reputations.[11] He assumed that any African American person listed in either of these two books was automatically a top-tier, high-status professional figure, hence the book's title.

The second work I referred to was written by an African American businessman from Atlanta named A. B. Caldwell, who was also a part-time amateur historian—a kind of race achievement chronicler, one might say. Focusing on the time period of the late Emancipation era through the first two decades of the twentieth century, Caldwell produced eight large volumes of biographical portraits of professional-class individuals among African Americans in eight southern states. He solicited hundreds of brief biographical accounts from southern African American professionals, which he then rewrote or reprinted as presented to him. Next to the biographical accounts, Caldwell included high-quality photographs from which it was possible to discern skin color. These eight volumes, published in 1923 under the title *History of the American Negro,* are a truly unique source of basic sociodemographic information on the small but expanding population of African American professional individuals living in southern states.[12]

I chose to focus particularly on volume 7, *West Virginia Edition.* Inasmuch as West Virginia is a geographically marginal southern state, I assumed that, all things being equal, African American citizens of that state experienced fewer institutionalized racist barriers to modern social mobility than elsewhere in the South. I also assumed that the social mobility data derived from Caldwell's West Virginia volume would be analytically richer than similar data in the other seven volumes.

It should be noted here that the Caldwell and Bardolph works on the evolving twentieth-century African American professional stratum complement each other. While Caldwell's West Virginia volume concentrates on state-level development of the black professional class, Bardolph's book focuses mainly on national-level developments. However, in *The Negro Vanguard,* Bardolph also intertwines social data on state-level black-elite patterns with that on national-level patterns.

Given the fact that Caldwell and Bardolph present sociodemographic materials on the early-development phases of the African American professional stratum mainly in narrative form, I undertook the somewhat arduous task of translating those materials into a series of tables (Tables 1.1–1.3). Although my tabular translation of the Caldwell and Bardolph materials is impressionistic, nevertheless some degree of systematic veracity can be derived from them.

Data in Table 1.1 summarizing the Caldwell data represent fifty-four professional persons randomly selected from the 118 total in Caldwell's

West Virginia volume. Ten of these fifty-four black West Virginians were born before the 1863 Emancipation Proclamation, and three were born before the Civil War ended; the vast majority were born under freedom, at the dawn of African American free citizenship status.

For Bardolph's *The Negro Vanguard,* I constructed three sets of tabular translations of his narrative materials on eighty-seven top-tier African American professionals, presented in the appendix to this volume, following Bardolph's conceptual classification categories: "Out-of-Bondage Black Elite, 1865–1900," "Black Educator Elite, 1920s–1940s," and "Creative and Media Black Elite, 1920s–1940s." I also constructed two tables summarizing Bardolph's data: Table 1.2 relates data on the "Out-of-Bondage Black Elite," and Table 1.3, on the "Black Educator Elite."

I've already mentioned that Caldwell's volume provides photographs for most of the 118 biographical entries, which made it possible to obtain a measure of the range of skin color among the formative-phase black professional class in West Virginia. Similarly, Richard Bardolph's *The Negro Vanguard* also presents evidence on skin color among eighty-seven top-ranked national-level African American professionals. Bardolph obtained his skin-color evidence through a combination of published biographical materials, photographs, and interviews. Just as the sociodemographic data on the out-of-bondage elite (see Table 1.2) reveal the central role that Negro colleges played in educating that group, the data in Table 1.1 similarly reveal that forty-six of the fifty-four West Virginians selected from Caldwell's book attended Negro colleges; only six attended white higher education institutions.

Regarding the African American social system in the late nineteenth and early twentieth centuries, the fifty-four West Virginia black professionals from Caldwell's volume had a clear middle-class family advantage: among the forty-two for which there was family background evidence, only seven came from working-class families, whereas thirty-five had a middle-class family background; of these, fifteen had farmer family backgrounds, eight artisan, four business, four clergy, one teacher, one clerk, and two agrarian foreman backgrounds. What these data suggest, then, is that during the nascent appearance of an African American professional class during the Emancipation era, some degree of wealth above the weak agrarian and working-class ranks was likely required if one were

Table 1.1. Summary of class attributes of black elite persons in West Virginia, 1880s–1920s (n=54)

Family background		Education background		Occupation			
					Light skin (n=16)	Brown skin (n=20)	Dark skin (n=18)
Farmer	15	Black college	41	Doctor	6	9	4
Artisan	8	White college	1	Lawyer	2	2	3
Business	4	White/black college	5	Teacher	2	2	2
Barber		Self-educated	1	Academic	2	2	1
Caterer		Grammar school	3	College president	2		
Chef				Clergy	1	5	7
		Apprentice and correspondence	3				
Manager				Business	1		1
Clergy	4						
Teacher	1						
Clerk	1						
Foreman	2						
Worker	7						
Not available	12						

Source: Data from A. B. Caldwell, History of the American Negro: West Virginia Edition, vol. 7 (Atlanta: Caldwell Publishing, 1923).

to attend any of the early Negro colleges, such as Atlanta University (Georgia), Hampton Institute (Virginia), Howard University (Washington, D.C.), Lincoln University (Pennsylvania), Livingston College (North Carolina), Shaw University (North Carolina), Spelman College (Georgia), Talladega College (Alabama), Tuskegee Institute (Alabama), Virginia Union University, West Virginia State Teachers College, and Wilberforce University (Ohio).

In addition to revealing the importance of family background in the emergence of the formative-phase African American professionals in West Virginia, the data in Table 1.1 also show another important factor at work: the skin-color attribute associated with one's late nineteenth- and early twentieth-century African American family background. For example, sixteen of Caldwell's fifty-four West Virginia black professionals had "light skin," and twenty "brown skin"—these two skin tones were basic elements of African American's high-rank social class stratum during the Emancipation era and into the first several decades of the twentieth century.

Finally, data in Table 1.1 show the favorable occupational status for persons with light or brown skin. This was the case for individuals in the medical profession and also for individuals in administrative posts in Negro colleges. It is important to note, however, that eighteen of the fifty-four individuals selected from Caldwell's volume fell in the dark skin range; among them, four became medical doctors, three lawyers, and seven clergymen.

Table 1.2 shows the social class attributes of top-ranked black professionals during the Emancipation era that Richard Bardolph profiled in *The Negro Vanguard*. Of those born before the Civil War, quite a few had white planter-class fathers. White fathers often provided their black sons special funds to pursue education in the Emancipation era, which in turn provided them a social mobility related to the light-skin/brown-skin color dynamic.

The massive evidence of white male parentage of African American offspring during the long epoch of the American slavocracy cannot be overemphasized. Take, for example, the tale that Mary Chesnut, the privileged wife of a plantation owner and politician, relates in her famous Civil War diary.[13] Chestnut relates the American slave system's extensive "sexual miscegenation." She points out that, by the Civil War, white plantation owners had fathered so many offspring with their female slaves that the wives of the planters could easily identify the fathers

Table 1.2. Summary of class attributes of Bardolph's "Out-of-Bondage Black Elite, 1865–1900" (n = 28)

Family background	Education	Occupation		
		Light skin (20)	Brown skin (2)	Dark skin (6)
12 White plantation father	9 Black college	9 Reconstruction official	1 College president	
1 White professional father	4 White college	1 Lawyer	1 Politician	1 Newspaper owner
1 Clergy	2 White/black college	1 Teacher		5 Clergy
1 Barber	10 Mission school	6 Clergy		
3 Artisan	3 High school	3 Business		
1 Farmer		Grocer		
2 Domestic servant		Tailor		
4 Field hands		Hotelier		
3 Not available				

Source: Data from Richard Bardolph, *The Negro Vanguard* (New York: Rinehart, 1959), chaps. 1 and 2.

Note: Also see Table A.1 for the names of the professionals and the sociodemographic evidence associated with these individuals.

of numerous light-skinned and brown-skinned slave children among neighboring plantations.

As shown in Table 1.2, twenty-two of the twenty-eight persons listed among Bardolph's out-of-bondage black elite had light or brown skin. In white social class terms, twelve on Bardolph's list had upper-class planter fathers, and one had a professional-class white father; thus, thirteen of the twenty-eight were offspring of a white parent. Five of the twenty-eight had middle-class black family background. Nine attended Negro colleges, four attended white colleges, and two attended both a black and white college. Finally, regarding occupational outcomes, among the twenty-one light- or brown-skinned individuals on Bardolph's list, nine became Reconstruction officeholders, a position of power for anyone at the time, but particularly for an African American.

In Table 1.3 the time frame moves out of the late nineteenth century into the first several decades of the twentieth. Of the thirty-nine individuals that Bardolph characterized as the "black educator elite" (out of a total eighty-seven persons studied), a majority had middle-class family backgrounds. Only eight of the thirty-nine came from working-class families: three had domestic-servant family backgrounds; four, field-hand; and one, coal-miner. In a similar vein, four had farmer family background.

Thus, overall, twenty-seven of Bardolph's thirty-nine black educator elite individuals for the 1920s–1940s period were from middle-class or professional-class families. Those individuals' family occupations were as follows: six clergy, four teachers, three businessmen, one lawyer, two professionals, three barbers, one hotel porter, one butcher, two launderers, one messenger, one butler, one carpenter, and one plantation foreman.

It was especially regarding professional occupations held by Bardolph's black educator elite of this period where the social class prominence of light skin color stood out. As shown in Table 1.3, out of thirty-nine black educators that Bardolph randomly selected from *Who's Who in America* for the 1920s–1940s period, twenty had light skin. Of those twenty, five were academics, one was a high school principal, one was a college dean, and thirteen were college presidents. Also listed in Table 1.3 are thirteen individuals with brown skin, among whom eight were academics and five were college presidents. An additional six persons fell in the dark-skinned category, two of whom were academics, three were college presidents, and one was a college dean.

Based on these data, I suggest that there is a systemic social class message regarding the salience of skin-color dynamics in the composition of Richard Bardolph's black educator elite. Above all, regarding the professional positions of college president and faculty member at Negro colleges during their high-noon period, from the 1920s through the 1950s, professional-class African Americans with light or brown skin possessed a distinct advantage. In Bardolph's sample, they claimed eighteen college presidents, one college dean, and thirteen faculty positions at Negro colleges.

It happens that I attended a Negro college during the high-noon period of black institutions of higher education, so I can attest to the disproportionate representation of African American faculty and administrators at my alma mater—Lincoln University—who had light or brown skin. The president of Lincoln University, Horace Mann Bond (father of the NAACP official Julian Bond), was a member of this high-status light-skin/brown-skin category, as was the dean of students, James Bonner McRae. So, too, were the following African American faculty at

Table 1.3. Bardolph's "Black Educator Elite, 1920s–1940s" (n = 39)

Family background

Occupation		Class category	
Farmer	4	Middle class (17 LS, 8 BS, 2 DS)	27
Field hand	4	Working class (2 LS, 2 BS, 4 DS)	8
Domestic servant	3	Agrarian (1 LS, 3 BS)	4
Coal miner	1		
Launderer	2		
Plantation foreman	1		
Hotel porter	1		
Businessman	3		
Barber	3		
Butcher	1		
Lawyer	1		
Teacher	4		
White professional	2		
Clergy	6		
Messenger	1		
Butler	1		
Carpenter	1		

Occupation

	Light skin (20)	Brown skin (13)	Dark skin (6)
College president	13	5	3
Academic	5	8	2
College dean	1		1
School principal	1		

Source: Data from Richard Bardolph, The Negro Vanguard (New York: Rinehart, 1959), chaps. 2 and 3.
Note: See also Table A.2 for the names of the professionals and the sociodemographic evidence associated with these individuals.

Lincoln University in the 1950s: Norman Gaskin in chemistry, John Aubrey Davis in political science, Henry Cornwell in psychology, James Frankowsky in mathematics, Peter Hall and Kenneth Sneed in biology, Samuel Washington in accounting, Orrin Suthern in music, Alfred Farrell in English, and university treasurer Austin Scott. Only two of Lincoln University's African American faculty had dark skin: Laurence Foster in sociology and Joseph Newton Hill in English, who was also dean of the college. The rest of Lincoln's faculty members during my undergraduate years (1949–1953) were white Americans. They taught foreign languages (German and French), classical languages (Greek and Latin), philosophy, physics, economics, English literature, and history.

An anecdotal note regarding the dean of the college, Joseph Newton Hill, might highlight the broader representational cultural dynamics at a leading black institution of higher education during my undergraduate years. When Hill was given full-professorship rank along with the deanship of Lincoln University in 1932, he was the first African American to acquire that faculty rank there, even though the university was founded for Negro youth by a liberal branch of the white Presbyterian Church in the mid-nineteenth century. Hill had dark skin, stood about five feet, ten inches tall, and was very handsome, with a courtly bearing. Added to his striking personal demeanor was Hill's manner of speech—a distinctive upper-class British accent. Inasmuch as Hill's native diction was forged in a Negro agrarian community, the courtly manner and cosmopolitan speech he fashioned in his adult years might be viewed as a "new identity counterweight" to his agrarian roots. Be that as it may, Hill was recognized by Lincoln University students as an academic of intellectual depth in the fields of English studies and Afro-American literature, as well as a faculty member who deeply respected Lincoln students. The university, by the way, was his alma mater.

In addition to Bardolph's valuable sociodemographic evidence on the top tier in the formative-phase African American professional class, *The Negro Vanguard* also provides important material on the evolving twentieth-century black intelligentsia's social class patterns, especially what can be dubbed "elite consolidation dynamics." Bardolph focuses mainly on marriage patterns in his discussion of these formative-phase black intelligentsia status patterns. What Bardolph calls "family dynastic marriage practices" played a prominent role in shaping the black professional stratum's social class formation from the 1880s to the World War II era. Bardolph's discussion reveals that *during this three-generation period, these dynastic marriages solidified into institutionalized patterns.* It is this developmental facet of family dynastic marriages, then, that I have in mind when I use the term "black elite consolidation dynamics." Here's how Bardolph initially formulates his understanding of the issue:

> Many contemporary Negro leaders inform the writer [through interviews] that the increasing complexity of the Negro status system in recent years [1950s] has reduced the importance of family connection as a qualification for status [in the black elite] . . . , but few deny that it was in earlier days a major determinant.
> That it was a decisive factor in the rise of many who [during] 1936–1959 stood at the head of the [Negro] race is more than hinted by the extraordinary links between this and the previous generations. After compiling the roster of Negro notables of the past half century [from *Who Who's in America* and *Who's Who in Colored America*], we can . . . trace out an intricate web of family relationships that [represent] a high degree of [family] intermarriage.[14]

A rather curious feature of Bardolph's discussion of the importance of family dynastic marriage among the evolving twentieth-century black intelligentsia is that the skin-color issue remains implicit, not explicit. For instance, when Bardolph elaborates on aspects of what he calls "an intricate web of [elite] family relationships," he writes: "One notable feature of the [dynastic family] pattern is the emergence of a number of families, who, now in their third generation since the Civil War, have produced an extraordinary number of outstanding leaders in a variety of fields since the founders of the clans came to prominence in the mid-nineteenth century. People like the Bonds of Tennessee, the Huberts and the Nabrits of Georgia, the Tanners of Pennsylvania, the Clements and the Delanys and Jones[es] of North Carolina, the Churches of Memphis."[15]

Interestingly, Bardolph's foregoing characterization of dynastic black families who passed on professional- or upper-class status to their children underplays the important fact that professional-class African American families like the Nabrits, Delanys, Tanners, and Bonds all had light or brown skin. Put another way, *from the late nineteenth century into the first four decades of the twentieth century, the cross-generational transmission of bourgeois status among African Americans was a significantly color-caste dynamic.*

Take the aforementioned Bond family. In Bardolph's "Black Educator Elite," he lists Horace Mann Bond and J. Max Bond, who had light or brown skin. They were the sons of the Reverend James M. Bond, a leading African American Presbyterian clergyman educated in religious studies at Oberlin College in the late nineteenth century. J. Max Bond attended a black college, earned a Ph.D. in 1936 from the University of Southern California, and married into the elite Clement family of Louisville, Kentucky, whose family head was an African Methodist Episcopal Zion bishop. The Clement family had light and brown skin as well.

As for Horace Mann Bond, he also attended a black college (Lincoln University), graduating at the top of his class in 1923, and earned a Ph.D. in 1934 from the University of Chicago. Horace Mann Bond married into the elite Washington family of Nashville, Tennessee; the head of this family was a leading black Congregational clergyman whose congregation was almost exclusively middle and professional class. The Washington family also had light or brown skin.

When he elaborates the status-system dynamic of these dynastic family marriage patterns, Bardolph's account emphasizes the crucial role of cross-generational top-tier professional attainment within what he calls the "intricate web of [black elite] family relationships." Here is an example of one of Bardolph's descriptions:

> Children of [college president] David D. Jones and Susie Williams Jones are married to children of Louis T. Wright [leading surgeon] and Mordecai Johnson [appointed in 1926 as the first black president of Howard University]; William H. Dean [black economist at the United Nations] was the son-in-law of Channing Tobias [first black national YMCA official], and the younger [A.M.E. clergy] Archibald Carey's sister married Shelton Hale Bishop [a leading A.M.E. bishop]. Julian Lewis [leading chemist and first black faculty member at the University of Chicago] is the son-in-law of Anthony Overton [a black banking/insurance millionaire]. . . . [Furthermore], Judge [Hubert] Delany's first wife was a daughter of Emmett J. Scott [Booker T. Washington's secretary]. . . . [Newspaper owner] Lester Walton's wife is the daughter of Fred R. Moore [owner of the *New York Age* in Harlem] . . . , [and] Frederick D. Patterson married the daughter of R. R. Moton before succeeding him as president of Tuskegee Institute.[16]

I should mention again that, as was the case with Bardolph's earlier description of dynastic family marriage patterns among the evolving twentieth-century African American professional class, in the foregoing description Bardolph neglects to mention the skin-color dynamic. As it happened, all but one of these professional-class persons had light or brown skin. In fact, Mordecai Johnson, Channing Tobias, and Archibald Carey (the son of the A.M.E. bishop Archibald Carey Sr. in Chicago) were ultra-fair-skinned individuals and could have passed as white.

The only person named by Bardolph who did not have light or brown skin was Dr. Robert Moton, who was appointed president of Tuskegee Institute following Booker T. Washington's death in 1915. Moton had very dark skin; in fact, he was what old black folks in the Pennsylvania mill town where I grew up called "bone black." Frederick Patterson, however, who was Moton's son-in-law and his successor as president of Tuskegee Institute, belonged to the light-skin category.

Thus, on the basis of materials I have presented from A. B. Caldwell's book on the West Virginia black professional stratum and from Richard Bardolph's book on the early twentieth-century black professional stratum, it is clear that skin-color dynamics influenced many attributes of the early black elite's class system. Accordingly, by the 1930s, skin-color orientations resulted in what might be called an "elite consolidation process" among light-skinned and brown-skinned families in the top tier of African American society.

Importantly, however, this powerful trend toward a skin-color-based elite-consolidation dynamic, which began in the late Emancipation era, always confronted countervailing or oppositional trends among the liberal sector of the evolving twentieth-century African American intelligentsia. Furthermore, those oppositional trends eventually translated into full-fledged social democratization dynamics regarding color elitism's influence in the top tier of African American society. As shown in Table 1.4, the 1910 U.S. Census Bureau data show that 20 percent of the 1,700,800 African Americans in the South, and 26.6 percent of the 273,559 African Americans in the North, belonged to the light-skin/brown-skin sector (the sector classified as "mulatto element" by the U.S. Census Bureau). As these 1910 census data reveal, the light-skin/brown-skin sector constituted a sizable minority of the African American total population in the South and North (one-fifth and one-fourth, respectively). What's more, the bulk of the high school and college graduates among black Americans in both the South and North belonged to the

Table 1.4. Mulatto segment of U.S. black population, 1870–1910

Region	Dark skin			Light or brown skin		
	1870	1890	1910	1870	1890	1910
South	3,931,107	5,816,997	6,988,567	489,704 (11%)	924,944 (13%)	1,700,800 (20.1%)
North	300,744	504,506	754,115	92,074 (20%)	196,512 (28%)	273,559 (26.6%)
West	4,109	16,477	34,495	2,271 (35%)	10,004 (39.2%)	16,267 (32.1%)
Total black population	1870 (4,820,009)	1890 (7,469,440)	1910 (9,767,803)			

Source: Data from U.S. Department of Commerce, Bureau of the Census, Negro Population 1790–1915 (Washington, DC: Government Printing Office, 1918). See p. 25 for total Negro population data summary from 1790 to 1910; see also pp. 212–213 for data on what the U.S. Census Bureau labeled the "mulatto element," which represented 20.9 percent of the total Negro population in the 1910 U.S. Census—nearly equal to the "mulatto element" of 20.1 percent in the South but less than the 26.6 percent in the North and the 32.1 percent in the West.

Note: The U.S. Census Bureau's Negro Population 1790–1915 offers the following explanation for how the "mulatto element" was tabulated: "At the census of 1910 enumerators were instructed to indicate the color or race of each person in the Negro population in accordance with the definition following: For census purposes the term 'black' includes all persons who are evidently full-blooded Negroes, while the term 'mulatto' includes all other persons having some proportion or perceptible trace of Negro blood" (207).

light-skin/brown-skin sector—what the U.S. Census Bureau dubbed the "mulatto element."

Interestingly enough, during the time period when color-caste dynamics were still prominent features of the formative-phase African American professional class, there were emergent signs of countervailing ideological forces. In other words, the color-elitist ranks of the formative-phase black intelligentsia stratum were being challenged from within. This was mainly an attitudinal and ideological challenge, the goal of which was to vanquish skin-color obsessions and related color-caste dynamics (Bardolph's "intricate web of family relationships") within the black elite of the time, thereby replacing color elitism with liberal and progressive orientations toward blackness in African American life and society in general.

Beginning in the 1920s and gaining maturity from the 1930s onward, this challenge from within amounted to a counterelitist rebellion. Its overall goal was to fashion what might be called a black-consciousness activism pattern within the ranks of the evolving twentieth-century African American elite. Above all, the counterelitist activism was defined ideologically and operated behaviorally in a manner that favored (and sometimes celebrated) the dark-skinned agrarian and working-class Negro masses.

Before elaborating on aspects of the counterelitist activism pattern from the 1920s onward, I want to emphasize the depth of skin-color obsessions and related color-caste pretensions among the formative-phase African American elite between the 1880s and 1930s. University of Arkansas historian Willard Gatewood's pioneering 1991 book on color-caste patterns, *Aristocrats of Color: The Black Elite, 1880–1920*, presents a vivid analysis of the tenacity of this behavior. While Gatewood covers a variety of urban black communities like Philadelphia, Atlanta, Cincinnati, Chicago, and New York, he also presents a core focus on a group of four hundred black elite families in Washington, D.C., delineating their rigid color-elitist sociocultural practices. These families were given the nickname "the black 400" by liberal African American critics in the Washington community.

Among these critics was a progressive African American civil rights activist lawyer, Archibald Grimké, who graduated from one of the oldest Negro colleges—Lincoln University in Pennsylvania—in the 1870s and later became one of the first African American graduates of Harvard

Law School. Along with W. E. B. Du Bois and Monroe Trotter, Grimké joined ranks with the Niagara Movement and was a founding member of the NAACP in 1909. In 1916, Grimké, while head of the NAACP branch in Washington, D.C.—the most influential of all NAACP branches—traveled to Lincoln University to inaugurate an early NAACP branch at a Negro college.[17]

In an article in the *People's Advocate*—Washington, D.C.'s leading African American newspaper in the early 1900s, edited by lawyer John Wesley Cromwell, one of the founders of the American Negro Academy in 1897—Grimké chastised Washington's black elite for its "preoccupation with 'pomp and trappings.'" In describing the article, Gatewood says that "[Grimké singled out] the fierce competition of numerous 'social factions and cliques' [that] precluded the cohesiveness necessary to advance the [Negro] race in general." Gatewood went on: "Grimké reminded his fellow aristocrats that it was their responsibility 'always to lift the lower classes upward.' 'Noblesse oblige,' he continued, 'is an infinitely nobler motto . . . than that of Eat, Drink and be Merry.'"[18]

Grimké was joined in the ranks of a small number of Washington's early twentieth-century liberal-oriented black elite by his equally liberal brother, the Reverend Francis Grimké. They were the sons of a South Carolina plantation owner and one of his female slaves, and in the 1870s their white father sent them north to be educated at Lincoln University in Pennsylvania. Lincoln University was the first institution for the education of black people. It was founded by a small group of antislavery-oriented upper-class white Presbyterians just before the Civil War in 1854.

Both of the Grimké brothers used the social mobility advantages that their fair skin afforded them to fight for and advance the needs of the dark-skinned agrarian and working-class Negro masses, rather than either to "pass" as whites or to fashion exclusive color-elitist enclaves that separated them from the massive problems endured by black folks. In fact, it might be said that among the light-skin/brown-skin sector of the formative-phase African American intelligentsia, *the Grimké brothers inaugurated the liberal pattern of fair-skin African Americans using their elite capabilities to advance the social status of the dark-skinned Negro masses.*[19] Along with other light-skinned/brown-skinned African American professionals in the early twentieth century—such as W. E. B. Du Bois, Anna Julia Cooper, Monroe Trotter, James Weldon Johnson, Walter

White, and Mary Church Terrell—the Grimké brothers rejected the accommodationism of Booker T. Washington and his Tuskegee machine. Thus, they joined progressive organizations like the Niagara Movement and the NAACP that challenged America's white supremacist practices head on. As it happened, many subsequent graduates of the Grimké brothers' alma mater, Lincoln University, who fell into the light-skin/brown-skin category—including high-achieving graduates like Horace Mann Bond (sociologist/educator), Langston Hughes (poet, essayist, and activist), Monroe Dowling (accountant), Thurgood Marshall (civil rights lawyer), and Roscoe Lee Brown (poet and actor)—might have been influenced by the progressive example set by Archibald and Francis Grimké during the African American intelligentsia's early twentieth-century phase.

Be that as it may, as Gatewood elaborates his analysis of color-elitism patterns in *Aristocrats of Color*, he points out that the skin-color-obsessed elements in the black elite in Washington, D.C., during the early twentieth century were quite naive regarding the Negrophobic viciousness of the racist oligarchy in American society. The color-caste segment of the black elite in the nation's capital assumed that the combination of their upward mobility and their virulent disrespect for the dark-skinned Negro masses would render this privileged sector favorable in the eyes of upper-class whites. However, by World War I, says Gatewood, this belief turned out to be a fantasy: "Whatever success the colored aristocrats in the city [Washington, D.C.] have had in disassociating themselves socially from the surrounding black community," Gatewood writes, *"they were unable to escape the disabilities and proscriptions imposed upon all blacks by a racist society—a society that adhered to the notion that 'one drop' of African blood is sufficient to place a person in the 'inferior caste.'"*[20]

Nonetheless, the "aristocrats of color" clung to the erroneous belief that their disassociation from the Negro masses would render white Americans friendly toward and perhaps allies of "the aristocrats of color." Thus, as new progressive ideological forces debuted among the early twentieth-century African American intelligentsia—forces that eventually formed the so-called New Negro Movement—the new forces challenged the Negrophobic color-caste patterns represented among some top-tier elements in African American society. As it happened, W. E. B. Du Bois played a groundbreaking role in shaping the progressive discourse that challenged color-caste ideology and the conservative ac-commodationist patterns connected with that ideology.

In chapter 10 of his seminal 1903 work *The Souls of Black Folk,* titled "Of the Faith of the Fathers," Du Bois ruminates on the characterologi-cal nature of capitalist American civilization at the very time that the modern African American intelligentsia is appearing on the stage of American history. This formative era in the life cycle of the African American intelligentsia is portrayed by Du Bois as "a time of intense ethi-cal ferment, of religious heart-searching and of intellectual unrest." With this preliminary portrayal of modern capitalist American civilization, Du Bois was suggesting to the fledging black intelligentsia that it should oppose what he called "pretense and hypocrisy" and instead turn to-ward "radicalism."[21] Of course, the "radicalism" that Du Bois had in mind was of a constitutionalist bent, as it were, because Du Bois and his circle of progressive colleagues believed in pragmatic civil rights activ-ism, not in revolutionary radicalism.

In the same chapter, Du Bois proposes two possible ideological strands, or leadership paradigms, for the nascent black intelligentsia: "[We] have two great and hardly reconcilable streams of thought and ethical striv-ings," he writes. "The one type of Negro . . . is wedded to ideals remote, whimsical, perhaps impossible of realization; the other [type of Negro] forgets that life is more than meat and the body more than raiment. . . . *To-day the two groups of Negroes . . . represent these divergent ethical [ideological] tendencies, the first tending toward radicalism, and the other toward hypocritical compromise.*"[22]

The twentieth century was barely under way when Du Bois penned this keen and prescient formulation of the generic ideological strands that were vying for hegemonic status among the fledgling African Amer-ican intelligentsia. But two decades would pass—a full generation—before Du Bois' incisive formulation realized political salience. From the 1920s into the 1940s, a variety of elements on the progressive side of the African American ideological spectrum contributed to challenging the sway of conservative color-caste patterns in African American society. One of those elements comprised a cadre of light-skinned and brown-skinned African American intellectuals who hailed from bourgeois families that had par-ticipated in color-caste pretensions and patterns themselves.

As it happened, a sizable segment of those who, by the 1920s, were known as the New Negro Movement intellectuals were sons and daughters of color-caste-oriented families. Their movement was a genuine social and cultural rebellion. It was through affiliation with the New Negro Movement that, *by the 1940s, thousands of African American professionals from color-caste-obsessed families redefined their ideological and political identity.*[23] Above all, through their affiliation with the New Negro Movement, many offspring of color-caste-obsessed families were announcing two crucial things about themselves. First, they rejected color-caste pretensions as being dishonorable to black folks—dishonorable to blackness—thereby denouncing what my African Methodist clergy great-grandfather, the Reverend Joseph Martin, called "mulatto arrogance." Second, by joining the New Negro Movement from the 1920s into the 1940s, light-skinned/brown-skinned African American intellectuals were affirming belief in the intrinsic capacity of Negro people's cultural and institutional forms to contribute to fashioning modern civilization and its nation-state societies.[24]

Put another way, through affiliation with the New Negro Movement from the 1920s into the 1940s, black professionals were rejecting the self-hating beliefs of their color-caste-oriented bourgeois families, especially beliefs that white people were intrinsically better at producing the institutional, intellectual, aesthetic, and knowledge forms of modern civilization. Thus, if in 1935 you came into the United States as a professional of African descent from West Africa, Haiti, or the Caribbean when the National Negro Congress was being formed in Chicago, you would have become aware of a phalanx of prominent African American professionals who were challenging Negrophobic color-caste ideology and practices through the New Negro Movement.

The following list of well-known professionals with light or brown skin who were associated with the New Negro Movement by the middle 1930s is by no means complete, but the names on it are impressive: W. E. B. Du Bois (sociologist and editor of the NAACP's journal, the *Crisis*), James Weldon Johnson (essayist and executive director of the NAACP), Charles S. Johnson (sociologist and professor at Fisk University), Arna Bontemps (literary scholar and professor at Howard University), Alain Locke (philosophy scholar at Howard University), Langston Hughes (poet and playwright), Ira Reid (sociologist and editor of the National Urban League's magazine *Opportunity: Journal of Negro*

Life), Nella Larsen (novelist), Jesse Fauset (editor and poet), Aaron Douglas (artist and professor at Howard University), Sadie Mossell Alexander (economist and lawyer), Charles Hamilton Houston (founder of the
NAACP Legal Defense Fund), James Nabrit and William Hastie (Howard
University law professors), Horace Mann Bond (sociologist and professor
at Dillard University), J. Max Bond (sociologist and field analyst for the
Tennessee River Valley Authority), Raymond Pace Alexander and Hubert
Delany (civil rights lawyers), Otelia Cromwell (literature scholar and
professor at Miners Teachers College), Allison Davis (social psychologist
and professor at Dillard University), John Aubrey Davis (political scientist and professor at Lincoln University), Carter G. Woodson (historian
and director of the Association for the Study of Negro Life and History),
St. Clair Drake (anthropologist and professor at Dillard University), Elmer Henderson (staff lawyer at the NAACP Legal Defense Fund), Robert
Weaver (economist in the federal government), Rayford Logan (historian
and professor at Howard University), R. R. Wright (A.M.E. bishop and
editor of *Encyclopedia of African Methodism*), A. Philip Randolph (editor
of *Messenger*, a socialist journal), John P. Davis (lawyer and a founder of
the National Negro Congress), Sterling Brown (literary scholar and professor at Howard University), Benjamin Quarles (historian and professor
at Morgan State College), Irene Diggs (anthropologist at Atlanta University), Adam Clayton Powell (clergyman at Abyssinia Baptist Church in
Harlem), and Reverdy Ransom (A.M.E. bishop and editor of the A.M.E.
Church's leading journal, the *A.M.E. Church Review*). This list represents the "best and brightest" of that second and third generation of
twentieth-century African American professionals, who ideologically and
politically transformed themselves through the New Negro Movement.[25]
They transformed themselves into an "intellectual weapon," as it were,
against the Negrophobic color-caste patterns that were practiced by a
sizable segment of the evolving black elite during the late nineteenth century and early decades of the twentieth century.

When eventually stripped of their ideological and normative legitimacy within the intelligentsia stratum, the proponents of color elitism's
denigration of blackness lost their authority. In operational terms, this
meant that advocates of color elitism also lost their position as gate-
keepers to professional-stratum networks throughout African American
society. Thus, as African American society moved into the post–World
War II era (the period when the fourth generation of African American
youth entered black colleges), the hegemony of Gatewood's aristocrats

of color had diminished significantly. Following this change, the path for the full-fledged social democratization of the African American intelligentsia was nearly free of pathological skin-color and color-caste impediments.

It should be mentioned, however, that during the period between the two World Wars, the progressive professional elements in the African American intelligentsia were not alone in challenging color-elitism patterns in the evolving twentieth-century African American society. There was also a coexisting challenge that contributed to the demise of color elitism patterns in African American society. That challenge emanated from a working-class-based black-populist leadership dynamic.

The black populist contribution to the decline of color-elitism patterns in African American society was initially manifested through Negro folk-culture agencies like Holiness-type churches (e.g., Pentecostal, Spiritualist, Apostolic, and Primitive Baptist churches). These churches differed in important respects from the lower-middle-class and middle-class-based Negro churches like the African Methodist Episcopal Church, the African Methodist Episcopal Zion Church, the Colored Methodist Episcopal Church, and the National Baptist Church. Commencing in the 1910s and the World War I period into the 1940s, a broad range of poor working-class-based Holiness-type churches evolved among millions of illiterate Negro agrarian migrants from the South to northern cities. In the sanctuaries of thousands of Holiness-type churches—most of which were flimsy in their structural mode—a mainly self-trained black clergy fashioned what might be called a Negro-masses-friendly religio-ideological discourse. In his 1944 book *Black Gods of the Metropolis*, the African American anthropologist Arthur Huff Fauset produced the first major study of Negro Holiness-type churches and their discourse. Fauset probed how the Holiness churches and clergy fashioned Negro theological and church patterns that strengthened the normative legitimacy of "blackness"—by which I mean respect for the "organic legitimacy of Negro folkways."[26]

Moreover, this important normative and ideological transformation was executed by a kind of second-tier working-class-based African American leadership that evolved along with the development of the first-tier middle-class-based African American leadership. This parallel second-tier African American leadership realm coexisted for much of the period when the mainstream African American intelligentsia's civil rights political leadership predominated in the evolving twentieth-century African American society. What was unique about this parallel realm was that *its leadership figures rose not from college-educated ranks—not from Du Bois' Talented Tenth—but directly from the Negro masses.*

Here again I use Richard Bardolph's *Negro Vanguard* as a jumping-off point for my discussion of black populist leadership. In his book, Bardolph's discussion of the period's African American professional class proceeds from a "top-down" perspective—he barely acknowledges that there were "bottom-up" forces affecting the evolving twentieth-century African American leadership development as well. Indeed, Bardolph doesn't even refer to the existence of a black populist leadership pattern until the end of his book, where he includes a rather dismissive footnote about the phenomenon: "Mention of such men as 'Father Divine,' 'Prophet Jones,' 'Daddy Grace,' and other leaders of exotic cults has been omitted [in *The Negro Vanguard*] because they are almost never mentioned in lists of distinguished Negroes compiled by persons of color [or by whites]," writes Bardolph. "Elijah Muhammed [*sic*], a Chicago leader of Muslim Negroes has in 1959 a considerable following, but I have encountered little mention of him in the literature I surveyed."[27]

As Bardolph informs his readers in the foregoing endnote, he determined the "type" of black American to list in what he calls the "vanguard stratum" of the black intelligentsia by their inclusion in the main documentary sources he used to write his book: *Who's Who in America* and *Who's Who in Colored America*. However, had Bardolph used supplementary sources, he *would have discovered* that second-tier working-class black populist leaders coexisted alongside the top-tier black middle-class leadership. In short, Bardolph would have encountered figures like Daddy Grace, head clergy of the United Church of Prayer, through which he led thousands upon thousands of mainly black working-class congregants across several major urban areas on the East Coast, from Boston to Raleigh. Daddy Grace was not alone—Bardolph would have also been exposed to other working-class-based Holiness-type leadership figures, including Prophet Jones in Detroit and Father Divine in Philadelphia and New York City.[28]

Of course, what was developmentally unique about the black clergy in the Holiness-type churches was that they did not boast credentials from black higher education institutions, as did the vast majority of the top-tier or mainstream African American leaders of the time. Instead, the Daddy Graces and Father Divines learned their leadership capabilities through what might be called black popular-society grassroots agencies, which is to say, from working-class civic groups and artisan associations, and especially from storefront churches operated by self-made clergy.[29]

It was then through these black grassroots agencies where, during the interwar era, working-class black populist personalities mastered viable leadership attributes. For example, they mastered the operational use of the English language. They gained basic numerical calculation skills that grew into sizable moneymaking skills, which in turn blossomed into full-blown business acumen. Most significant, perhaps, they acquired basic theological discourse skills that eventually translated into political mobilization capabilities. As a result, working-class black populist leadership figures like Father Divine, Daddy Grace, Elder Michaux, Prophet E. R. Killingworth, and Elder Lucy Smith fashioned a *genuine second-tier African American leadership realm.*

In general, during the era between the two world wars, the sociocultural milieu of the black church generated a broad variety of black populist leadership. I base this proposition on the thinking of the most prominent sociological analyst of African American life during the interwar era, Charles S. Johnson, who taught at Fisk University in Nashville in the 1930s and became its president in 1948. Writing in his classic 1940 book *Growing Up in the Black Belt,* Johnson reflected on the generic social system character of the Negro church as follows: "It has a far wider function than to bring spiritual inspiration to its communicants. . . . It is a complex institution meeting a wide variety of needs."[30]

As millions of agrarian African Americans left the South for the North from 1910 into the 1940s in what historian Isabel Wilkerson recently dubbed the Great Black Migration (comprising some six million people),[31] their spiritual and soul-healing needs were met most often by black churches and clergy. By the World War I era, two main types of black churches had evolved in cities outside the South. Type I churches comprised "mainline" black churches, led by seminary-educated black clergy who ministered to congregants of middle-class and blue-collar families. The National Negro Baptist and African Methodist churches were the main religious denominations of type I churches, with the latter having four main branches: the African Methodist Episcopal Church, the African Methodist Episcopal Zion Church, the Colored Methodist

Episcopal Church, and the African Union Methodist Protestant Church. Type I churches were historically the oldest institutionalized black churches, especially the African Methodist denominations that originated in the early 1800s. Accordingly, by the 1930s, the type I African Methodist churches possessed viable infrastructure attributes and thus greater institutionalizing capabilities.[32]

Type II churches comprised "theistic" black churches. These were urban Negro churches that evolved during the World War I period and were characterized as Holiness churches and Spiritualist churches by sociological analysts of the black church, among them Arthur Huff Fauset, Ira Reid, Miles Mark Fisher, and St. Clair Drake. Led largely by self-educated black clergy, by the 1920s these churches had congregations mainly from the weak working-class and poor sectors of urban African Americans in the North. Whereas the physical edifice of type I churches involved brick or stone, the physical structures of type II churches were fragile and temporary in nature, described by social analysts as "store-front" churches. The sociologists St. Clair Drake and Horace Cayton contrasted the structural character of type I and type II churches in the 1940s as follows: "There are five churches in Bronzville [Black Chicago] seating over 2,000 persons and claiming more than 10,000 members, and fifty church buildings seating between 500 and 2,000 persons," they wrote. "Seventy-five per cent of Bronzville's churches are small 'store-front' or house-churches, with an average membership of fewer than twenty-five persons. Many of these represent survivals from the Great Migration. Others are the result of leadership conflicts within the larger churches."[33]

Similarly, in his 1971 book *Harlem: The Making of a Ghetto*, social historian George Osofsky describes the fragile social realm of a plethora of storefront-type churches in Harlem in the 1920s: "An investigator found 140 [type II] churches in a 150-block area in Harlem in 1926. Only about a third—fifty-four—of Harlem's churches were housed in regular church buildings. . . . The rest held services in stores and homes and appealed to Harlem's least educated people."[34]

A view of the broad denominational range of black churches in the city of Chicago during the period between World War I and World War II is provided by data shown in Table 1.5, which are based on a survey by Drake and Cayton published in their pioneering 1945 book *Black Metropolis: A Study of Negro Life in a Northern City*. Among the type I

Table 1.5. Black church denominations in Chicago, 1928

Church denomination	Number	Percent (%)
Mainline Baptist	98	33.2
Missionary Baptist	30	10.2
Primitive Baptist	5	1.7
African Methodist Episcopal	24	8.2
African Methodist Episcopal Zion	5	1.7
Colored Methodist Episcopal	6	2.0
Methodist Episcopal	8	2.7
Episcopal	3	1.0
Presbyterian	3	1.0
Congregational	2	0.7
Disciples of Christ	2	0.7
Seventh-Day Adventists	2	0.7
Catholic	1	0.3
Lutheran	1	0.3
Community Churches, Inc.	3	1.0
Catholic of God in Christ—Pentecostal	24	8.2
Church of Christ—Holiness	3	1.0
Church of Christ	5	1.7
Church of the Living God—Holiness	2	0.7
Church of God—Holiness	1	0.3
Church of God—Pentecostal	6	2.0
Church of God and Saints of Christ	1	0.3
Apostolic and Pentecostal	11	3.8
Pentecostal Assemblies of World	2	0.7
Old Time Methodist	1	0.3
Spiritual and Spiritualist	17	5.8
Cumberland Presbyterian	2	0.7
African Orthodox (Garvey Movement)	1	0.3
Liberal Catholic	1	0.3
Others	25	8.5
Total	295	100

Source: Data from St. Clair Drake and Horace R. Cayton, *Black Metropolis: A Study of Negro Life in a Northern City,* vol. 2 (New York: Harper & Row, 1945), 414.

Note: Percentages do not total 100 due to rounding.

churches, the Negro Baptist denomination had the largest number of black churches in Chicago in 1928: some ninety-eight churches, or one-third of all black churches. The African Methodist denominations (i.e., African Methodist Episcopal, African Methodist Episcopal Zion, Colored Methodist Episcopal)—also type I churches—had thirty-five churches, or 12 percent of the total. And the Pentecostal/Holiness/Spiritualist churches—type II churches—claimed sixty-six churches, or 23 percent of the total.

On the basis of a variety of studies of the type II church from the 1920s to the 1940s by such analysts as Fauset, Reid, Fisher, and Drake, the theological mode within such churches ranged from hyperemotionalist "other-worldly soul-saving" ritualism to an evangelical "this-worldly benefits" ritualism. Moreover, between the two world wars, a wide variety of black-populist type leadership figures—mainly males but also females—functioned as clergy in type II churches.[35]

A prominent example of the hyperemotionalist otherworldly soul-saving clergy was the Reverend R. C. Lawson, who pastored the Apostolic Church of Christ in Harlem from the 1920s to the 1940s. According to George Osofsky, Lawson called himself "the only real Apostolic–Holy Ghost Bible preacher." Furthermore, says Osofsky, Lawson "decried the lack of emotionalism in the more established [mainline] urban [Negro] churches . . . and offered recent migrants a touch of fire and brimstone and personal Christianity characteristic of religion in the rural South."[36] Throughout the interwar period, there were many other examples of Lawson's variant of the type II church. Among them were Prophet Martin's and Prophet Joseph's Apostolic churches in Washington, D.C.; Prophet E. R. Killingworth's so-called Kodesh Church in Philadelphia, Elder Lucy Smith's All-Nations Pentecostal Church in Chicago, and another All-Nations Pentecostal Church, pastored by Mother Rose Horne, in Evanston, Illinois.

Furthermore, during the 1930s and the 1940s there was a variant of the type II church that pursued, on the one hand, an evangelical other-worldly soul-saving ritualism, while simultaneously practicing a this-worldly benefits ritualism, and the latter facet of this Janus-faced Holiness ritualism afforded this type II church and its leader a social problem-solving orientation. Perhaps the most prominent black clergyperson of this theological mode was Elder Lightfoot Solomon Michaux. His ministry began in the early 1920s in Newport News, Virginia, where he had been a fish peddler. By the late 1920s Michaux had moved his church to Washington, D.C., where he erected a large stone edifice that seated some seven hundred congregants.

Michaux called his church the Apostolic Church of God, and by the mid-1930s his type II church had organized several farms in Maryland. According to one study, Michaux's church mounted a food program that fed "some 25,000 people monthly . . . provided clothes for thousands and operated four settlement homes. His *Happy News* [monthly newspaper] advertises five 'Happy Are We' five-and-ten-cent meat markets in Washington, D.C."[37]

Other type II churches that pursued Michaux's form of the evangelical this-worldly benefits ritualism also had business endeavors. Prominent among such type II churches was Father Divine's Peace Mission Church, which operated a hotel in Philadelphia and restaurants in New York City, Philadelphia, and Baltimore. The food was priced to accommodate the typical wages earned by working-class urban blacks.[38]

Besides the type II church clergy during the interwar years who employed religious features of everyday Negro folkisms to advance black-populist type leadership, there also surfaced in several large urban areas a politically oriented working-class-based black populist leadership. The Universal Negro Improvement Association (UNIA), which was founded in 1918 in New York City by Marcus Garvey, was perhaps the most prominent organization representative of this type of black populist leadership during these years.

Popularly known as the Garvey Movement, its leader had very dark skin with pronounced Negro features, and he articulated an assertive pro-Negro cultural ideology that historical analysts labeled "black nationalism."[39] Above all, during the 1920s and 1930s, the Garvey Movement's mode of working-class-based black populist leadership militantly challenged the mainstream African American intelligentsia that prevailed in black leadership organizations like the NAACP, the National Urban League, the National Council of Negro Women, the Brotherhood of Sleeping Car Porters, and the National Negro Congress. As studies on the Garvey Movement have documented, Garvey charged the mainstream civil rights organizations with being anti-Negro and elitist, owing to the prominence of light-skinned and brown-skinned professionals among them. The Garvey Movement's skillful black-nationalist challenge of the mainstream African American leadership helped the UNIA to amass the largest following among African American leadership groups during the 1920s and 1930s.

However, this massive following (estimated by historians at over 200,000) declined precipitously after Garvey's deportation to Britain by the U.S. government in 1935.[40] Yet, as significant as the Garvey Movement was as a secular example of working-class-based black populist leadership during the 1920s and 1930s, it was exceptional as a variant of black-populist-type leadership during the interwar period, and geographically, it was mainly limited to New York. For the most part, black populist leadership during the interwar era thrived primarily among proletarian-based Negro folkisms–oriented clergy, who pastored mainly Pentecostal, Holiness, and Spiritualist urban black churches that were located not merely in big cities but also in medium and small cities.

Between World War I and World War II, the Negro folkisms–oriented clergy often grappled with trauma-laden sociocultural issues relating to the dark-skinned citizens in urban communities. During this period, the black populist leadership comprising type II church clergy taught millions of black folks to adapt to urban realities through pragmatic sociocultural uses of Blackways, Negro folk patterns.[41]

Thus, as World War II came to a close, it can be said that the populist clergy had contributed to the demise of color elitism's ideological hegemony during the formative phase of twentieth-century African American society. Above all, perhaps, the wide presence of type II black church clergy, serving millions of migrant working-class African Americans in urban areas in the North, *strengthened the cultural authoritativeness of Negro folk patterns among the lower-class black masses.* Having made this important contribution to sustaining the cultural legitimacy of Blackways among the urban African Americans by the time World War II ended, I suggest that, in turn, the black-populist-type leadership between the 1920s and 1950s also facilitated social democratization dynamics in the top tier of African American society. Above all, as working-class African American families entered the postwar period, it became increasingly apparent that Gatewood's "aristocrats of color" and their Negrophobic ideology and status pretensions could no longer denigrate the black masses as they once did. In short, African America's aristocrats of color were now culturally dethroned.

Accordingly, as African American society entered the 1950s, a new "black-ethnic" modality within the overall patterns of African American political activism commenced: *a full-fledged radicalization of civil rights activism.* Moreover, this full-fledged radicalism differed from African American political mobilization patterns during the 1920s through the 1940s. Above all, it entertained ideas relating to African American participation in overall mobilization for systemic reformation in American society, quite beyond issues relating to racial barriers against black folks. Antiwar activism, for example, was one such new systemic reformation now advanced by top-tier African American activist leadership. Prominent among the postwar-era African American political organizations that contributed to the radicalization of civil rights activism were the Congress on Racial Equality (headed by James Farmer), the Southern Christian Leadership Conference (headed by the Reverend Martin Luther King Jr.), and the Student Nonviolent Coordinating Committee (headed by James Lawson and others).

Finally, owing to the full-fledged radicalism ethos that emerged among the post–World War II African American civil rights leadership, African American society was guaranteed the demise of the Negrophobic status pretensions that characterized color elitism among the aristocrats of color of the pre–World War II era. By the end of the 1960s, color elitism among the mainstream social groups of African American society was anathema—color elitism and its bourgeois proponents could no longer muster any semblance of a significant presence in African American life.

But what about latent color-elitism patterns within the African American intelligentsia in the years ahead? I think that latent, backwater nooks and crannies of skin-color-obsessed elements among the African American elite will persist, which is to say, as the old adage about the poor in our society puts it, "They'll always be with us."

2

BLACK INTELLIGENTSIA
LEADERSHIP PATTERNS

THE CENTRAL LEADERSHIP task of the evolving African American intelligentsia from the late nineteenth century and into the twentieth was this: How do you challenge and eventually reverse the undemocratic and oppressive impact of America's white-supremacist system on its Negro citizens? From the end of the post–Civil War Reconstruction programs onward, the social, economic, political, and cultural status of African Americans was broadly oppressed, demeaned, and marginalized in the American democratic system.

When viewing this question from today's vantage point, we can say that the African American intelligentsia has been fairly successful in fulfilling this task. After all, Barack Obama, an African American president, now sits in the White House, and he was elected to a second term in November 2012. Moreover, there is now a full-fledged African American political class made up of ten thousand elected officeholders in counties, cities, state legislatures, and Congress, and many thousands more African American administrative and technical officials at state and federal levels. Nevertheless, in spite of these recent and impressive achievements, the historical road to the making of a viable African American political leadership was arduous, to say the least.[1]

Furthermore, when the numbers constituting the political class are viewed in combination with the nearly four million African Americans recorded by U.S. Census Bureau surveys in 2002 and 2006 as holding top-tier white-collar occupations (a topic I discuss further in Chapter 4), we have evidence of a fairly sizable African American intelligentsia or professional stratum. When contrasted with W. E. B. Du Bois' figures that recorded a total of 1,996 black American college graduates during 1899–1900—the last year of the Emancipation era—this represents an important transformation in the life cycle of the African American intelligentsia.

Du Bois reported these figures in his pioneering essay "The Talented Tenth," which appeared in Booker T. Washington's *The Negro Problem* in 1903. However, Du Bois' first reference to the "Talented Tenth" appeared in chapter 6 of his 1903 *The Souls of Black Folk,* which was published six months before. In it, Du Bois refers to the Census Bureau data on the small number of "college-bred Negroes" (his usual term when writing about African Americans who attended colleges or universities), after which he elaborates: "Here, then, is the plain thirst for training; by refusing to give this Talented Tenth the key to knowledge, can any man imagine that they will lightly lay aside their yearning and contentedly become hewers of wood and drawers of water?"[2]

Fast upon the defeat of the secessionist southern states after the Civil War in 1865, the federal government instituted a policy to politically incorporate the formerly enslaved Negro population into the American social and political order. The socioeconomic implications for all aspects of southern society were enormous. In his book *1861: The Civil War Awakening,* the Washington College historian Adam Goodheart explains the massive monetary significance of slavery to the antebellum South: "Slaveholding was now woven so tightly into the South's culture and economy—indeed into the whole nation's economy—as to be almost inextricable. Even its foes acknowledged this." In 1858, Goodheart wrote, "Lincoln himself noted in a speech that the region's four million slaves were valued at no less than two billion dollars. (Most recent historians have put the figure even higher.) *This was an absolutely mind-boggling sum, greater than the value of all the nation's factories and railroads, North and South combined.*"[3]

Inevitably, then, the federal Reconstruction policy—officially called the Reconstruction Act of 1867—revolutionized the South's social and political order. As Du Bois demonstrated in his great work of 1935, *Black Reconstruction in America, 1860–1880,* Reconstruction policy provided the formerly enslaved Negroes their first experiences with democratic practices.[4] And in South Carolina, where Negro voters were in the majority, democratic practices under Reconstruction policy were operating on the highest level, as the University of Chicago historian Thomas Holt demonstrates in his brilliant book *Black over White: Negro*

Political Leadership in South Carolina during Reconstruction. South Carolina's Reconstruction period saw numerous black officeholders at both the state and federal level, as well as broad-based black voter participation.[5]

Regarding the South's Reconstruction period generally, Eric Foner, the leading contemporary historian on Reconstruction, informs us that it was Du Bois' seminal book *Black Reconstruction in America* that first probed the broad democratic range of Reconstruction policy. "Writing at a time when racial inequality was deeply embedded in American life," says Foner, "Du Bois insisted that Reconstruction must be understood as an episode in the struggle for genuine democracy—political and economic—in the United States. He pointed to the contest over access to land and control of the labor of the emancipated slaves as the crucial issue of Reconstruction, and explored the ramification of Reconstruction's failure for the future course of American development."[6]

By the early 1880s, however, when federal support of Reconstruction had ended (i.e., when the Union Army withdrew from southern states as a protector of black people's democratic and human rights), what might be called a white-supremacist authoritarian deluge—maybe "tsunami" is a better word—crushed those very rights that had been so recently granted to blacks. Authoritarian, violent, and terrorist southern restorationist forces gained full hegemony.[7] Owing to the federal government's unwillingness to sustain and protect the voting, participatory, and basic human rights for black people hard won under Reconstruction policy, the gains that blacks had made in terms of participation in the democratic process under Reconstruction between 1867 and 1877 were obliterated.

It should be mentioned, moreover, that a special federal government agency called the Freedmen's Bureau was critical during Reconstruction to the administration of the processes of democratic incorporation for black Americans. As the University of Virginia political historian Lawrie Balfour has observed, "The Freedmen's Bureau represents for Du Bois an institution that held out the promise of a lasting independence from the domination of the planters for poor Southerners, black and white."[8] In *The Souls of Black Folk*, Du Bois cogently articulated his fervent commitment to the crucial and salient role of the Freedmen's Bureau: "The Freedmen's Bureau was the most extraordinary and far-reaching institution of social uplift that America has ever attempted. It had to do, not simply with emancipated slaves and poor whites, but also with the property of Southern planters. It was a government guardianship for the relief and guidance of white and black Labor from a feudal agrarianism to modern farming and industry."[9]

In states outside the South, where by 1920 nearly 10 percent of black citizens had settled, a state-supported mode of America's racist oligarchy was not established. Nevertheless, a broad range of what might be called "white hegemonic maneuvers"—both in the racist social system and in the political system—prevailed in the North. This northern racist pattern resulted in massive deficiencies in both the social and political development in twentieth-century African American society at large, as Du Bois had been the first to identify in his pioneering 1899 book *The Philadelphia Negro: A Study.*[10]

Furthermore, the combination of authoritarian southern restorationist forces, on the one hand, and northern white hegemonic maneuvers, on the other, resulted in social and political deficiencies in the development of the evolving twentieth-century African American society and its leadership.[11] Not least of these deficiencies was a five-generation delay in the emergence of a full-fledged African American modern political class in both the South and the North. For example, not until the passage of major Civil Rights legislation and federal policy practices in the 1960s (e.g., the 1964 Civil Rights Act and the 1965 Voting Rights Act) did the typical African American citizen gain full citizenship rights and electoral participation rights. Put another way, *it was nearly a century following the end of Reconstruction before the 10 percent of American citizens who were black gained genuine voter participation status and access to public office.*

Ironically, however, during the same five-generation period between the 1870s and 1960s, the politically oppressed black citizens provided a major part of the labor force for southern agricultural and industrial capitalist production. Needless to say, African Americans did not enjoy the economic fruits of their labor. To offer just a sketch of the core socioeconomic condition of the Negro masses during this period, I turn to a description, published in 1953, of the crucial role black workers played in the South's economy from the late nineteenth century into the first half of the twentieth century. This account comes from a study by the economic historian Victor Perlo, titled *The Negro in Southern Agriculture:*

The importance of Negro labor becomes more apparent if attention is concentrated on the large commercial farms and plantations—less than 5% of the total—which account for roughly 60% of the value of marketed farm production. These decisive farms depend mainly on wage laborers and croppers. . . . The Negro people supply almost two-thirds of this basic labor force. . . . Not only do the Negro people supply the majority of the labor for commercial agriculture in the South, but they are the most exploited, and supply an even greater portion of the total profit. . . . If agriculture is the leading industry in the South generally, it is peculiarly the leading industry of the Negro.[12]

Furthermore, as shown by data in Table 2.1 for ten selected southern states, by 1930 some half-million black males worked for manufacturers. This indicates a significant dependence by the South's manufacturing sector on black workers compared with white workers.

From the early 1880s until the 1950s, the agriculture industry was also heavily dependent on a Negro labor force, the recruitment of which was officially intertwined with southern states' prison systems. Called the convict lease labor system, this was an American version of authoritarian labor recruitment, despite the official existence of an American democratic polity. In his 2008 book on this antidemocratic phenome-

Table 2.1. Black and white male employees in manufacturing industries in select southern states, 1930

State	White males		Black males	
	Number	Percentage	Number	Percentage
Alabama	105,746	21.4	55,009	19.6
Arkansas	51,312	12.8	17,331	11.7
Florida	76,611	24.9	36,110	25.6
Georgia	124,258	23.0	64,149	20.6
Louisiana	85,976	22.1	43,013	18.3
Mississippi	40,789	13.7	30,339	9.6
North Carolina	167,711	27.1	46,840	19.0
South Carolina	79,814	29.8	31,969	15.0
Tennessee	128,001	20.8	32,583	22.1
Texas	236,168	18.0	38,607	14.5

Source: Data from Horace Mann Bond, *The Education of the Negro in the American Social Order* (New York: Prentice Hall, 1934), 211.

Note: Percentages are of all white and black males employed in manufacturing industries in each state.

non, *Slavery by Another Name: The Re-enslavement of Black Americans from the Civil War to World War II,* historian Douglas Blackmon describes how this prison-based labor system of black workers functioned for three-quarters of a century throughout the South, in every manner of agriculture and industrial production, most prominently cotton and tobacco, various food crops (tomatoes, melons, corn, etc.), iron ore/coal/lime mining, iron and steel production, railroad production, brickmaking, and wood processing.

Blackmon extensively documents the cruelty and brutality of the massive official and unofficial armed force applied to control the post–Reconstruction era prison-based labor system well into the twentieth century. Black prisoners, like their enslaved ancestors only a generation or two before them, worked for no pay for white overseers who profited handsomely. This system, in its origins, was the draconian, authoritarian underbelly of America's industrial robber-baron era, so to speak, and it generated vast industrial and commercial wealth in states like Georgia, Alabama, Arkansas, Mississippi, South Carolina, and North Carolina.[13]

Thus, one cannot overemphasize the core fact that *the late-nineteenth and early twentieth-century context of an emergent African American modern leadership and the socially ravaged black masses it represented was widely oppressive and beleaguered.* While books written at the time by progressive activist intellectuals like Jacob Riis and Upton Sinclair revealed the subhuman conditions faced by white immigrant workers in late nineteenth- and early twentieth-century robber-baron industrial America, books like Blackmon's and others' (e.g., David Oshinsky's 1996 work *Worse than Slavery: Parchman Farm and the Ordeal of Jim Crow*) elucidate the even more gruesome plight of black workers during the same era in the South, where the vast majority of African Americans resided.[14]

Coterminous with the desperate economic situation of black folks of this period loomed a devastating 90 percent illiteracy rate and nearly zero-level political participation status, not to mention that judicial protection of the black folks' human rights was nearly nonexistent. Vigilante harassment and violence by whites against blacks went unchecked. Worst of all was the widespread lynching of black men; many thousands of lynchings occurred, some officially recorded and some not. The sociologist Gunnar Myrdal minced few words when, in the Carnegie

Foundation's 1944 book *An American Dilemma: The Negro Problem and Modern Democracy*, he summarized the wide-ranging and vicious violation of the basic human rights of black folks in the South from 1880 to the 1950s: "It is the custom in the South to permit whites to resort to violence and threats of violence against the life, personal security, property and freedom of movement of Negroes. . . . There is a whole variety of behavior, ranging from mild admonition to murder, which the white man may exercise to control Negroes. . . . *Any white man can strike or beat a Negro, steal or destroy his property, cheat him in a transaction and even take his life without much fear of legal reprisal.*"[15]

This is a useful juncture at which to mention a few core aggregate sociodemographic attributes of black Americans as that ethnic community entered the twentieth century. As shown in Table 2.2, there were 9.8 million Negroes in the American population by 1910, with the vast majority—some 8.7 million—living in the South. By the 1930 U.S. Census, what the historian Isabel Wilkerson calls the "Great Black Migration" in her 2010 book, *The Warmth of Other Suns*, resulted in a major black population shift to the North, with 2.4 million residing there out of a total 11.8 million Negroes nationwide. The number of blacks living in the North had more than doubled in twenty years' time. Furthermore, as the African American sociologist Horace Mann Bond observed in his pioneering 1934 book *The Education of the Negro in the American Social Order:* "The migration of Negroes to the North has been a cityward movement. . . . In these cities, 1,513,834 Negroes [are] living. Nearly 90 percent of the Negro population of the North was located in urban centers. . . . In 1930, the number of Negroes living in urban areas [nationwide] had increased to 5,193,913. This number represents 43.7 percent of the Negro population for the entire country."[16]

As the fledgling modern African American social system entered the twentieth century—just a generation and a half after the Civil War—the black intelligentsia or professional stratum confronted a perplexing and monumental issue: How do you fashion modern leadership processes for the formerly enslaved black Americans?

We can approach this monumental issue by hypothesizing two essential functions for modern ethnic-group leadership in American society. One generic leadership function can be characterized by the term that anthropologists often use: "social organization." What might be called

Table 2.2. U.S. black population by region, 1910, 1920, and 1930

Region	1910	1920	1930
South	8,749,427	8,912,231	9,361,577
North	1,027,674	1,472,309	2,409,219
West	50,662	78,591	120,347
Total	9,827,763	10,463,131	11,891,143

Source: Data from Monroe N. Work, *The Negro Year Book: An Annual Encyclopedia of the Negro, 1931–1932* (Tuskegee, AL: Negro Yearbook Publishing, 1932), 338.

the *social-organization leadership function* is concerned with building up the institutional infrastructure of modern ethnic-group development by nurturing or cultivating agencies such as churches, mutual-aid societies, artisan organizations, agrarian organizations, trade unions, and fraternal/sororal associations. Through the development and expansion of its own institutional infrastructure, a modern ethnic group can realize its growth in civil society.

A second generic leadership function for modern ethnic-group development on a national level is to fashion-status-enhancing benefits and rights-enhancing benefits for an ethnic group. Thus, this might be called a *mobilization-type leadership function*. Accordingly, in the post–Reconstruction era of the evolution of African American society, it was through processes associated with the mobilization-type leadership function—especially what historians dubbed civil rights activism processes—that status-enhancing and rights-enhancing goals for black Americans were realized.

It happened that for African Americans generally, the federal government's betrayal of Reconstruction policy from the 1880s onward erected a nearly insurmountable barrier to the natural growth of mobilization-type leadership processes. In the South, where the vast majority of black people lived between 1900 and the 1950s, mobilization-type leadership was brutally restricted by authoritarian racist practices, police practices, and especially vigilante terrorism. One of the many debilitating consequences of the South's authoritarian practices against blacks was that by 1940, only 5 percent of voting-age African Americans there had been allowed to become registered voters.[17] For all intents and purposes, they were denied participation in the electoral process.

During this same period, although nakedly authoritarian constraints against African Americans did not exist in the North, or at least were not blatantly institutionalized, numerous white-hegemonic social and political practices resulted in grave deficiencies in modern development among northern black communities. In fact, by the 1960s, a massive intervention by the federal government—through federal legislation and administrative practices—was required to break down the overwhelming obstacles to modern development that bedeviled African American society during the first half of the twentieth century. Prior to federal intervention, however, most African Americans living in southern states had to rely almost exclusively on the embryonic form of modern ethnic-group leadership—*social-organization-type leadership*. Only in the North during the first half of the twentieth century were some aspects of the mobilization-type ethnic-group leadership available to African Americans. Meanwhile, all white groups, whatever their ethnicity, had access to mobilization-type leadership, which meant their citizens were full-fledged political participants who could compete for public office in cities, counties, and states and at the federal level.

The key African American personality associated with the social-organization-type leadership pattern from the late 1880s until his death in 1915 was Booker T. Washington, who was educated at Hampton Institute in Virginia and was the founder and president of Tuskegee Institute in Alabama. At the forefront of the mobilization-type ethnic-group leadership pattern, in stark contrast to Washington, stood the Fisk University and Harvard University–educated founder of African American progressivism W. E. B. Du Bois. Beginning in 1905 with the birth of the Niagara Movement and lasting through the next several decades, the ideological contours of the black intelligentsia were shaped by competition between these two generic paradigms for modern ethnic-group leadership.

It was the persona of Booker T. Washington that generated the modern black leadership ideas that inspired the first major ideological fissures within the nascent twentieth-century black intelligentsia. Historians have attached the term "political accommodationism" to Washington's methodology, which essentially espoused a "don't-challenge-America's-racist-oligarchy" message.

If we could transport ourselves back 117 years to Atlanta, Georgia, in 1895, we could experience for ourselves an extraordinary event for black Americans, an event that ultimately shaped the contours of political leadership dynamics for the emerging African American society from the late 1890s through the 1940s. That event was the Cotton States and International Exposition in Atlanta—commonly called the Atlanta Exposition—and the keynote speaker was Booker T. Washington. In what historians have dubbed his historic "Atlanta Compromise" address, Washington told an audience of white capitalists—the leading figures of an exploding American industrial economy—that, regarding a troublesome American working class, all they had to worry about was the white proletariat. As for the black working class, Washington assured his audience that, under his ideological influence, black workers would remain politically quiescent.

At the time of Washington's Atlanta Compromise address, the Negro working class was totally excluded from full citizenship rights and thus from the American social contract. By the early twentieth century, more than half of the Negro working class comprised an agrarian proletariat. It was a Negro peonage-agrarian class that endured authoritarian domination within the mainly cotton and tobacco agriculture industry in the South, and *this class produced the bulk of the massive wealth derived from southern capitalist agriculture from the 1880s to World War II.* The remainder of the Negro working-class sector consisted of millions of unskilled domestic laborers in middle-class and elite white homes in the South and North, as well as many more millions of unskilled subproletarian black factory workers.

And what exactly did Washington tell the capitalist elites at the 1895 Atlanta Exposition about the future status of these African Americans, 90 percent of whom were ravaged by poverty and disenfranchisement as America was entering the twentieth century? First, Washington belittled the possibility of advancing the development of the country's poor black proletarians through the application of democratic citizenship and political rights. This no doubt cheered the industry leaders in the audience.

Second, Washington addressed black Americans generally. He advised them to forget about citizenship rights and political rights: leave them alone! Or, to use Washington's homespun language, "Start . . . a dairy farm or truck garden." And in case his meaning wasn't clear enough to all in attendance, Washington resorted to more florid language—he performed, so to speak. He raised his hands and proclaimed that *in matters of political rights and citizenship rights, white folks and black folks will be "as separate as the fingers on my hands."*[18]

Four years later, Booker T. Washington, writing in his 1899 book *The Future of the American Negro,* elaborated on the conservative accommodationism he encouraged black people to embrace: "I believe that the past and present teach but one lesson—to the Negro's [white] friends and to the Negro himself—[namely,] that there is but one hope of solution [to the race problem]: and that is for the Negro in every part of America to resolve from henceforth that he will throw aside every nonessential [citizenship and human rights] and cling only to essential—that his [the Negro's] pillar of fire by night and pillar of cloud by day shall be property, economy, education, and Christian character. To us [Negroes] just now these are the wheat, all else the chaff."[19]

In response to this Bookerite accommodationism leadership methodology, Du Bois and his allies in the black intelligentsia fashioned a black leadership methodology based on civil rights activism. Whereas Washington's accommodationism was a form of what I earlier characterized as the social-organization-type leadership function, the Du Boisian civil rights activism leadership methodology was a form of the mobilization-type leadership function. This was the leadership function concerned with *status-enhancing benefits and rights-enhancing benefits for black people, who were oppressed by America's racist oligarchy.*

Du Bois' circle of allies included a talented cadre of African American intelligentsia personalities, among them William Monroe Trotter (editor of the Negro weekly the *Boston Guardian*), Archibald Grimké (a lawyer), Reverdy Ransom (an African Methodist Episcopal clergyman), and F. H. M. Murray and L. M. Hershaw (two federal civil servants who in 1907 helped Du Bois found the Niagara Movement's unofficial magazine, *Horizon*).[20]

Inasmuch as Du Bois was a precocious and assertive intellectual member of his circle, it was he who first formulated in print the ideological and political precepts underlying the mobilization-type black leadership methodology. This Du Bois did initially in 1903 in *The Souls of Black Folk*—the quintessential text of African American progressivism. In chapter 3, "Of Mr. Booker T. Washington and Others," Du Bois refers to his activist colleagues in the intelligentsia as "the other class of Negroes who cannot agree with Mr. Booker T. Washington." He then proceeds to lay out a bold mobilization-type black leadership methodology that challenged Bookerite accommodationism head on. Though first magnanimously expressing that his activist circle "of men in black leadership honor Mr. Booker T. Washington for his attitude of conciliation toward the white South," Du Bois goes on to identify the indispensable principles of a progressive black leadership nexus with the poor Negro masses.

That nexus, Du Bois believed, was premised on fidelity with black people's honor. Du Bois writes that he and his colleagues "insist that the way to truth and right lies in straightforward honesty, not in indiscriminate flattery; [it lies] . . . in remembering that only a firm adherence to their higher ideals and aspirations will keep those ideals within the realm of possibility." Du Bois then elaborates this anti-Washingtonian perspective: "They [Du Bois' activist circle] are absolutely certain that the way for a people to gain their reasonable rights is not by voluntarily throwing them away and insisting that they do not want them; that the way for a people to gain respect is not by continually belittling and ridiculing themselves; that, on the contrary, *Negroes must insist continually, in season and out of season, that voting is necessary to modern manhood, that color discrimination is barbarism, and that black boys need education as well as white boys.*"[21]

Thus, for Du Bois in 1903, these core ideological ingredients of a progressive leadership nexus with the poor Negro masses amounted to a moral imperative. As such, they defined what might be called the "obligation-and-responsibility" contours of the evolving twentieth-century African American intelligentsia. As Du Bois formulates this crucial issue in chapter 3: "[By] failing . . . to state plainly and unequivocally the legitimate demands of their people, . . . the thinking classes of American Negroes would shirk a heavy responsibility—a responsibility to themselves, a responsibility to the darker races of men whose future depends so largely on this American [Negro] experiment."[22] In operational terms, therefore, Du Bois was openly calling for a leadership methodology that was the diametric opposite of the Bookerite accommodationism leadership methodology.

Accordingly, as Du Bois is about to close chapter 3, he draws a line in the sand vis-à-vis Washington's accommodationism. He proclaims firmly and candidly that his activist leadership circle could never accept Washington's accommodationist proposition of "reconciliation" with the American racist oligarchy. After all, such a reconciliation would require black people to put on hold indefinitely the acquisition of full citizenship status, political rights, and human rights. As Du Bois formulated this crucial issue in 1903: "If that [Bookerite] reconciliation is to be marked by the industrial slavery and civic death of . . . black men, with permanent legislation into a position of inferiority, then those black men, if they are really men, are called upon by every consideration of patriotism and loyalty to oppose such a course by all civilized methods, even though such opposition involves disagreement with Mr. Booker T. Washington. *We have no right to sit silently by while the inevitable seeds are sown for a harvest of disaster to our children, black and white.*"[23]

It can be mentioned here that Cornel West, in his seminal collection of essays *Democracy Matters,* writes that it was this decree that defined Du Bois as an "Emersonian democratic intellectual." West uses that term to refer to a generic attribute of the progressive humanist ethos in American intellectual culture, to wit, the attribute of unmasking and challenging inequality. "For Emerson, to be a democratic [intellectual] is to speak out on uncomfortable truths," West explains. "To be an active player in public discourse is to be thrown into life's contingency and fragility with the heavy baggage of history and tradition, baggage like the American legacies of race and empire."[24]

Thus, when Du Bois challenged Washington's accommodationist leadership methodology by delineating the principles of his progressive alternative, he was unmasking and challenging racist inequality against black folks. Or, in West's words, Du Bois was "lift[ing] the veil over the invisibility of black individuals, community, and society [who were] denied by white supremacist America."[25]

When he was writing *The Souls of Black Folk,* the young Du Bois was probably unaware that he was functioning as a so-called Emersonian democratic intellectual. Nevertheless, his discourse in *Souls* paved the way for what in two years would be the 1905 Niagara Movement. As it happened, at that historic gathering at Niagara Falls more than a hundred years ago, where twenty-nine progressive black intelligentsia personalities convened—on the Canadian side of the falls because no white hotel on the American side would house them—the principles of what became "Du Boisian progressivism" were formalized.

The civil rights activism principles drafted by Du Bois for the Niagara conference resolutions were as follows: "We will not be satisfied to take one jot or tittle less than our full manhood rights. We claim for ourselves every single right that belongs to a freeborn American, political, civil, and social; and until we get these rights we will never cease to protest and assail the ears of America. The battle we wage is not for ourselves alone, but for all true Americans. It is a fight for ideals." Among the specific goals sought by those attending the 1905 Niagara Movement conference:

First. We would vote; with the right to vote goes everything.
Second. We want discrimination in public accommodation to cease.
Third. We claim the right of freemen to walk, talk and be with them that wish to be with us.
Fourth. We want our children educated.
Fifth. We want the laws enforced against rich as well as poor; against Capitalist as well as Laborer; against white as well as black.
These [then] are some of the chief things we want. How shall we get them? By voting where we may vote; by persistent unceasing agitation; by hammering at the truth; by sacrifice and work.[26]

Though each of the Niagara Movement's policy resolutions likely had equivalent status, the fourth—"We want our children educated"—can be viewed as particularly important. Why? Because by the year 1905, black Americans possessed a minuscule literate and educated community— especially at the college level—from which a viable modern leadership cadre could evolve. As the Emancipation era closed and the twentieth century commenced, the paucity of college-educated black Americans was underscored by Du Bois in his pathbreaking 1903 essay "The Talented Tenth," in which he presented data showing that fewer than two thousand "college-bred Negroes" graduated in the 1899–1900 academic year. This meant that the road to an effective modern African American leadership sector capable of challenging America's racist oligarchy would be a rocky one.

What have been the key dimensions of the Du Boisian civil rights activism leadership legacy? The legacy was multidimensional, which is to say this legacy, from the Niagara Movement in 1905 to the 1940s, was more than the public policy of integration associated with the national-level goals of the NAACP. Above all, the Du Boisian civil rights activism leadership legacy had what might be called black-communitarian leadership dimensions.

I use the term "black-communitarian leadership" to refer to middle-class African Americans' activist use of their social-class capabilities to advance interclass black civil society mobilization—a mobilization mode that emphasizes the needs of the African American working-class sector as commensurate with the overall interests of middle-class African Americans. This, I suggest, is the core ideological and moral predilection that undergirds Du Bois' foundational design of twentieth-century African American progressivism—a black progressivism that he broadly articulated in his classic *The Souls of Black Folk*.

Although it is not adequately recognized among analysts of Du Bois' leadership legacy, Du Bois actually entertained a kind of two-tier black leadership orientation. On the top tier, Du Bois articulated his civil rights integration–black leadership orientation at official NAACP gatherings and through the pages of the organization's journal, the *Crisis,* which he founded and edited from 1910 to 1934. For the second tier of Du Bois' black leadership orientation, he simultaneously propagated a black-communitarian activism leadership outlook, which held that middle-class African Americans and their civil society agencies (that is, churches, civic associations, women's organizations, business groups, and professional groups) *had a special obligation and responsibility to engage in outreach to the black working-class sector, thereby assisting its modern social advancement.*

Du Bois first articulated the ingredients of a black-communitarian leadership ethos in 1903 in *The Souls of Black Folk*. He expressed those ingredients not in the social-science language of black-communitarian leadership that I'm using here but, rather, using the marvelously haunting and lyrical English prose he first experimented with in writing this classic book.

The following passage from *Souls*—from chapter 4, "Of the Meaning of Progress," perhaps its most intellectually deft and humanitarianly forceful—reveals the young Du Bois' conversion to something akin to a black-communitarian leadership ethos. First, he delineates a portrait of the environmental and agrarian social system existing in the post–Reconstruction era southern state of Tennessee in the summer of 1886:

> Once upon a time I taught school in the hills of Tennessee, where the broad dark vale of the Mississippi begins to roll and crumple to greet the Alleghenies. I was a Fisk student then, and all Fisk men thought that Tennessee—beyond the Veil—was theirs alone, and in vacation time they sallied forth in lusty bands to meet the county school-commissioners. Young and happy, I too went, and I shall not soon forget that summer, seventeen years ago. First there was a Teachers' Institute at the county-seat . . . [where]

distinguished guests of the superintendent taught the teachers fractions and spelling . . . white teachers in the morning, Negroes at night.

. . . There came a day when all the teachers left the Institute and began the hunt for schools. . . . I secured [a school]. . . . The schoolhouse was a log hut, where Colonel Wheeler used to shelter his corn. It sat in a lot behind a rail fence and thorn bushes, near the sweetest of springs. There was an entrance where a door once was, and . . . a massive rickety fireplace. . . .

Furniture was scarce. A pale blackboard crouched in the corner. My desk was made of three boards . . . and my chair, borrowed from the landlady, had to be returned every night. Seats for the children . . . [were] rough plank benches without backs.[27]

Second, still in lyrical cadence, the young Du Bois relates his deeply emotional and spiritual nexus with the frightful plight of the South's socially ravaged Negro agrarian masses in the Emancipation era. He reveals a spiritual quest for outreach to assist this oppressed population, whom he meets face-to-face in the summers of 1886 and 1887—hence the term "black communitarian" that I use to characterize Du Bois' fervent desire to identify with and assist the Emancipation-era Negro.

It was a hot morning late in July when the school opened. I trembled when I heard the patter of little feet down the dusty road, and saw the growing row of dark solemn faces and bright eager eyes facing me. . . . There they sat, nearly thirty of them, on the rough benches, their faces shading from a pale cream to a deep brown, the little feet bare and swinging, the eyes full of expectation, with here and there a twinkle of mischief, and the hands grasping Webster's blue-back spelling book. I loved my school, and find the faith the children had in the wisdom of their teacher was truly marvelous. . . . *For two summers I lived in this little world.*[28]

It is clear, I think, that the foregoing passage intimates something like a black-communitarian leadership aesthetic dwelling in Du Bois' soul. To be more precise, it suggests a core ethno-ideological predisposition that informed nascent black-communitarian feelings that dwelled within Du Bois during the summers of 1886 and 1887. Those ethno-ideological predilections, in turn, became manifest on "a hot morning late in July [1886] when [Du Bois' public school] opened." As one reads the passage in which he describes the children and their "dark solemn faces," Du Bois' epiphany-like response is palpable.

That epiphany, in turn, eventually shaped the political contours of the evolving twentieth-century Du Boisian political mobilization leadership dynamic. Central to that dynamic was, above all, the intermeshing of the Talented Tenth's accumulated capabilities, on the one hand, with the overall modern development needs of the working-class black masses, on the other. Thus, it is suggested that a Du Boisian black-communitarian leadership motif is a narrative aesthetic theme throughout *The Souls of Black Folk*.

Later, in a series of articles in the *Crisis* during 1933 and 1934, Du Bois elaborated on his black-communitarian leadership ethos. There he discussed the need for what he called the "race-conscious black cooperating together in his own institutions and movements [so as to] . . . organize and conduct enterprises." He went on to say that what might be called black-communitarian activism was nothing new or radical for black folks. Why? Because, said Du Bois, "the vast majority of the Negroes in the United States are born in colored homes, educated in separate colored schools, attend separate colored churches, marry colored mates, and find their amusements in colored YMCAs and YWCAs."[29]

Now, Du Bois used the everyday milieu of the nooks and crannies of black civil society agencies to propagate his black-communitarian activism leadership orientation. He did this via black churches, civic associations, professional organizations, women's organizations, and the campuses of Negro colleges. I first encountered Du Bois at the Mary Dod Brown Memorial Chapel at Lincoln University in the spring term of my freshman year. The president of Lincoln University, Horace Mann Bond, invited Du Bois, along with Mary McLeod Bethune, a founding official of the National Council of Negro Women in the 1920s, to address the Sunday convocation, and one of the topics mentioned by Du Bois related to the black-communitarian leadership dynamic. New York University historian David Levering Lewis' seminal 2000 biography of Du Bois, *W. E. B. Du Bois: The Fight for Equality and the American Century, 1919–1963,* includes accounts of Du Bois' numerous trips around the country during the 1920s and 1930s for the purpose of addressing black civic and cultural agencies. In those speeches Du Bois often addressed the black-communitarian leadership pattern.

One occasion when Du Bois articulated a version of the black-communitarian leadership outlook occurred in the 1920s during a visit to the black community in Charleston, South Carolina. As reported in Rochester University anthropologist Karen Fields' coauthored memoir of her hundred-year-old grandmother, Mamie Gavin Fields, Du Bois expressed a black-communitarian leadership perspective during an automobile tour of Charleston:

> Once Charleston did have a black-owned hotel [said Mamie Fields], called the Hotel Hametic. The Hametic was on Drake Street and East Bay, near the Cross River. W. E. B. Du Bois was the first person of note we entertained there. I was on the committee that drove him around to see various places. We took him, as we thought, for a "grand tour" of our city—the Custom House (from before the Civil War), the old Slave Market, the Provost's Dungeon (from the days before the Revolution), and so forth and so on. I can see now that we weren't thinking very well. Most of those places that we showed off with all our city pride had to do with slavery, which brought our people to South Carolina in the first place. And then we drove past in the car, explaining that this was this and that was that, because colored people were no allowed to go inside. In the car, Dr. Du Bois got restless. After a while, he set us straight: "All you are showing me is what the white people did. I want to see what the colored people of Charleston have built." So then we took him to the Negro "Ys", and what do you think? That didn't satisfy him. He said the "Y" was under national auspices.... [A] city like Charleston [and its black folks] ought to be able to do more locally than it was doing. I never forgot that lesson. Oh, Du Bois was hard on us, but it woke us up. He was telling us to take pride in our accomplishments, and he wanted us to strive to do more. So we took him to our churches, our civic organizations, and our black businesses. Of course, he was staying in one of them.[30]

From the 1920s through the 1950s, middle-class agencies in black civil society fashioned black-communitarian leadership patterns that assisted overall African American social uplift. In doing so, many middle-class African Americans in both the North and South entwined their social-class capabilities with the social mobility needs of working-class African Americans. By the 1930s, an important segment of middle-class African Americans in the North had employed their churches, civic, and professional associations in this manner.

Some of the earliest evidence of the middle-class black-communitarian leadership dynamic was reported in Carter G. Woodson's pioneering 1934 study *The Negro Professional Man and the Community*. Woodson's book, which was produced by the Association for the Study of Negro Life and History, which he founded in 1915, presents data on the scale and forms of the communitarian-type leadership role by the African American middle class by the 1930s. Woodson also presents

U.S. Census Bureau data on African American professional occupations by the 1930s. These data are shown in Table 2.3, and data for selected cities are shown in Table 2.4. In an overview observation on the black-communitarian type leadership role of African American medical doctors by the 1930s, Carter Woodson remarks as follows:

> Black physicians . . . have not restricted their social uplift efforts merely to matters of health. They have seen other needs of the community and have done much to meet them. They have been especially interested in the program of the Y.M.C.A., Y.W.C.A., and the Urban League. In almost all these cases these institutions have been made up in part of the Negro professional class or they have depended to a great extent on the support which they have obtained from Negroes thus established. The Negro physicians, like the Negro dentists, lawyers, pharmacists, and nurses, have played their part in such efforts. . . . The data compiled [by Woodson's survey of 1,051 doctors] show that 39 percent of the physicians support these institutions [Y.M.C.A., Y.W.C.A., Urban League] as contributing members and some in addition as directors.[31]

Table 2.3. White-collar occupations held by blacks, 1890–1930

Occupation	1890	1900	1910	1920	1930
Architect, draftsman, inventor	44	52	154	195	230
Artist, art teacher	150	236	329	259	381
Author, editor, journalist	134	210	220	251	406
Chemist, metallurgist	—	—	123	207	331
College faculty	—	—	242	1,063	3,131
Clergy	12,139	15,228	17,996	19,571	24,560
Dentist	120	212	478	1,019	1,748
Doctor	909	1,743	3,409	3,885	3,770
Lawyer	431	728	915	950	1,230
Librarian	—	—	15	22	150
Music teacher, musician	1,881	3,915	5,606	5,902	10,583
Photographer	190	247	404	608	411
Social worker	—	—	501	1,231	1,313
Teacher	15,100	21,267	29,432	35,442	54,439
Nurse	—	—	2,433	3,331	5,589

Source: Data from Carter G. Woodson, *The Negro Professional Man in the Community* (Washington, DC: Associated Publishers, 1934), 33.

Table 2.4. White-collar occupations held by blacks in select cities, 1930

Occupation	Atlanta	Baltimore	Chicago	Cleveland	Detroit	New York	Philadelphia
Clergy	285	265	388	121	193	398	382
Dentist	14	31	134	37	42	145	101
Doctor	55	82	281	41	78	185	142
Lawyer	7	29	175	38	51	106	30
Teacher	534	888	452	101	103	638	553
Nurse	195	126	236	30	92	734	153

Source: Data from Carter G. Woodson, *The Negro Professional Man and the Community* (Washington, DC: Associated Publishers, 1934), 335–340.

On the basis of a survey of 1,051 African American medical doctors, Woodson's research project reported a broad range of social-advancement connections that those doctors (nearly two-fifths of them) had with African American community agencies during the 1930s: 9.2 percent had ties with health groups and clinics; 7 percent, with antituberculosis organizations; 9.4 percent, with the Y.M.C.A; 10.7 percent, with the NAACP; 12.5 percent with welfare leagues; 3 percent, with the Boy Scouts; 5.3 percent, with community centers, settlement houses, and social agencies; and 3 percent, with black public hospitals and the National Negro Health Movement.[32]

Another important aspect of the professional individuals studied by Woodson's research project requires mention here: the vast majority of African Americans who had obtained college-level education by the 1930s did so not at white-majority but at black-majority public and private institutions of higher education. A select list of black-majority institutions of higher education by the 1930s is shown in Table 2.5.

Indeed, when my age cohort of African American high school students entered college in the post–World War II period as I did—being the fourth generation of twentieth-century college-going African Americans—some 90 percent were still entering Negro colleges. Virtually no white higher-education institution in the South admitted African American students in 1949 (save Berea College in Kentucky), and in the North, neither public universities—where most white students attended college—nor private institutions admitted a significant number of African American students. For example, Penn State University, Pennsylvania's main public university, admitted fewer than forty African Americans in 1949. To put this number in perspective, when I entered Lincoln University as a freshman

Table 2.5. Attributes of select black colleges in the 1930s (average per year)

Colleges	Location	Church association	Students	Faculty	High school enrollment*
Allen University	Columbia, SC	M.E.	150	36	250
Benedict College	Columbia, SC	Baptist	239	29	120
Bishop College	Marshall, TX	Baptist	388	28	41
Clark University	Atlanta, GA	M.E.	306	30	184
Fisk University	Nashville, TN	Cong.	521	35	—
Hampton Institute	Hampton, VA	—	788	125	282
Howard University	Washington, DC	—	2,183	196	—
Johnson C. Smith University	Charlotte, NC	Presb.	304	23	—
Knoxville College	Knoxville, TN	Presb.	280	21	28
Lane College	Jackson, TN	C.M.E.	242	22	—
LeMoyne College	Memphis, TN	Cong.	166	20	212
Lincoln University	Oxford, PA	Presb.	341	20	—
Livingston College	Salisbury, NC	A.M.E.Z.	219	29	21
Morehouse College	Atlanta, GA	Baptist	369	24	73
Morgan College	Baltimore, MD	M.E.	474	24	—
Morris Brown University	Atlanta, GA	A.M.E.	178	27	179
New Orleans College	New Orleans, LA	M.E.	455	35	209
Saint Augustine's College	Raleigh, NC	Episcopal	158	25	125
Samuel Houston College	Austin, TX	M.E.	376	24	32
Shaw University	Raleigh, NC	Baptist	317	22	—
Spelman College	Atlanta, GA	Baptist	239	37	148
Straight College	New Orleans, LA	Cong.	319	31	317
Talladega College	Talladega, AL	Cong.	256	64	135
Texas College	Tyler, TX	C.M.E.	170	17	157
Tuskegee Institute	Tuskegee, AL	—	466	253	720
Virginia Union University	Richmond, VA	Baptist	585	25	48
Wilberforce University	Wilberforce, OH	A.M.E.	280	81	155
Wiley College	Marshall, TX	M.E.	426	32	—

Source: Data from Monroe N. Work, *The Negro Year Book: An Annual Encyclopedia of the Negro, 1931–1932* (Tuskegee, AL: Negro Yearbook Publishing, 1932), 233.

Note: Many black colleges were founded by religious denominations, which contributed to their annual budgets. Church associations are denoted as the following: M.E., White Methodist Episcopal Church; Baptist, Negro Baptist Church denomination; Cong., White Congregationalist Church; Presb., White Presbyterian Church; C.M.E., Colored Methodist Episcopal Church; A.M.E.Z., African Methodist Episcopal Zion Church; and A.M.E., African Methodist Episcopal Church.

*Many black colleges from the 1870s to World War II operated high schools for black youth in southern states, and they were often of top-tier quality.

in 1949, I joined some six hundred other African American students. In 1949 when the novelist Toni Morrison, the psychologist Florence Ladd, and the playwright Le Roi Jones (later, Amiri Baraka) entered their first year at Howard University, they joined several thousand African American students enrolled there. In short, *until the 1970s the evolving twentieth-century African American society depended largely on black-majority institutions of higher education for the ranks of its middle-class and professional-class sector.* This was especially so at the level of under-graduate education and also for professional training in such fields as law, medicine, dentistry, pharmacy, and nursing during the first sixty years of the twentieth century.[33]

Interestingly enough, there was one important social development outcome during the first-half of the twentieth-century African American society that stemmed from the fact that black-majority colleges shoul-dered an important part of the burden of training most of the African American middle class. That social development outcome was that many African American professionals functioned within the social realm of Af-rican American life. Accordingly, many of the intellectual, science, techni-cal, organizational and modern-systemic skills they acquired at black institutions of higher education became available to assist the social ad-vancement needs of the overall African American society. Eventually, with the success of African Americans' political mobilization leadership led by the NAACP in generating political pressures in the 1960s for fed-eral antisegregation laws, broad opportunities became available for a new egalitarian stage in structuring black people's status in American life, namely, the stage of viably integrating the African American profes-sional sector.

It should also be mentioned that after gaining their first degrees at black institutions of higher education, a good number of those college-trained African Americans pursued postgraduate degrees at mainstream white-majority universities for professional training. In 1957, the soci-ologist Horace Mann Bond published a study of postgraduate degrees gained by graduates of Lincoln University in Pennsylvania, where Bond was president from 1945 to 1957. The data from Bond's study are shown in Table 2.6. Bond's data start with the Lincoln graduation class of 1912 and conclude with the class of 1953. Of the fifty Lincoln Uni-versity graduates with doctorate degrees listed in Bond's data, seventeen gained their doctorates in the sciences (biology, chemistry, mathematics,

pathology, parasitology, and physics), representing one-third of the doctorates gained by Lincoln graduates at white universities between 1912
and 1953.[34]

This achievement, I suggest, was solid evidence of the academic strength
of the top tier of black institutions of higher education during the first sixty
years of the twentieth century. I have in mind black institutions of higher
education like Atlanta University (Georgia), Clark University (Georgia),
Dillard University (Louisiana), Fisk University (Tennessee), Hampton Institute (Virginia), Howard University (Washington, D.C.), Lincoln University
(Pennsylvania), Morehouse College (Georgia), Morgan State College
(Maryland), Morris Brown College (Georgia), Spelman College (Georgia), Talladega College (Alabama), Tuskegee Institute (Alabama), Virginia Union University, West Virginia State University, Wilberforce
University (Ohio), Wiley College (Texas), and Xavier University (Louisiana). During the first sixty years of the twentieth century, a good

Table 2.6. Doctoral degrees of Lincoln University graduates, 1912–1953

Name	Lincoln class	Doctorate degree	University (field)	Year received
J. S. Price	1912	D.Ed.	Harvard (education)	1940
A. S. Beckham	1915	Ph.D.	New York University (psychology)	1934
F. C. Summer	1915	Ph.D.	Clark University—Massachusetts (psychology)	1920
H. D. Gregg	1916	Ph.D.	University of Pennsylvania (education)	1936
F. T. Wilson	1921	D.Ed.	Columbia University (education)	1937
Horace Mann Bond	1923	D.Ed.	University of Chicago (education)	1936
R. S. Jason	1924	Ph.D.	University of Chicago (pathology)	1932
H. A. Poindexter	1924	Ph.D.	Columbia University (parasitology)	1932
W. E. Farrison	1926	Ph.D.	Ohio State University (English)	1936
M. S. Briscoe	1926	Ph.D.	Catholic University (biology)	1950
Laurence Foster	1926	Ph.D.	University of Pennsylvania (anthropology)	1931
J. S. Lee	1927	Ph.D.	University of Michigan (biology)	1939
J. L. Scott	1927	Ph.D.	University of Pittsburgh (education)	1942
J. O. Hopson	1927	Ph.D.	University of Pittsburgh (English)	1948
F. S. Belcher	1928	Ph.D.	Yale University (English)	1946
J. E. Dorsey	1928	D.Ed.	Columbia University (music education)	1945
J. L. Williams	1929	Ph.D.	University of Pennsylvania (entomology)	1941
Mark Parks	1929	Ph.D.	New York University (biology)	1953

Table 2.6 (continued)

Name	Lincoln class	Doctorate degree	University (field)	Year received
Toye G. Davis	1930	Ph.D.	Harvard University (zoology)	1940
William Fontaine	1930	Ph.D.	University of Pennsylvania (philosophy)	1936
T. B. O'Daniel	1930	Ph.D.	University of Ottawa (English)	1956
J. H. Taylor	1930	Ph.D.	University of Delaware (chemistry)	1953
F. A. De Costa	1931	Ph.D.	University of Pennsylvania (education)	1954
J. M. Smith	1931	Ph.D.	University of Iowa (philosophy)	1941
G. W. Hunter	1931	Ph.D.	Penn State University (chemistry)	1946
J. O. Lee	1931	Th.D.	Union Seminary–Virginia (theology)	1946
L. D. Johnson	1931	Ph.D.	University of Pennsylvania (chemistry)	1954
O. J. Chapman	1932	Ph.D.	Ohio State University (education)	1940
H. E. Wright	1932	Ph.D.	Ohio State University (psychology)	1947
F. R. Brown	1932	D.Ed.	Columbia University (religious studies)	1956
Henry G. Cornwell	1933	Ph.D.	University of Pennsylvania (psychology)	1952
H. Alfred Farrell	1934	Ph.D.	Ohio State University (English)	1948
G. W. Keilholtz	1935	Ph.D.	University of Washington (physics)	1946
A. H. Wheeler	1936	Ph.D.	University of Michigan (public health)	1949
C. J. Reynolds	1936	D.Ed.	Harvard University (education)	1951
Charles Blalock	1937	Ph.D.	University of Pennsylvania (social work)	1955
Julius Taylor	1938	Ph.D.	University of Pennsylvania (physics)	1948
I. G. Newton	1939	Ph.D.	University of Pennsylvania (political science)	1956
J. E. Closter	1941	Ph.D.	University of Pittsburgh (economics)	1955
G. S. Shockley	1942	D.Ed.	Columbia University (education)	1946
J. N. Okongwu	1942	D.Ed.	Columbia University (education)	1946
William Fitzjohn	1943	D.Ed.	Columbia University (education)	1946
T. J. Edwards	1948	Ph.D.	Temple University (education)	1955
A. R. Young	1949	Ph.D.	University of Pennsylvania (chemistry)	1955
Lonnie Cross	1949	Ph.D.	Cornell University (mathematics)	1955
E. O. Awa	1951	Ph.D.	New York University (political science)	1955
N. Uka	1952	Ph.D.	University of Southern California (education)	1956
James A. Scott	1952	Ph.D.	Yale University (religion)	1957
A. N. Abai	1953	Ph.D.	New York University	1957

Source: Lincoln University Bulletin (Spring 1957). Data gathered by Horace Mann Bond, president of Lincoln University. Copies of the *Bulletin* are in Lincoln University Archives at the Langston Hughes Memorial Library.

number of graduates of these institutions of higher education gained professional degrees in medicine, dentistry, veterinary science, business administration, accounting, and law. Thus, such achievers of professional degrees among college-educated African Americans during the first half of the twentieth century contributed significantly as what Woodson dubbed the "Negro professional" in his *Negro Professional Man and the Community.*

Mention should also be made of the thousands of African American women who gained professional degrees in nursing. Between the 1890s and the 1950s, nursing education for black folks was attained almost solely at medical hospitals organized by African American medical doctors. One such hospital was the Frederick Douglass Memorial Hospital founded in 1895 in Philadelphia by Dr. Nathan Mossell, a graduate of Lincoln University in 1879 and later of the Howard University School of Medicine.[35] Along with African American doctors and dentists, African American nurses helped to advance the black-communitarian leadership dynamic in African American society during the first half of the twentieth century.

Interestingly enough, although there was a massive need for nurses in the U.S. armed forces during World War II, it took an arduous struggle by the nine-thousand-member National Association of Colored Graduate Nurses and the association's leader, Mabel Keaton Staupers, to convince the Roosevelt administration's War Department to draft black nurses in the Army Nurse Corps. (American nurses totaled 200,000 by World War II.) According to Northwestern University historian Darlene Hine, Staupers was a skillful civil rights leader who, by late 1944, had persuaded Eleanor Roosevelt to lobby Congress and the War Department in behalf of drafting black nurses.[36] Staupers produced a memoir on her leadership career, in which she relates how tenacious the racist impediments to drafting African American nurses in the Army Nurse Corps were. Eventually, the enlistment of African American nurses officially occurred in January 1945, as World War II was winding down.[37] The World War II manpower recruitment by the American armed forces also included thousands of African American female technicians in the U.S. Women's Army Corps (WAC), a subject that Howard University historian Martha Putney studied in her 1992 book *When the Nation Was in Need: Blacks in the Women's Army Corps during World War II.* Putney, by the way, was a lieutenant in the Women's Army Corps during

World War II, among nearly seven thousand African American women who served in the American armed forces.[38]

Now let me expand the range of this discussion of the black-communitarian leadership dynamic during the first half of the twentieth century. Vanderbilt University historian Dennis Dickerson provided evidence of this kind of black-communitarian interclass social development between the 1920s and the 1950s, which was published in the *A.M.E. Church Review* (April–June 2004). In his article "Medicine for the Masses: The Health Commission of the [Negro] Elks, 1927–1952," Dickerson describes the medical clinic program of the hundred-thousand-member Negro Elks organization. He discovered that there were nearly seven hundred Negro Elks branches in roughly the same number of black communities, and each branch supported a medical clinic program. To my knowledge, nothing like this Black Elks outreach to black masses representing the black-communitarian leadership dynamic exists in the early twenty-first century.

Another interesting case of the black-communitarian leadership pattern occurred between the 1930s and 1980s in the eastern Pennsylvania steel-producing city of Coatesville. The 1920 U.S. Census data for Coatesville recorded 1,881 black citizens living among 12,633 white citizens. By the 1930s, the black population reached 2,222, representing 15 percent of the city's population—a proportion that was sustained into the World War II years and beyond.[39] In 1925, an African American graduate of the Howard University School of Medicine named Whittier Atkinson gained his medical degree and, having read in a Negro weekly newspaper about the medical needs of black communities in Pennsylvania's urban areas, said in an interview about his professional career, "I came here [Coatesville] in 1927 because they [black folks] needed a colored doctor."[40]

As a member of Coatesville's small African American middle-class sector, Atkinson, who was a bachelor, joined ranks with several local middle-class associations, such as the Prince Hall Masons and the Alpha Phi Alpha fraternity. He exhibited a yearning to function as a facilitator of modern social development among Coatesville's working-class black citizens, not merely as just another self-serving bourgeois professional-class African American. The notion of a "self-serving black American bourgeoisie" was the rather cynical view of African American professionals during the first half of the twentieth century that was advanced in the 1950s by the prominent Howard University sociologist E. Franklin Frazier—a view that the discussion in this chapter rejects.[41]

As it happened, Atkinson was not an example of Frazier's cynical outlook toward middle-class and professional African Americans, and neither were many thousands of other bourgeois African Americans during the first half of the twentieth century. By the middle 1930s, Atkinson publicly expressed his antipathy toward the racism-riddled conditions that Coatesville's black citizens faced regarding medical care. As Atkinson informed his *Philadelphia Inquirer* obituary writer, Andy Wallace: "Several attempts to join the staff of Coatesville Hospital were rejected. He also had trouble getting patients into the hospital. When he did, the doctors there would not consult him about their treatment." Thus, Atkinson, exasperated by the kind of daily racist tormenting of black folks' medical needs, decided to organize a black community hospital in 1936.

Initially drawing on his own resources, Atkinson "built a five-bed hospital next to his home at 824 E. Chestnut Street," reports his *Philadelphia Inquirer* obituary. And according to Virginia Coad Armsted, Atkinson's nurse for many years, "his primary goal was to see a hospital [established] during those early years. *He was interested in establishing some place black people could go and be treated as human beings and with dignity. He started without help from anyone.*"[42] Moreover, by 1945 Atkinson had mobilized enough resources to enable him to expand his black community hospital to sixty beds.

As was often the case among black-communitarian leadership-oriented African American professionals during the first half of the twentieth century, such personalities were the taskmaster–type professionals, so to speak. While this meant that they were demanding toward their staff workers, they were also demanding toward themselves. This was true of Atkinson, who often overlooked financial remuneration from his patients when their circumstances were on the edge, and Atkinson's own work obligations were fulsome. As his *Philadelphia Inquirer* obituary puts it: "When his patients were broke, he was paid in eggs and vegetables. [Furthermore, he] spent long hours on duty. The Hospital was joined by a hallway to the kitchen of the two-story brick home he had built earlier, making it easy for him to make emergency calls in lab coat and pajamas at 3 A.M." An old folk expression has it that "hard work won't kill you," and this was true for Dr. Whittier Atkinson, who lived until his ninety-seventh year, passing in 1991.[43]

Additional instances of the black-communitarian leadership dynamic among the evolving twentieth-century black intelligentsia might also be noted here. The University of California historian Vincent Franklin, editor of the *Journal of African American History,* probes a variety of cases of the black-communitarian leadership pattern in his 1979 book *The Education of Black Philadelphia,* for example:

> The Deltas [during the 1930s into the 1960s] brought speakers to the city [of Philadelphia] for free lectures and sponsored an annual Education Week similar to that of the [Negro] Elks. The annual "Go to High School—Go to College Campaign" of Alpha Phi Alpha fraternity was supported by the organization's national and local membership. The campaign in Philadelphia usually consisted of a week of activities for children and their parents stressing the educational benefits of secondary and higher education. Such prominent persons as A. Philip Randolph [trade union leader], Carter G. Woodson [historian], Raymond Pace Alexander [civil rights lawyer], and W. E. B. Du Bois spoke during these educational campaigns. . . . This sampling of activities and organizations indicates . . . the commitment of these [civic and professional] groups to informing black youth about the need to improve themselves through education.[44]

Interestingly enough, several hundred miles across Pennsylvania during the 1920s into the 1960s, other cases of the black-communitarian leadership dynamic were evolving in the Greater Pittsburgh area. From World War I onward, in the Greater Pittsburgh area the black clergy and church were crucial agents of black-communitarian-oriented social development patterns among the black masses. Vanderbilt University historian Dennis Dickerson takes an in-depth look at this subject in his seminal 1986 book, *Out of the Crucible: Black Steelworkers in Western Pennsylvania, 1875–1980.*

First, some basic social demographic facts about the black proletarian community in Pittsburgh and western Pennsylvania generally during the early twentieth century: By 1910 there were twenty-five thousand black people in Pittsburgh and thirty thousand in the overall western Pennsylvania industrial belt, making blacks 5 percent of Pittsburgh's population and 3 percent of the overall industrial-belt towns. By 1930 the black population in Pittsburgh had doubled to fifty-five thousand (8 percent of the city) and almost eighty thousand (or 7 percent) in the overall industrial belt.

Dickerson discusses two particular crisis areas in the social system that constrained the social mobility of working-class blacks in and around Pittsburgh and hampered their political rights. One such crisis concerned "color-elitism" practices by light-skinned and brown-skinned black families against dark-skinned families. The second crisis was related to housing discrimination practiced by whites against working-class blacks.

The problem of color-elitism patterns was internal to the Pittsburgh black community and was practiced widely in middle class–dominated African American churches. It surfaced precisely when a sizable number of poor, dark-skinned working-class families moved into the Pittsburgh area by World War I. "Some Black churches in the Pittsburgh area were inhospitable [toward such families]," Dickerson writes. "A few of [those churches], such as Bethel African Methodist Episcopal Church, Grace Memorial Presbyterian Church, and Holy Cross Episcopal Church, all in Pittsburgh, were elitist and [practiced] a color line which disfavored darker-skinned Blacks. They also discovered that the style of worship in some existing congregations differed from traditional Southern Black religion, and in some instances they could not exercise their denominational preferences."[45]

This color elitism, by the way, was common in the mainline black churches in the North during the early twentieth century. In his 1976 book *A Ghetto Takes Shape: Black Cleveland, 1870–1930*, Temple University historian Kenneth Kusmer provides a perceptive analysis of color elitism in several middle-class black churches during the 1920s into the 1940s. Regarding two prominent churches, St. Andrew Episcopal Church and Mt. Zion Congregational Church, Kusmer relates a vivid color elitism pattern. "Neither church," explains Kusmer, "was interested in accepting working-class Negroes as members, and most recent migrants from the South would have found the staid . . . services that both provided rather uninviting. [The churches were] restricted to 'old elite' families."[46]

As it happened in the Pittsburgh industrial area, a young generation of liberal-oriented black clergy appeared on the scene during the 1920s and 1930s, and within a decade they transformed the religious culture in mainline black churches along the lines of the social gospel activist Christian theology. Table 2.7 provides data on the growth of black churches in the Greater Pittsburgh area between 1890 and 1930. Among these churches is John Wesley African Methodist Episcopal Zion Church, one of the liberal social gospel–oriented African American churches founded in the 1920s. The pastor at this church articulated a variant of the black-communitarian social advancement ethos. Dennis Dickerson relates how the John Wesley Church often allied on social issues with activist secular organizations of this period, including Marcus Garvey's Universal Negro Improvement Association.

Dickerson also examines the black-communitarian leadership dynamic that was practiced in another major Pittsburgh area African American church, the Ebenezer Baptist Church, which was founded in the 1920s in the Pittsburgh area. Its pastor, the Reverend J. C. Austin, provided assertive social gospel–oriented leadership in an effort to destroy color-elitism patterns in black churches throughout Greater Pittsburgh. However, Austin left Pittsburgh in the mid-1930s for Chicago, where he pastored the Pilgrim Baptist Church, transforming it into one of the

Table 2.7. Black church growth in the Greater Pittsburgh area, 1889–1929

Church denomination	City	Year founded
Bethlehem Baptist Church	McKeesport	1889
Payne Chapel African Methodist Episcopal	Duquesne	1891
Mt. Sinai Baptist	Johnstown	1917
Bethel African Methodist Episcopal	Johnstown	1917
Colored Methodist Episcopal	Pittsburgh	1917
First Baptist Church	North Vandergrift	1918
Ebenezer African Methodist Episcopal	Aliquippa	1920s
John Wesley African Methodist Episcopal Zion	Pittsburgh	1920s
Blackwell African Methodist Episcopal Zion	Homestead	1920s
Church of the Living God-Pentecostal	Duquesne	1920s
Church of God in Christ-Pentecostal	Coraopolis	1925
Carter Chapel African Methodist Episcopal	Pittsburgh	1926
Cleaves Temple Colored Methodist Episcopal	Pittsburgh	1926
Beebe Colored Methodist Episcopal	Pittsburgh	1926
New Hope Baptist Church	Coraopolis	1929

Source: Data from Dennis C. Dickerson, *Out of the Crucible: Black Steelworkers in Western Pennsylvania, 1875–1980* (Albany, NY: SUNY Press, 1986), 65–69, 111, 114.

premier black-communitarian social development–oriented African American churches in the country.[47]

Regarding the housing crisis that constrained the social advancement of black working-class families in the Greater Pittsburgh area, Dickerson reports that some 82 percent of black families rented their living quarters by 1930, compared with 44 percent of white families. In other words, less than 20 percent of the Pittsburgh area's working-class black families were homeowners by 1930. Two progressive black clergy, the Reverend Austin and the Reverend H. G. Payne, mobilized their churches—the Ebenezer Baptist Church and the African Methodist Episcopal Church, respectively—in an effort to help blacks moving to the area locate decent housing. As Dickerson informs us, the Reverend Austin "organized a Home Finder's League in the early 1920s to pursue this objective. Reverend H. G. Payne . . . made a similar attempt. In 1923 he led his congregation in establishing a real estate agency to secure homes to sell or rent to 'colored' people . . . on low monthly installments."[48] Furthermore, by 1924, Austin's Ebenezer Baptist Church took a similar entrepreneurial approach as well, mobilizing his church's five-thousand-member congregation as a business institution by launching a bank for the Pittsburgh black community. The bank facilitated the opening of a home-loan association and, in addition to providing mortgages, also financed a home rehabilitation program for black families.

In short, numerous examples of the black-communitarian leadership dynamic among the African American middle class were replicated broadly in black urban communities during the first half of the twentieth century. A wide range of studies on black urban communities during this period attest to this. Among those studies are the following: Robert Warner's study on New Haven, Connecticut; St. Clair Drake's and Alan Spear's on Chicago; David Levering Lewis' on Harlem; Kenneth Kusmer's on Cleveland; Joe W. Trotter's on Milwaukee; Harold McDougall's on Baltimore; Nick Salvatore's on Detroit; Robert Gregg's on Philadelphia; Henry Louis Taylor's on Cincinnati; Megan Shockley's on Richmond, Virginia; and Gretchen Eick's on Wichita, Kansas, just to mention a few major studies.[49]

Mention should also be made of Cara Shelly's seminal study of the black-communitarian leadership pattern associated with the clergy of the Second Baptist Church in Detroit's black community between 1910 and 1946.[50] The clergyman involved was the Reverend Robert L. Bradby, who was trained at two black institutions of higher education: Virginia Theological Seminary and Wilberforce University. Bradby's extraordinary leadership capability transformed the Second Baptist Church from a miniscule 250 congregation at the start of his ministry in 1910 to some four thousand by the middle 1940s.

Shelly describes how during this period Bradby's church developed a set of mechanisms to assist both the job-placement needs and urban acculturation of thousands of unskilled and semiliterate black migrants from the South. Bradby mobilized the financial resources to fund a monthly newspaper, the *Second Baptist Herald*. It performed two interrelated modern development functions: (1) propagating middle-class norms and values as an instrument of urban acculturation and (2) advancing hands-on advice regarding self-employment and money management, using a monthly "Question and Answer" section for this purpose.

> "Should you go into business for yourself?" a reader asked the Herald's "Question and Answer" department. "Yes," the paper responded, "if you are able to work hard [and] save your money. . . ." A number of back enterprises advertised in the *Herald*, and [it] frequently made a point encouraging the congregation to patronize these businesses, explain that "We want to help those who are . . . building up the race by their business endeavors." Beginning a series of articles on the professionals and businessmen in the congregation, the editors hoped that these pieces would "serve as a guide to Race pride uplift and appreciation."[51]

Looking back across a century of black intelligentsia activist strands, it is useful to have a schema for differentiating these various strands. I propose a threefold classification: (1) political mobilization activists, (2) black consciousness activists, and (3) black bourgeois activists. I would classify Du Bois and the 1905 Niagara Movement organizers as a quintessential example of political mobilization leadership. The 1920s–1930s New Negro Movement discussed in Chapter 1 represented the evolving twentieth-century African American intelligentsia's first major black consciousness leadership strand. This strand's prominent intelligentsia personalities included Langston Hughes (poet/essayist); Charles S. Johnson (sociologist and editor of the National Urban League's magazine *Opportunity: Journal of Negro Life*); A. Philip Randolph (editor of the *Messenger,* a black socialist magazine); Alain Locke (literary critic and Howard University scholar); Jessie Fauset (essayist/editor); W. E. B. Du

Bois (sociologist and editor of the NAACP's journal, the *Crisis*); Aaron Douglas (painter); Paul Robeson (classical singer); and Sterling Brown (literary critic/poet and Howard University scholar), to mention just a prominent few.

I now want to discuss the attributes of the third generic leadership strand that evolved among the African American intelligentsia during the twentieth century: the black bourgeois activists. Perhaps the core attribute of the evolving twentieth-century African American intelligentsia personalities whom I classify as black bourgeois activists is that they were politically paradoxical. By this characterization I mean that, *although black bourgeois activists expressed some commitment to advancing political rights for black people, they also clung ideologically to establishmentarian bourgeois ideals.* For example, they were staunchly "capitalist friendly" in their politics and usually opposed progressive public policies that regulate the excesses of business. Thus, when bourgeois activist personalities occasionally embraced a facet of the Du Boisian activism leadership pattern during the first half of the twentieth century, *they usually did so along one-dimensional lines, not along broader, multifaceted political lines.* Accordingly, I use the term "black bourgeois activists" to characterize a section of the evolving twentieth-century black intelligentsia who might best be dubbed "reluctant" black activists, which is to say, they were intelligentsia personalities who usually sat on the fence politically, but under special circumstances—such as when black folks' honor was insulted and demeaned—they assumed a genuine activist demeanor.

Put another way, we can characterize the black bourgeois activists as professional persons who entertained doubts regarding Bookerite accommodationism (such as its indifference to the human rights of black folks), while simultaneously agreeing with some of Washington's black leadership praxis—such as supporting his National Negro Business League. So in order to manage this awful dilemma, the black bourgeois activists fashioned for themselves *just enough* black ethnic commitment to prevent them from being ideologically dominated altogether by Booker T. Washington's accommodationist leadership.

Several early twentieth-century black bourgeois activist leadership personalities tilted occasionally though strategically in favor of Du Boisian civil rights activism and warrant discussion here. One fascinating such figure was Madam C. J. Walker, the cosmetics-industry millionaire. Another was Raymond Pace Alexander, the Philadelphia business lawyer. Still another was Charles Clifton Spaulding, the North Carolina businessman. And the last black bourgeois activist personality I'll mention was the Reverend Francis Grimké, a Lincoln University–educated clergyman who pastored the era's leading black Presbyterian church in Washington, D.C.

The entrepreneur Madam C. J. Walker—the wealthiest African American woman of her time, who made her fortune in the cosmetics industry and who sat on the board of Booker T. Washington's National Negro Business League—was a quintessential example of the black bourgeois activist leadership personality. In August 1918, Walker hosted the League's annual convention at her Hudson River estate in New York, during which she delivered a welcome address in which she lambasted white vigilante attacks against Negro soldiers in towns that bordered U.S. Army bases during World War I. Not long after the address, she received sharp criticism from powerful white members of the board of trustees of Tuskegee Institute, where the National Negro Business League was located. It was the late Booker T. Washington's secretary and confidante Emmett Scott, who attended the league's 1918 convention and who later informed the Tuskegee Institute's board members about Walker's address, characterizing it as incendiary.

A letter of criticism from Colonel William Jay Schieffelin, a white board member of Tuskegee Institute, especially inflamed Walker. One might say it violated her fierce sense of black people's honor. In a first-rate biography of Walker by her great-great-granddaughter A'Lelia Bundles, a graduate of Harvard College, we learn that in a January 1919 letter to Schieffelin, Walker stood her ground. She firmly defended the need for professional-class African Americans like herself to critique Booker T. Washington's accommodationism in cases where the human and civil rights of black people were violated. Here are Walker's words, which amounted to her black bourgeois activist epiphany, one might say:

> The Negro in the South had been denied the use of firearms . . . and has been no match for the fiends and brutes who have taken advantage of his helplessness. [Having] bravely, fearlessly bled and died [in Europe] . . . they [black soldiers] will soon be returning. *To what? Does any reasonable person imagine to the old order of things? To submit to being strung up, riddled with bullets, burned at the stake? No! A thousand times no!*
>
> They will come back to face life like men, whatever is in store for them, and like men to defend themselves, their families, their homes. . . . Please

understand that this does not mean that I wish to encourage in any way a conflict between the races. Such a thing is farthest from my mind. . . . My message to my people is this: *Go live and conduct yourself so that you will be above the reproach of anyone. But should but one prejudiced, irrational boast infringe upon [your] rights as men—resent the insults like men . . . and if death be the result—so be it.* An honorable death is far better than the miserable existence imposed upon most of our people in the South.

I have tried very hard to make you see the thing through the eyes of a Negro, which I realize is next to impossible. . . . Your talks [about my speech] would do a far greater good if you would point out to the white people just what their duties to the Negro are.[52]

Another intelligentsia personality belonging to the black bourgeois activist leadership during the period between the two world wars was Raymond Pace Alexander. Alexander was one of four black Harvard Law School graduates in 1923, along with Benjamin Davis, William Hastie, and Charles Hamilton Houston. Davis, the son of Benjamin Davis Sr., who was the wealthiest black business figure in Atlanta during the 1920s, settled in New York City and became the leading African American figure in the Communist Party.[53] William Hastie became a civil rights lawyer in Washington, D.C.; he was a founding figure in the New Negro Alliance organization based there and was the first African American appointed to a federal court.[54] And Charles Hamilton Houston became a law professor at Howard University and then dean of its law school and founded the NAACP Legal Defense Fund in 1929.[55]

During the 1920s, Alexander established a law practice in Philadelphia and married attorney Sadie Tanner Mossell, the granddaughter of Bishop Benjamin Tanner, a leading late nineteenth-century African Methodist Episcopal church clergyman and the daughter of a prominent African American medical doctor in Philadelphia.[56] That marriage afforded Alexander entrée to Philadelphia's black elite society from the 1920s onward. As the leading African American lawyer in Philadelphia, Alexander devoted a part of his legal career to rendering legal service to black organizations. As related in Vincent Franklin's book *The Education of Black Philadelphia*, Alexander spent several decades assisting—both legally and financially—black schoolteachers and the NAACP in challenging the notoriously racist practices in Philadelphia's public school system, as well as in the school systems in neighboring Chester County, where the shipbuilding city of Chester had a sizable black population. Moreover, Alexander was a leading figure for a half century in the Association for the Study of Negro Life and History. He assisted its general finances and the publication of the association's monthly *Negro History Bulletin,* which was distributed nationwide to black schoolteachers.[57]

Charles Clifton Spaulding, the owner of the North Carolina Mutual Life Insurance Company, also gained renown in the 1930s and 1940s among the black bourgeois activist leadership. Spaulding was the wealthiest black person in Durham, North Carolina, during the interwar years. In the course of being publicly humiliated by a white store clerk in Durham's largest department store—he was prevented from trying on a suit—Spaulding had an epiphany that propelled him toward a "subterranean" resistance to racism. In the early 1930s he contacted the civil rights activist editor of Durham's black newspaper, offering to lend it financial support, and in 1940 he agreed to do the same for Durham's main civil rights–oriented black civic association—a radical event for a bourgeois gentleman like Spaulding, who, like Madam C. J. Walker before him, commenced his business career as a devotee of Booker T. Washington's accommodationism.[58]

The black Presbyterian clergyman Reverend Francis Grimké was a graduate of Lincoln University in the 1880s and later of Princeton University Theology School. Grimké initially celebrated Booker T. Washington's role in organizing and advancing the Tuskegee Institute. But it was Washington's dramatic failure to publicly condemn the murderous anti-Negro Atlanta riot in 1906 and the equally vicious Springfield, Illinois, riot in 1908 that turned Grimké firmly against Washington's leadership. In an obituary he wrote for a black newspaper in Washington, D.C., Grimké observed:

> His [Booker T. Washington's] attitude on the rights of the Negro was . . . anything but satisfactory. He either dodged the issue when he came face to face with it, or dealt with it in such a way as not to offend those who were not in favor of according . . . [the Negro] full citizenship rights. *He never squarely faced the issue, and, in a straightforward, manly spirit declared his belief in the Negro as a man and a citizen, and as entitled to the same treatment as any other man.*
>
> His death will be a loss to Tuskegee, but will not be to the [Negro] race. *The race will not in any way suffer from his death. It will not suffer in its higher aspirations, nor in its efforts in behalf of its rights, as it did in the*

death of Frederick Douglass. In neither of these respects did Mr. Washington make himself felt.[59]

Thus, the foregoing experiences of several elite African American personalities whom I classify as members of the "black bourgeois activist leadership strand" demonstrate the importance of what the University of Massachusetts sociologist Richard Robbins calls "sidelines activists" in the evolving twentieth-century African American intelligentsia.[60] A crucial function of such sidelines activists among the evolving twentieth-century black intelligentsia personalities was, I suggest, to demonstrate that an establishmentarian-oriented perspective toward America's racist patterns was not a dead end—that black bourgeois activist personalities were not Uncle Toms. On the contrary, sidelines activists like Walker, Alexander, Spaulding, and Grimké demonstrated that, as establishmentarian-oriented elite African Americans, they were also "worth their salt" when it came to defending black folks' honor against white supremacist patterns. In this regard, then, it can be said that, during the evolving twentieth century, members of the "black bourgeois activist leadership strand" fashioned their own special variant of the black-communitarian leadership dynamic.

Although the twentieth-century African American political mobilization leadership groups persuaded America's federal government by the early 1970s to fashion public policies outlawing formal segregation practices against black folks, *the future efficacy of the Du Boisian black-communitarian leadership dynamic within African American society unexpectedly became problematic.* My belief is that, today, the status of the black-communitarian leadership pattern in African American society has declined relative to its viable status during the first sixty years of the twentieth century. No doubt, the reasons for this situation are numerous. One of the basic reasons has been the black middle-class flight from inner-city black communities, a development that commenced in the 1970s and exploded by the middle 1980s. This black middle-class migration, however, occurred in the context of a broader urban decline dynamic in American society generally—a decline that was sparked by capital and industrial flight from urban to suburban areas in the 1960s, eventually culminating in the "deindustrialization" of American cities.[61] These systemic changes, furthermore, contributed to a full-fledged joblessness crisis that has plagued large segments of the African American urban working class into the twenty-first century. Although this crisis initially fueled the urban riots by working-class African Americans during the late 1960s into the 1970s, after the urban riots subsided a persistent joblessness also fueled extensive social crises among black folks, causing a broad range of deplorable conditions, including the awful fact that some 35 percent of African American children live in poverty today.

From 1980 onward, urban riots had been replaced by lower-class black internecine mayhem, often called "black-on-black" violence and crime. This aspect of black urban decline was intensified by the so-called war on drugs. However, this was actually a war on working-class African American males—a perverted war on drugs that, commencing in 1982–1983, became an institutionalized state and federal policy during the administration of President Ronald Reagan. Moreover, political conservatism among a sizable segment of white voters made it difficult for black leadership groups (the NAACP, the National Urban League, the Children's Defense Fund, and the Congressional Black Caucus, among others) to forge viable legislative alliances that could reverse the justice system's draconian practices associated with the perverted war on drugs since the 1980s.[62]

For example, by 2011 there was a sizable incarceration rate of one in twelve among African American males between eighteen and sixty-four years of age, compared with one in eighty-seven for whites in this age bracket and one in thirty-six for Hispanics.[63] This situation has led the New York University public policy analyst Michelle Alexander to pen a persuasive critique of incarceration practices related to the war on drugs in her 2010 book *The New Jim Crow: Mass Incarceration in the Age of Colorblindness.* In an analysis that criticizes the manipulation of arrests as a post–Jim Crow era method of pubic control over working-class African American males, Alexander recommends the replacement of the "war on drugs" by a federal-level drug rehabilitation program.[64]

Because the war on drugs has had a rather long public policy lifetime—from the 1980s into the twenty-first century—it resulted in broad patterns of social crises in urban black communities. One consequence of this one-generation-and-half development was that, *by the middle 1980s, the functioning of a black-communitarian leadership pattern in African American urban communities reached its nadir.*

This awful outcome in the late twentieth-century evolution of the African American society leads me to conclude this chapter with reflections on the metamorphosis of a nationwide decline in a viable black-communitarian leadership dynamic in numerous African American communities. My reflections stem from a personal tale of my experience with, on the one hand, a viable black-communitarian leadership pattern in an urban neighborhood in Philadelphia during the 1940s and 1950s and, on the other hand, a broad black-communitarian decline in that same neighborhood owing to black middle-class flight during the 1970s and 1980s.

As I remarked earlier in this chapter in commenting on Vincent Franklin's research on a vibrant black-communitarian leadership dynamic in Philadelphia from the 1920s to the 1960s, that period was one during which broad areas of Philadelphia's black community benefited from the prevalence of stable working-class and middle-class neighborhoods nestled among a large community of poor working-class and poor black families. My tale focuses on one such sociologically mixed but stable black neighborhood in Philadelphia from the 1930s into the 1970s.

During my childhood some three-quarters of a century ago in a small black community in Ambler, Pennsylvania, a mill town about thirty miles outside Philadelphia County, the black community at large in Philadelphia was served by several black-run community centers for male youth. Two of these centers were operated by the YMCA; (prominent among them was the Christian Street YMCA), and one was operated under the auspices of the Boys' Club Federation of America. The latter, the Wissahickon Boys' Club, was supported financially by a group of upper-class white families of Quaker religious background (especially the John T. Emlen family), who resided in the section of north Philadelphia known as Germantown during the period between the two world wars. The edifice of the Wissahickon Boys' Club was located in a sociologically mixed black neighborhood of Germantown, on the corner of Coulter Street and Pulaski Avenue.

Geographically, the Germantown area of Philadelphia actually bordered Montgomery County, the county in which my hometown of Ambler was located. So it was possible for black youth living in Montgomery County areas near Philadelphia to attend institutions like the Wissahickon Boys' Club, which is precisely what I and my younger brother, Richard, occasionally did. To get there, we rode a rickety bus that traveled along the Bethlehem Pike between Germantown and towns on the edge of Philadelphia County, such as Lansdale, Fort Washington, Flourtown, and Springfield. Through our occasional attendance at the Germantown Wissahickon Boys' Club, my brother and I were able to spend two weeks during one summer at Camp Emlen. The camp was operated by the Wissahickon Boys' Club director, William T. Coleman Sr., and was located in a bucolic rural Mennonite farming village in Morwood, Pennsylvania, nestled on the northern tier of Montgomery County, nearly eighty miles from Philadelphia.[65]

Coleman was a typical representative of the emergent twentieth-century African American professional class when he was chosen in 1915 by the Boys' Club Federation of America (BCFA) as director of the Germantown Wissahickon Boys' Club. He had studied at Hampton Institute in Virginia, where he earned a degree in sociology and social work, and also did further study at the University of Pennsylvania. After his first year as director of the Wissahickon Boys' Club, the BCFA recognized Coleman's professional talent and hired him as a field director, whose occasional function was to be a traveling inspector of the BCFA's clubs for African American youth.

William Coleman had a son, William T. Coleman Jr., who worked as a summer youth counselor at Camp Emlen. The son attended the University of Pennsylvania and was admitted to the Harvard Law School, from which he graduated in 1946. A distinguished career followed, during which he occasionally participated as a civil rights lawyer for the NAACP Legal Defense Fund under the direction of Thurgood Marshall, who was later the first African American appointed a Supreme Court justice. Coleman Jr. went on to become one of the first top-tier African American corporation lawyers—responsible for the Ford Motor Company's legal affairs—and was appointed secretary of transportation in President Gerald Ford's cabinet.[66]

My recollection of the Wissahickon Boys' Club and its sociologically mixed African American neighborhood during the 1940–1945 period was revived through the 2000 publication of *Philadelphia, 1639–2000*, a book of photography by Temple University historian Charles Blockson. The book contains a photograph of the Wissahickon Boys' Club as it was when I first saw the building in 1940, nestled among a mixed working-class and middle-class black neighborhood.[67]

Now fast-forward to the 1980s, when I was teaching at Harvard University. I was visiting a former Lincoln University classmate who lived in Germantown, and he and I visited the Coulter Street–Pulaski Avenue area where the original club had been located. I was shocked by what I saw. Many houses in the neighborhood were rundown, some were boarded up, and the marvelous brick building that had housed the original Wissahickon Boys' Club at the corner of Coulter Street and Pulaski Avenue was dilapidated and shuttered. Through inquiries around the neighborhood, I learned that the name of the original club had been changed to Wissahickon Boys' and Girls' Club, and it had been relocated to a new middle-class Germantown neighborhood. In short, beginning in the middle 1970s, there was a slow but steady flight of middle-class black families from the old, socially stable neighborhood around the original boys' club, with the fleeing families relocating in black communities in counties bordering Philadelphia, such as Delaware and Montgomery Counties. Within a decade, middle-class flight produced a nationwide variant of black urban neighborhood decay that had proliferated unchecked in Germantown's Coulter Street–Pulaski Avenue area.

Put another way, the black communitarian leadership–oriented citizens who had fashioned a stable, sociologically mixed African American neighborhood in the Coulter Street–Pulaski Avenue area between the 1920s and the 1970s had ceased functioning from the late 1970s onward. In short, by this period the once vibrant black-communitarian leadership dynamic in this Germantown neighborhood had lost its black middle-class bloodstream, as it were. Furthermore, throughout the remainder of the twentieth century and into the twenty-first century, this pattern of declining black-communitarian leadership dynamic became endemic throughout black urban communities nationwide, as a variety of sociological studies have documented.

As the African American intelligentsia or professional class has entered the twenty-first century—armed with advanced social and political capabilities—it remains to be seen whether or not there can be a revitalization of a black-communitarian leadership pattern in the working-class and poor sector of African American communities. Be that as it may, it is my belief that in light of the development of what might be called a two-tier African American class system during the last several decades of the twentieth century and into the first decade of the twenty-first century, there is clearly a pressing need for a revitalization of the black-communitarian leadership pattern.

After all, the existence today of a two-tier class system (what the Harvard University sociologist William Julius Wilson has characterized as "black haves" and "black have-nots")[68] in African American society means that literally millions of African American citizens are having their life prospects stymied by a kaleidoscope of social crises. Thus, I view it as a moral imperative for today's variant of Du Bois' Talented Tenth to mobilize its new socioeconomic and political resources to help ameliorate some of the social crises that now plague about 40 percent of African American families. Insofar as the Du Boisian leadership legacy contributed significantly to the development of today's viable African American professional sector, I believe that sector has a special moral obligation to facilitate a renewal of some features of the black-communitarian leadership dynamic. The goal of a black-communitarian leadership revitalization is within the resource capabilities of the twenty-first-century African American elite sector. I offer further reflections on this issue in the final chapter in this book.

3

IDEOLOGICAL DYNAMICS AND THE
MAKING OF THE INTELLIGENTSIA

I N THIS CHAPTER, I address more extensively a topic that I have
already discussed briefly in Chapter 2. There, I remarked that "for
Du Bois in 1903, [the] core ideological ingredients of a progressive
leadership nexus with the poor Negro masses amounted to a moral imperative." Accordingly, W. E. B. Du Bois articulated a set of progressive
black-leadership propositions that lay out what might be called the contours of obligation and responsibility of the emergent twentieth-century
African American intelligentsia.

I argue in this chapter that Du Bois believed that in order to give operational substance to the obligation-and-responsibility contours of its
leadership nexus with the black masses, the African American intelligentsia required a black-ethnic commitment leadership orientation. By this
I mean something basic and straightforward: as a precondition for challenging America's racist oligarchy and for assisting the modern advancement of the socially ravaged late nineteenth-century Negro masses, the
nascent black intelligentsia needed a "Negro-masses-friendly" worldview.
Moreover, as Du Bois understood it, such a worldview would inspire the
long struggle to achieve full citizenship rights and human rights for African Americans.

Of course, Du Bois did not use the term "black-ethnic commitment
leadership orientation" when he initially fashioned for himself what might
be called a "black-communitarian nexus" with the agrarian black children that he taught in Tennessee in 1886–1887 during two summer ses-
sions while a student at Fisk University. Rather, Du Bois used the term
"Talented Tenth" when he first characterized his understanding of the

modern developmental relationship between college-trained Negroes like himself, on the one hand, and the Negro masses on the other. Indeed, for Du Bois, "Talented Tenth" was a very special term—a term fraught with a kind of transcendent modern-developmental aura for black people.

As far as I can determine, Du Bois first used the term "Talented Tenth" (always with capital "Ts" as I do in this book) in the context of a discussion defending the need to expand higher-education opportunities for Negro youth in the South. The reason behind this need in 1903 was, in Du Bois' eyes, patently clear: "For this is certain, [that] no secure [modern] civilization can be built in the South with the Negro as an ignorant, turbulent proletariat." Despite the oppression and socioeconomic backwardness imposed on black folks since the end of Reconstruction, Du Bois points out, Negro youth had continued—against the odds—in their quest for full-fledged higher education: "We ought not to forget that despite the pressure of poverty and despite the active discouragement and even ridicule of friends, the demand for higher training steadily increases among Negro youth: There were, in the years from 1875 to 1880, 22 Negro graduates from Northern colleges; from 1885 to 1890 there were 43, and from 1895 to 1900, nearly 100 graduates. From Southern Negro colleges there were, in the same three years, 143, 413, and over 500 graduates."[1]

It is immediately after this paragraph that Du Bois uses the famous term "Talented Tenth": "*Here, then, is plain thirst for training: by refusing to give this Talented Tenth the key to knowledge, can any sane man imagine that they will lightly lay aside their yearning and contentedly become hewers of wood and drawers of water?* No. The dangerously clear logic of the Negro's position will more and more loudly assert itself in *that day when increasing wealth and more intricate [modern] social organization preclude the South from being, as it so largely is [today], simply an armed camp for intimidating black folk.*"[2]

Soon after Du Bois used the term in the April 1903 printing of *The Souls of Black Folk* by Chicago's A. C. McClurg Company, he had a second opportunity to discuss this topic in Booker T. Washington's *The Negro Problem*. In the chapter he titled "The Talented Tenth," Du Bois provides a table listing the number of college-educated black Americans between 1880 and 1900. From our twenty-first-century vantage, it is rather difficult to think that for the year 1899–1900, higher education institutions produced fewer than two thousand "college-bred Negroes"—Du Bois' favorite term for characterizing college-educated black Americans.[3]

In 1903, what was Du Bois' intellectual and operational understanding of the leadership obligation of this unique American Negro social stratum? By 1903, he articulated a two-tier conception of the Talented Tenth's responsibilities toward the overall African American society. Its first leadership task was to acquire for itself *a viable understanding of the post–Emancipation era southern social and economic order.* In chapter 9 of *The Souls of Black Folk,* titled "Of the Sons of the Master and Man," Du Bois remarks that because of the defeat of the slavocracy in the Civil War, by the 1890s systemic power in the South was controlled by a new white power class: "The rod of empire that passed from the hands of Southern gentlemen in 1865 . . . has passed to those men who have come to take charge of the industrial exploitation of the New South—the sons of poor whites fired with a new thirst for wealth and power [joined by] thrifty and avaricious Yankees, and unscrupulous [European] immigrants. Into the hands of these men the Southern laborers, white and black, have fallen; and this to their sorrow. . . . *But among the black laborers all this is aggravated . . . by a race prejudice which varies from a doubt and distrust among the best element of whites, to a frenzied hatred among the worst. And . . . it is [also] aggravated by the wretched economic heritage . . . from slavery.*"[4]

As Du Bois viewed it, once the Talented Tenth gained a viable understanding of the character of systemic power in the "New South," its second and major leadership obligation was to assist the advancement of the Negro masses into "modern civilization," another of Du Bois' favorite terms. In chapter 9, Du Bois writes: "Today no one seriously disputes the capability of individual Negroes to assimilate the culture and common sense of modern civilization, and to pass it on . . . to their fellows. If this is true, then here is the path out of the [oppressive] economic situation, and here is the imperative demand for trained Negro leaders of character and intelligence. Men of skill, men of light and leading, college-bred men, black captains of industry, and missionaries of culture; *men who thoroughly comprehend and know modern civilization, and can take hold of Negro communities and raise and train them by force of precept and example, deep sympathy, and the inspiration of common blood and ideals.*"[5]

Here, then, Du Bois is providing in 1903 an operational understanding of how the Talented Tenth might exercise leadership in the new century. Thus, my conception of the "black ethnic-commitment ethos" as a guidepost for the evolving twentieth-century black intelligentsia is an extrapolation of Du Bois' own conception of the leadership interface of the nascent black elite—the Talented Tenth—with the Negro masses. In Du Bois' overall conception of the Talented Tenth, there is a presumption that a progressive segment of that elite must take on a special task in the evolving twentieth-century black leadership. The progressive segment of the black intelligentsia was called upon to assist both the modern social advancement of the Negro masses and their full-fledged citizenship rights.

In this respect, the progressive segment of the evolving twentieth-century African American intelligentsia differed fundamentally from the conservative or accommodationist segment, whose leadership contours were influenced by Booker T. Washington. The ideological and operational distinction between these two branches of the nascent African American intelligentsia was first delineated by Du Bois in 1903 in chapter 3 of *The Souls of Black Folk,* titled "Of Mr. Washington and Others." There, Du Bois refers to his own inner circle as "the other class of Negroes who cannot agree with Mr. Booker T. Washington," and after making this crucial point, he outlines the core principles of a progressive black leadership nexus with the poor Negro masses. Those principles, I suggest, lay at the heart of the Du Boisian black-ethnic commitment leadership orientation.

Accordingly, it was in opposition to the Booker T. Washington's accommodationist leadership methodology ("[Washington's] attitude of conciliation toward the white south")[6] that Du Bois delineated his perspective on the leadership obligations of a progressive-oriented black intelligentsia. As Du Bois wrote in chapter 3 of *The Souls of Black Folk:* "The way for a people [Negroes] to gain their reasonable rights is not by voluntarily throwing them away and insisting that they do not want them . . . [which was Washington's approach]; on the contrary, Negroes must insist continually, in season and out of season, that voting is necessary to modern manhood, that color discrimination is barbarism, and that black boys need education as well as white boys."[7]

Besides focusing on the importance of what Du Bois called the Negro's "reasonable rights" (for example, voting and education), the

Du Boisian black-ethnic commitment leadership orientation would enable the evolving black intelligentsia to challenge what might be called
the Negro masses' systemic marginalization. *It was especially this feature of America's white-supremacist oligarchy that Du Bois believed the
Talented Tenth must strive to overcome.* Why? Because such systemic
marginalization would amount to what Du Bois called "a harvest of disaster to our children." Du Bois elaborates on the danger of the systemic
marginalization as follows: "If that [Bookerite] reconciliation [leader-
ship] is to be marked *by the industrial slavery and civic death of . . .
black men,* with permanent legislation into a position of inferiority, then
black men, if they are really men, are called upon by every consideration
of patriotism and loyalty to oppose such a course by all civilized methods, even though such opposition involves disagreement with Mr.
Booker T. Washington. *We have no right to sit silently by while the inevitable seeds are sown for a harvest of disaster to our children."* [8]

It is notable here that, in 1903, Du Bois used two core terms to describe black folks' systemic marginalization: "industrial slavery" and the
political-culture corollary "civic death." In the phrase "industrial slavery
and civic death . . . of black men," Du Bois anticipated by a century the
historian Douglas Blackmon's use, in 2008, of the term "slavery by another name" to characterize nearly eighty years of widespread capitalist
dependence on prison-based Negro labor in a brutal convict lease labor
system. [9]

There is little doubt that Du Bois' definitional imprimatur on the ideological and operational contours of a black-ethnic commitment leadership orientation afforded this leadership perspective a privileged status
among the evolving black intelligentsia. Accordingly, a variety of top-
tier early twentieth-century African American professional personalities
contributed to its legitimization within the ranks of the black intelligentsia. Among those professional figures were Alexander Crummell (a
founder of the American Negro Academy and president of Wilberforce
University), John Wesley Cromwell (lawyer and editor of the Washington, D.C., Negro weekly, the *People's Advocate*), Archibald Grimké (a
lawyer and a founder of the NAACP in 1909), African Methodist Episcopal Bishop Reverdy Ransom (a member of the Niagara Movement
and editor of the *A.M.E. Church Review*), Monroe Trotter (a member of
the Niagara Movement and editor of the Negro weekly *Boston Guardian*), Benjamin Mays (theology scholar and first black president of
Morehouse College), James Weldon Johnson (first black director of the

NAACP), and key black women's movement figures like Anna Arnold, Mary Church Terrell, and Mary McLeod Bethune (leaders of the National Association of Colored Women).

In general, from the 1920s through the 1960s, a black-ethnic commitment leadership ethos acquired wide acceptance among the ranks of the African American intelligentsia. There were, of course, many variations in regard to modality, style, and fidelity of articulation of the black-ethnic commitment ethos among African American professionals during the twentieth century. The intellectual range of those variations has been thoroughly probed in works by such scholars as William Banks, James Blackwell, John Bracey, Lawrence Jackson, James O. Young, John Hope Franklin and August Meier, Kevin Gaines, Dennis C. Dickerson, and Vincent P. Franklin, among others.[10]

It should also be noted that, commencing in the 1920s and 1930s, a handful of prominent African American intelligentsia personalities challenged the black-ethnic commitment leadership orientation. Foremost among them were William Stanley Braithwaite and George Schuyler. Braithwaite was a literary critic and poet who spent part of his career, from the 1930s to 1946, teaching at Atlanta University. Schuyler was a writer whose primary employment was as a columnist for a leading Negro weekly newspaper, the *Pittsburgh Courier,* from the late 1920s to the 1950s. Among black intellectuals in the period between the two world wars, Braithwaite was one of the earliest opponents of the black-ethnic commitment intellectual orientation, making him a pioneer black conservative intellectual.

A discussion of Braithwaite as such an intellectual can be found in Richard Bardolph's 1959 book *The Negro Vanguard.* Born in 1878, Braithwaite grew up in Boston in a middle-class, light-skinned black family, attended public schools, held an apprenticeship at the publisher Ginn and Company, and edited a Boston-based black magazine, the *Colored American Magazine.* His literary articles regularly appeared in Boston's leading daily newspaper, the *Boston Transcript.* In *The Negro Vanguard,* Bardolph provides a candid characterization of Braithwaite's aesthetic and intellectual orientation during the 1920s and how it riled many of his peers: "As a free-lance critic for the *Boston Transcript* [and] a lyric poet," Bardolph writes, Braithwaite "urged Negroes to disengage themselves from 'Negro writing,' lest they be judged by double standards, but the advice only offended Negro intellectuals [who were] exasperated by his 'repudiation' of his [Negro] 'heritage.' "[11]

Whereas Braithwaite attached himself to the cultural-aesthetic modality of intellectual discourse, George Schuyler focused on ideological and political issues. Oscar Williams' 2007 biography of Schuyler, *George Schuyler: Portrait of a Black Conservative,* suggests that he was, to put it mildly, an ideologically mercurial figure. In the early phase of his career, between the mid-1920s and World War II, Schuyler could be classified as a contrarian leftist intellectual. Amherst College historian Jeffrey Ferguson has also explored the ideological variability in Schuyler's intellectual persona.[12]

In the postwar era, however, Schuyler reinvented himself: he adopted a decidedly conservative ideological position, which was anti-leftist in general and anti–civil rights activism in particular. Schuyler's conservative writings gained him recognition in white conservative intellectual circles, which included recruitment to the editorial board of William Buckley's *National Review,* famous in America's conservative circles for its antipathy toward the Civil Rights movement. Schuyler's *Pittsburgh Courier* articles during the late 1950s and 1960s often attacked the Civil Rights movement, and in 1966 he was fired from the *Courier* after he published an article opposing the awarding of the Nobel Peace Prize to the Reverend Martin Luther King Jr.

Inasmuch as important parts of Braithwaite's and Schuyler's intellectual careers were antithetical to the influence of the Du Boisian black-ethnic commitment intellectual orientation, it can be said that these careers evolved outside the normative and ideological parameters associated with the mainstream sector of the twentieth-century African American intelligentsia. How, then, should we conceptualize the normative and ideological patterns they reflect?

I suggest that we can locate an understanding of Braithwaite's and Schuyler's intellectual careers in the contemporary writings of the Yale University intellectual historian Jonathan Holloway on the twentieth-century black intelligentsia. Thus, in the remainder of this chapter, by way of a critical exegesis on Holloway's discourse, I use Holloway's writings as a prism through which to delineate and expand on my own conceptual and analytical perspective toward the Du Boisian black-ethnic commitment leadership ethos in the metamorphosis of the African American intelligentsia.

Jonathan Holloway is an intellectual historian who teaches in the Departments of History and Afro-American Studies at Yale University. I became interested in Holloway's writings when I discovered an article titled "The Black Intellectual and the 'Crisis Canon' in the Twentieth Century," published in a 2001 issue of the *Black Scholar,* the African American studies journal. I recognized that Holloway's analysis of the developmental dynamics that characterized the mainstream African American intelligentsia's interface with the twentieth-century American white-supremacist oligarchy differed markedly from mine. Holloway views the African American intellectual as an intrinsically sovereign being, so to speak, who functions ideally when his or her intellect is unfettered by obligations emanating from racial or ethnic groups. My reading of Holloway's article suggests that, for Holloway, the evolving twentieth-century black intelligentsia personality inhabits a kind of "pristine intellectual-identity realm," which means that *given such a "natural-law-endowed" intelligentsia milieu, an intellectual's sovereignty cannot be qualified by claims put forth by his or her cultural, racial, or ethnic group.*

Thus, Holloway rejects the Du Boisian black-ethnic commitment orientation as a normative and ideological guidepost for the black intelligentsia's interface with American society's racist patterns. In his article, Holloway critiques the Du Boisian black-ethnic commitment intelligentsia orientation as generically flawed. For Holloway, it functions as a barrier to what he views as the ideal mind-set for the black intelligentsia's metamorphosis in twentieth-century American society, which might be called a "primal-individualism" mind-set. Holloway implies that this mind-set would have been more effective in the arc of black intelligentsia achievement, which is to say it would have been culturally superior—it would have enabled the evolving twentieth-century black intellectual to function, in Holloway's words, *"beyond the racial boundaries that have [historically] defined the black scholar's life."*[13]

Interestingly enough, however, Holloway's term "racial boundaries" takes on a rather ambiguous meaning inasmuch as it can be interpreted from several perspectives and therefore loses its interpretive and analytical specificity. First, "racial boundaries" could refer to white-imposed racial boundaries—that is, to racist barriers against African Americans. Second, the term could also refer to black cultural obligations that are fashioned within African American society as development guidelines for adoption by African American intellectuals. I suggest it is this second meaning that Holloway has in mind when he delineates his preference for the primal-individualism mind-set for the twentieth-century African American intelligentsia.

Accordingly, in Holloway's discourse it is not merely racist patterns during the evolving twentieth century but also, more significant, the Du Boisian black-ethnic commitment orientation that stymied viable intelligentsia development by African Americans. Holloway attempts to reinforce this argument by quoting disapprovingly one of Du Bois' observations in *The Souls of Black Folk,* in which Du Bois implores the Talented Tenth to assume "a heavy responsibility . . . to the struggling masses, a responsibility to the darker races of men." According to Holloway's discourse, what might be called Du Bois' black-ethnic moral injunction ("responsibility to the struggling masses [and] . . . the darker races of men") *amounts to a burdensome obligation for the nascent twentieth-century African American intelligentsia.*[14]

Holloway's discourse faults the Du Boisian black ethnic-commitment ethos not only for depriving black intellectuals access to a superior modern intelligentsia orientation—namely, the primal-individualism mind-set—but also for encouraging what Holloway calls the "crisis canon discourse." For Holloway, *"crisis canon discourse" overemphasizes the impact of the American racist system upon black intellectuals in particular, and upon black people in general.* Indeed, in Holloway's estimation, twentieth-century black intellectuals produced too many works that focused on American racism. As Holloway initially formulates this issue in his article: *"It is clear that the core concept of crisis continues to shape and distort our evaluation of blacks and black intellectual work to this day."*[15]

Early in Holloway's presentation of his "crisis canon" argument, he takes to task the early twentieth-century African American intelligentsia personalities who, by organizing the American Negro Academy in 1897, laid the institutional foundation of the black-ethnic commitment leadership orientation. The academy was conceived and fashioned by a pioneering African American intelligentsia figure, the philosophy and theology scholar Alexander Crummell. His cofounders were persons of stellar intellectual achievement: *People's Advocate* editor John Wesley Cromwell, Francis Grimké (pastor of a major black Presbyterian church in Washington, D.C.); William Sanders Scarborough (the first major African American classics scholar), Archibald Grimké (the first black graduate of the Harvard Law School in the early 1880s), and W. E. B. Du Bois. The academy was headquartered in Washington, D.C., and held its meetings at the John Wesley African Methodist Episcopal Zion Church.

At the historical moment when black folks were entering the twentieth century, Holloway's primal individualism–oriented discourse in his *Black Scholar* article argues that Crummell's organization of the American Negro Academy was a grave mistake. Why? Because, says Holloway, the academy erroneously fashioned "socially and historically specific expectations and institutional structures that constrain their [black intellectuals'] work. . . . *[B]lacks and whites alike have assumed that black intellectuals ought to speak for the black community; blacks [as intellectuals] have been presented with the obligation to represent to the white intelligentsia what all blacks think, do and feel. . . .* More often than not, black intellectuals have been discussed solely in a racialized context and considered experts or authorities only on those issues that deal with race."[16]

Contrary to Holloway, however, I suggest that a careful reading of the charter of the 1897 American Negro Academy reveals that its structure and goals were not conceived, in Holloway's words, "[to] constrain [black intellectuals'] work." Furthermore, Alfred Moss' seminal book on the American Negro Academy relates the serious endeavors by the academy and its members to facilitate scholarly discourse and production by the early twentieth-century African American intelligentsia.[17] Similarly, University of California historian William Banks' overview of the development of the twentieth-century African American intelligentsia provides further analysis of how the American Negro Academy and other African American cultural institutions (for example, churches, fraternities, sororities, civic associations) facilitated the black intelligentsia's viable modern development.[18] Both the Moss and Banks analyses refute Holloway's claim that the American Negro Academy—and, by extension, similar twentieth-century African American cultural institutions—constrain black intellectuals' work.

Moreover, it seems strange that in both his 2001 *Black Scholar* article and his 2002 book *Confronting the Veil*, Holloway's discourse on the development of the twentieth-century black intelligentsia minimizes the crucial role of African American cultural institutions in shaping the metamorphosis of the black intelligentsia along nonethnocentric lines. After all, it was precisely the endeavors of twentieth-century African American cultural institutions that cultivated a black-ethnic commitment leadership orientation among thousands of black intelligentsia personalities, *while also avoiding the spread of dysfunctional ethnocentric ideological patterns in the mainstream African American intelligentsia.*[19]

In fact, this nonethnocentric ideological metamorphosis among the twentieth-century African American intelligentsia was achieved in the same liberal nonethnocentric manner that a similar nonethnocentric ideological metamorphosis was realized among the mainstream white American intelligentsia, which is to say, among the white Anglo-Saxon Protestant (WASP) American, Irish American, Italian American, Jewish American, Polish American, and other ethnic groups' intelligentsia. Indeed, it was a major achievement of America's major cultural, religious, and ethnic groups to fashion, on the one hand, *ethnic-commitment orientations* among their evolving twentieth-century intelligentsia while, on the other hand, for the most part averting the institutionalization of ethnocentric-ideological patterns among their mainstream intelligentsia. That achievement, I suggest, has proved to be *a fundamental systemic-stabilizing process within the overall leadership sector of the modern post–Civil War era in American society.*

Accordingly, Holloway's endeavor to debunk the Du Boisian black-ethnic commitment leadership orientation's influence in the metamorphosis of the twentieth-century African American intelligentsia fails to understand this. Equally misplaced, I think, is Holloway's observation that "blacks and whites alike have assumed that black intellectuals ought to speak for the black community." For Holloway, this was a regressive assumption on the part of the evolving African American intelligentsia. My response to this observation is: Who else, pray tell, but the fledgling Negro Talented Tenth were the offspring of former slaves supposed to turn to as leaders and spokespersons for advice, guidance, and civil society agencies for constructing viable paths through the rugged terrain of the white-supremacist modern American society? Who?

I have another critical response to Holloway's formulations regarding black folks' expectations of their post–Emancipation era intelligentsia. In his preference for a primal-individualism orientation in shaping the character of the evolving twentieth-century African American intelligentsia, Holloway is governed by what I see as a flawed assumption that operates, as U.S. Supreme Court Justice Oliver Wendell Holmes once put it, like "an inarticulate major premise." Holloway presumes that a primal individualism–oriented intelligentsia-forming dynamic—an intelligentsia pattern free from cultural and ethnic-group obligations—was the norm among the emergent twentieth-century Irish American, Jewish American, Italian American, and other white intelligentsia. I suggest, however, that this assumption is invalid. As a matter of historical experience, the white intelligentsia among the Irish American, Italian American, Jewish American, and WASP communities were often viewed—albeit pragmatically not rigidly—by their cultural and ethnic communities in terms of obligations and responsibilities to these communities.

For example, during the late nineteenth century into the twentieth century, Catholic American communities (for example, Irish, Polish, Italian) and the Jewish American community fashioned what might be called cultural-disciplining agencies (both religious and secular) that influenced the relationship between their intelligentsia and the needs of their larger ethnic communities. This was also true for the WASP communities (Baptists, Presbyterians, Methodists, Congregationalists, Episcopalians, Lutherans) during the late nineteenth and evolving twentieth century. For example, this cultural- and attitude-disciplining function was undertaken among Massachusetts' WASP intelligentsia by the Massachusetts Immigration Society—a civic organization obsessed with anti-Catholicism—during the late nineteenth century and several decades into the twentieth. And a similar cultural-disciplining function was performed in southern states in the late nineteenth and the twentieth century by the Ku Klux Klan, whose Negrophobic militancy had a broad impact among the southern WASP intelligentsia. Whether we probe the Massachusetts Immigration Society, the Ku Klux Klan, or the Daughters of the American Revolution, those particular WASP cultural agencies articulated conservative expectations directed toward the WASP intelligentsia.

Accordingly, as a variety of scholars have informed us, some WASP cultural agencies during the period of the late nineteenth century and the twentieth century placed sociocultural expectations on the shoulders of the WASP intelligentsia.[20] As John Hope Franklin relates in his pioneering 1956 book *The Militant South, 1800–1861*, there were deep ideological and institutional roots underlying the WASP "culture of militancy" in the twentieth-century South. Furthermore, that culture of militancy was sociologically cross-class: both the intelligentsia and lower classes participated in organizations like the Ku Klux Klan from the 1880s to the 1960s and the white Citizen Councils from the 1960s to the 1980s. In short, there has been a long history of the influence of WASP cultural agencies upon the behavior of the WASP intelligentsia, in both the North and the South.

Thus, my analytical point here is plain enough: Holloway is mistaken in his claim that there was something culturally and intellectually illegitimate on the part of those late–Emancipation era black intelligentsia personalities who organized the American Negro Academy in 1897. It apparently matters little to Holloway that the American Negro Academy's guidelines (its "socially and historically specific expectations") eventually facilitated the democratic incorporation of black citizens into a racism-flawed American society. *It assisted the formerly enslaved four million African Americans in navigating the brutal seas of the white-supremacist American industrial civilization.*

Be that as it may, in a further elaboration of the parameters of his primal-individualism perspective, Holloway expands on the analytical meaning of what he calls "crisis canon discourse," giving this concept a formal definition: "This essay offers a consideration of the underlying significance of the black intellectual 'crisis canon'—*a term highlighting the fact that writing about black intellectuals almost always revolves around a crisis of the moment* or the crisis of living in a world where many believe the words 'black' and 'intellectual' are mutually exclusive. *It is clear that the core concept of crisis continues to shape and distort our evaluation of blacks* and black intellectual work to this day."[21]

I interpret Holloway's crisis canon argument as a rhetorical mask for his primal-individualism perspective toward the nascent African American intelligentsia. It is a rhetorical maneuver to make his argument more palatable. Furthermore, Holloway's crisis canon argument enables him to avoid a candid analytical encounter with the role of America's racist oligarchy in ravaging the citizenship status and social capabilities of black people in the early part of the twentieth century.

In this regard, of course, Du Bois' analytical posture toward America's racist oligarchy differed fundamentally from Holloway's analytical posture. Du Bois always confronted the nation's racist patterns head on. When he penned *The Souls of Black Folk* in 1903, he fully understood that the viable modern development of the Negro masses required both a candid analytical critique of and a civil rights activist assault on America's racist oligarchy. Put another way, Du Bois understood that the crucial leadership task of intellectually critiquing and politically challenging the American racist oligarchy that oppressed Negroes *was not going to be adopted as an obligation by a significant segment of America's white intelligentsia.* Thus, like the founders of the American Negro Academy in 1897, Du Bois understood intuitively that the ideological, intellectual, and political assault on the American racist oligarchy rested primarily on the shoulders of the evolving twentieth-century African American intelligentsia. Accordingly, when viewed from this analytical vantage, Holloway's crisis canon argument in his 2001 *Black Scholar* article offers very little elucidation. It fails to suggest possibilities for how beleaguered black people might challenge the American racist oligarchy, rather than remaining politically quiescent and inert.

So I arrive at the conclusion that Holloway has fashioned an intellectual discourse that is antithetical to the Du Boisian black-ethnic commitment intellectual orientation. It rejects, above all, what might be called an "uplift-the-race" black intelligentsia ethos that many evolving twentieth-century African American intellectuals were sympathetic toward. Holloway's voyage into the sea of twentieth-century black intelligentsia metamorphosis netted him some African American studies intellectual fish that he did not like, because they swam in "black-ethnic commitment waters," so to speak (for example, his 2001 *Black Scholar* article has a section critical of African American studies programs and scholars like Henry Louis Gates Jr. and Cornel West). Yet, interestingly enough, Holloway did net several twentieth-century black intellectuals he admired because they swam in what might be called "primal-individualism waters."

Those intellectuals were the economist Abram Harris, the sociologist E. Franklin Frazier, and the political scientist Ralph J. Bunche. Harris and Frazier were educated at Negro colleges and went to the University of Chicago for graduate study in economics and sociology, respectively. That was a typical route to professional training that many evolving twentieth-century black intellectuals and professionals took: undergraduate education at a Negro college followed by enrollment at a white university for graduate-level work. However, as an African American youth during the era between the two world wars, Bunche took what was partly a rare path to higher education. He earned his undergraduate degree at the University of California, Los Angeles—the only black in the class of 1926. For graduate school he went to Harvard University, earning a Ph.D. in 1934.

In his 2002 book *Confronting the Veil: Abram Harris Jr., E. Franklin Frazier, and Ralph J. Bunche, 1919–1941*, Holloway probes the academic careers of three prominent African American intellectuals during the era between the two world wars. He discusses the intellectual dynamics that characterized their metamorphosis during that period, focusing on the ways in which their metamorphosis diverged from those African American intellectuals who were associated with the Du Boisian black-ethnic commitment leadership orientation.

In some respects, it might be said that as interwar-era African American intelligentsia personalities, the intellectual careers of Harris, Frazier, and Bunche represented a kind of black intelligentsia anomaly. On the one hand, they were ideologically liberal and publicly known as leftists, while on the other hand *they were opposed to black ethnic-group-based political mobilization.* It was especially this attribute that rendered them favorable in Holloway's eyes as black intelligentsia personalities. After all, inasmuch as the mainline African American intelligentsia in the evolving twentieth century was broadly influenced by the Du Boisian intellectual and leadership legacy, Holloway viewed it as a positive intellectual attribute of Harris, Frazier, and Bunche that they did not suffer from this condition, so to speak, a condition that, for Holloway, amounted to a kind of "normative malady." Accordingly, Holloway uses one of Frazier's essays on Du Bois to support his perspective on Harris, Frazier, and Bunche: a rather testy critique of the Du Boisian leadership outlook that appeared in the 1935 debut issue of the Fisk University journal *Race*:

> Du Bois' racial [uplift] program needs not to be taken seriously. Cultural hybrids [such as Du Bois] often have "returned" to the minority race with which they were identified, glorified it and made significant additions to the artistic culture of the group. But Du Bois remains an intellectual who toys with the idea of the Negro as a separate cultural group. He has only an occasional romantic interest in the Negro as a distinct race. Nothing would be more unendurable for him than to live within a Black Ghetto or within a Black nation—unless perhaps he were king. . . . If a fascist movement should develop in America, Du Bois would play into the hands of its leaders through the development of his program for Negro racialism. As the situation is at present, the dominant social and economic forces in American life are destroying the possibility of the development of Negro nationalism.[22]

Note how dismissive the young sociologist Frazier is toward the older, progressive and black ethnic-group-friendly Du Bois. First, Frazier makes a disparaging reference to Du Bois' fair skin, labeling him a "cultural hybrid." He then indulges in young Turk–type posturing toward Du Bois that comes across as rather dismissive. After all, Du Bois had contributed Herculean service to the metamorphosis of the African American intelligentsia by the 1930s: he had inspired the Niagara Movement in 1905, was a founding member of the NAACP in 1909, inspired the several pan-African conferences of the 1920s that challenged the naked restoration of European colonialism in post–World War I Africa, and played a catalytic role in fashioning the core precepts of modern African American progressivism. Accordingly, from my analytical perspective, Frazier's 1935 commentary on Du Bois was mistaken.

The nearest Holloway got to a critical view of Frazier's 1935 article was his reference to "the stunning intensity of Frazier's critique."[23] Besides this reference, Holloway employs what can be considered a friendly tone as he informs his readers that Frazier's assault "certainly represented yet another attempt by a young intellectual to break free of the domination of his elders." Holloway continued thus: "Frazier's scorn also grew from his attempt . . . to distance himself from Du Bois' new racialist and 'romanticist' agenda. Where Frazier had only given hints of his class-driven worldview and tough mindedness in 'La Bourgeoisie Noire' [a 1929 essay], he now seemed unstoppable in his quest to find a proper solution to race problems in the United States. In addition to his invectives against James Weldon Johnson [head of NAACP], Du Bois, and Charles S. Johnson [Fisk University sociologist], Frazier amplified his argument regarding the economic basis of black oppression in the United States."[24]

It should be noted, moreover, that Holloway firmly endorses what he calls Harris, Frazier, and Bunche's "class analysis" perspective toward the issue that engaged a broad range of the evolving twentieth-century African American intelligentsia: ameliorating the racially oppressed status of black folks in American society. For Holloway, the "class analysis" perspective meant that Harris, Frazier, and Bunche were cool toward the black ethnic-group mode of political mobilization against American racism. As a prelude to his main discussion of their preference for class-based activism by African Americans, Holloway informs his readers of ties that Harris, Frazier, and Bunche had with Marxist intellectual networks during the 1930s. Both Frazier and Bunche were on the editorial board of a major left-wing academic journal, the *Modern Quarterly: A Marxist Review,* and Holloway draws upon Abram Harris' correspondence with its editor, V. F. Calverton, to illustrate Harris' commitment to Marxist class discourse regarding racial patterns in American society. Other studies on the careers of Harris, Frazier, and Bunche also relate their preference for Marxist class discourse regarding racial dynamics, one operational outcome of which was that they believed that joint black-white political mobilization was the indispensable route to vanquishing the American racist oligarchy.[25]

Moreover, Harris and Bunche were committed to this approach to black political mobilization more so than Frazier was. I have researched Bunche's relationship with civil rights activist organizations in Washington, D.C., during the 1930s and discovered that his preference for joint black-white political mobilization resulted in factious relations between Bunche and black ethnic-group activist organizations.[26] From 1933 until America's entry into World War II, a small cadre of civil rights–activist black professionals led by the political scientist John Aubrey Davis (along with the civil rights lawyers William Hastie, Belford Lawson, James Nabrit, and George Johnson) organized the earliest "Don't Buy Where You Can't Work" civil rights organization. Known as the New Negro Alliance (NNA), the organization had the goal of opening jobs for African Americans in white commercial businesses located in black neighborhoods. As a professor of political science at Howard University when the NNA was founded in 1933, Ralph Bunche had friendship ties with NNA leaders like Hastie, Nabrit, and Johnson, who also taught at Howard University. But inasmuch as the NNA was a black ethnic-group mode of political activism, Bunche kept his distance from it.

As University of California political scientist Charles Henry relates in his 1999 intellectual portrait of Bunche, during the 1930s Bunche adhered to a fervent Marxist vision of political mobilization for African Americans—a vision that differed in sociocultural terms from the black-ethnic-based activism promoted by the 1930s NNA movement.[27] Paralleling Henry's analysis, I analyzed this situation in a 2007 study I published on the NNA's founder, John Aubrey Davis, in the following terms:

Bunche believed that the racist oppression of African Americans should not be challenged merely along the lines of Black-ethnic activism and mobilization. Rather, he saw an alliance with the White American working class and its trade unions as a precondition for effective Black American civil rights activism. John Aubrey Davis, Hastie and other New Negro Alliance members rejected this position because there was no serious evidence that White workers were ready to challenge American racism; rather they were among its core practitioners. As Davis put it in correspondence to me: "Bunche was never a member [of the NNA], only a critic. . . . Bunche attacked the New Negro Alliance because he feared the division of the labor movement on the basis of race."[28]

Holloway also presents a keen assessment of Harris, Frazier, and Bunche's deep antipathy to the NNA's ethnic-group-based political mobilization against racist hiring practices by white-owned businesses in Washington, D.C. "The New Negro Alliance and the Amenia [1933 Conference] Delegates [which included Harris, Frazier, and Bunche] . . . shared the same general philosophy," writes Holloway. One would think, then, that Harris, Frazier, and Bunche would have at least expressed sympathy with the NNA's boycott, but this was not the case. "What separated the two groups," Holloway observes, "was the Alliance's belief that true reform would happen through intraracial [black ethnic-group] organization." Holloway then elaborates the core elements of this cleavage between the Marxist class approach and the NNA's black ethnic-group mobilization: "The leaders of the NNA advocated a platform of racial solidarity that Bunche and Harris could not accept. Because the NNA organized around the principle of replacing white workers with black (through normal labor turnover) in those stores that served a predominantly black population, Harris and Bunche viewed the alliance as unnecessarily antagonistic to the unification of white and black laborers."[29]

Interestingly enough, even the broad-based participation in the NNA's protests by prominent figures among Washington's leading middle-class black personalities did not abate Harris, Frazier, and Bunche's antipathy to the NNA. As Holloway puts it: "Even the most prominent black Washingtonians took part. Mary McLeod Bethune, head of the Negro Division of the National Youth Administration, leader of Franklin Roosevelt's so-called 'black cabinet,' and close friend of the First Lady, could be seen carrying NNA picket signs declaring 'Peoples [Drug Store] Unfair.

No Colored Clerks In Colored Neighborhoods. Stay Out!'"[30] Further-more, in an address Bunche delivered to a meeting of the NNA on March 17, 1935, he became rather shrill in articulating his disagreement with the NNA's black ethnic-bloc activism, arrogantly chastising the NNA's leaders—Davis, Hastie, Nabrit, and Charles Hamilton Houston—for what he called their "obvious short-sightedness, . . . petty opportunism . . . and babbitry." He then elaborated as follows:

> The blame for this must, of course, fall on the shoulders of the leadership of the organization; which is either entirely devoid of knowledge and under-standing of the dominant social facts and theories in American life today, and the relation of the Negro to them, or else dishonest and cowardly. My concern and interest are stirred not because of any importance of the work of the organization—for I think that relatively unimportant—but rather because the NNA is symbolic of a very vital aspect of Negro [activism] tech-nique and thinking in the U.S., and because it is such a fertile means of propagating another crop of Negro misleaders.[31]

Although Holloway mentions that, in this address, Bunche had un-necessarily "launched an attack on the black middle class in a [Washing-ton] neighborhood and to an audience that was comprised of the black middle class and middle-class aspirants,"[32] Holloway persists in his be-lief that the leftist interracial activism preferred by Harris, Frazier, and Bunche was a superior form of African American intelligentsia leader-ship. "Harris, Frazier, Bunche shared several common interests," writes Holloway: "Most significantly, they articulated an important vision in the evolving black intellectual tradition that militated against racialist [black ethnic-group] thought and advocated a class-driven worldview with a biracial workers' movement at its core. . . . Class [mobilization] was the answer, not race [black group mobilization]."[33]

Holloway's analytical schema leads him to the view that Harris, Fra-zier, and Bunche derived what he calls "logical benefits" owing to their rejection of black ethnic-group discourse and mobilization. By "logical benefits," Holloway means "superior analytical results" in their aca-demic writings, or, to use Holloway's words, "They were . . . convinced that their scholarship represented the best in objective, scientific reason-ing, and while they displayed a taste for ad hominem attacks on rivals, they maintained their faith in objectivity."[34] Following this favorable description of Harris, Frazier, and Bunche's preference for class-based rather than black ethnic-group-based discourse strategies, Holloway continues: "Such a stance [against black ethnic-group discourse] had logical benefits. . . . Because race was a constructed phenomenon and had no basis in objective reality, *whereas [with] class [analysis] . . . the social scientist could dismiss race's centrality as a causative social force.* By refusing race a defining role, the social scientist could devote attention to universal issues like health and welfare. Harris, Frazier, and Bunche attempted to do just this."[35]

I need hardly point out that the foregoing formulation by Holloway as a defense of his argument in favor of Harris, Frazier, and Bunche's antipathy to black ethnic-bloc political activism is analytically confusing. For one thing, Holloway thinks it is a valid proposition when he writes that "the social scientist could dismiss race's centrality as a causative social force." His reason or evidence for this proposition is his prior claim that "race was a constructed phenomenon and had no basis in objective reality." However, I would argue that this claim by Holloway is only true in biophilosophical terms. But in terms of real-world social-power systems and their historical dynamics, "race" has historically been and remains today what can be called an objectively power-linked phenomenon. In support of this observation, I refer to the fascinating 1998 book by Brandeis University historian Jacqueline Jones, *American Work: Four Centuries of Black and White Labor.* Jones is partly concerned with the racist structuring of the oppressed status of black people as laborers during several centuries of the formation of labor force and modern wealth in the American economy. She relates how various racial ideologies applied by whites systemically transformed peoples of African descent into a racial category that was culturally set apart from the white majority, on the one hand, but a source of wealth formation (largely for the benefit of white people), on the other. As Jones puts it:

> Racial ideologies are fluid, and reflective of shifting power relations over time. These ideologies in fact constitute strategies deployed for specific reasons; rhetoric more often than not follows function. By focusing on the idea of racial differences as one among any number of political weapons, it is possible to outline at least three historical contexts in which this has been used. First, groups of relatively powerful people have claimed "racial" superiority over other groups in order to enforce a certain kind of labor upon them. Second, people who perform the same kinds of work as people labeled "racially" inferior have seized upon racial ideologies to distance themselves

from the targeted group. For example, at certain times these ideologies proved useful to southern white sharecroppers and tenants, people who shared with blacks certain jobs . . . and feared that historic forces of economic inequality would condemn them to continue to work alongside blacks in the future. *These specific, strategic uses of racial ideologies remind us that emerging classes of whites have often used blacks as a counter-reference group, defining themselves as a unified group . . . not just on the basis of who they are, but also on the basis of who they are not—that is, "blacks."*[36]

Be that as it may, throughout both his 2001 *Black Scholar* article and his book *Confronting the Veil,* Holloway sustains his commitment to the class-linked social perspective on African American realities favored by Harris, Frazier, and Bunche, rather than the race-linked discourse favored by black-ethnic commitment-oriented intellectuals. Holloway expresses this preference as follows in *Confronting the Veil:* "It is important to realize that Harris, Frazier, and Bunche set standards for their [black] peers and protégés. If nothing else, their commitment to an anti-racialist, class-based agenda, even if some deemed it quixotic, proved that black intellectuals and their ideas could not be put into a single box, labeled 'Expert On All Things Black', to be opened or closed depending on one's whim."[37]

I think the foregoing formulation by Holloway is a quest to bestow something like a superior analytical and ethical imprimatur on the Harris-Frazier-Bunche sector of the black intelligentsia—superior, that is, to the black-ethnic commitment-oriented sector. In this quest, however, I think Holloway is analytically mistaken on this issue. For example, take Holloway's claim that "Harris, Frazier, and Bunche set standards for their [black] peers." By "standards," Holloway is referring to both "analytical standards" and "ethical standards." Here Holloway's discourse, in its ethical tilt, overlaps the so-called anti-essentialist discourse that rejects sociopolitical mobilization patterns that are structured through the agency of racial-ethnic groups and cultural groups (religious groups, gender groups, etc.). Basic to "anti-essentialist" discourse is the important concern that racial- or ethnic-inspired and cultural group–inspired political mobilization can easily assume—in nation-state societies—parochial "us-versus-them" xenophobic dimensions. After all, in Europe between the 1920s and the end of World War II, xenophobic essentialism was transformed monstrously into institutionalized pogroms and genocide carried out by fascist nation-states.

While as a liberal African American academic I have long shared the core concerns of anti-essentialist discourse, I also believe that this discourse contains a major analytical limitation when applied to black ethnic-based civil rights political mobilization against America's racist oligarchy. Such political mobilization by the mainstream African American intelligentsia against America's white-supremacist processes has been, throughout the twentieth century, overwhelmingly defined by and structured through constitutionalist and pluralist democratic modalities. This, I suggest, is due in part to the African American intelligentsia's long-standing roots in Christian social gospel activism—roots that extend back to black American abolitionists, especially to the clergy-based abolitionists like J. W. C. Pennington and John Sella Martin.[38]

Du Bois was an early enunciator of a constitutionalist and liberal-reformist black mobilization against America's racist oligarchy, and he practiced this doctrine in every black leadership organization he was associated with. Du Bois articulated this orientation in 1903 in *The Souls of Black Folk,* where he explains the ideological differences between his principles of civil rights activism and Booker T. Washington's principles of accommodationism. "If [Bookerite] reconciliation [with white supremacy] is to be marked by the industrial slavery and civic death of . . . black men, with permanent legislation into a position of inferiority," observed Du Bois in 1903, *"then those black men . . . are called upon by every consideration of patriotism and loyalty to oppose such a course by all civilized methods."*[39] Moreover, when Du Bois joined Monroe Trotter and several others as founders of the first early twentieth-century African American civil rights organization—the 1905 Niagara Movement, which was the progenitor of the 1909 NAACP—they firmly articulated their organization's intertwining of civil rights activism and constitutionalist-democratic norms. As the 1905 Niagara Movement's charter put it: "We will not be satisfied to take one jot or tittle less than our full manhood rights. We claim for ourselves every single right that belongs to a freeborn American, political, civil, and social; and until we get these rights we will never cease to protest and assail the ears of America. *The battle we wage is not for ourselves alone, but for all true Americans. It is a fight for ideals."*[40]

Of course, from the post–Civil War Emancipation era into the twentieth century, a variety of modes of activism against America's racist oligarchy vied for political hegemony among African Americans, groups like the Garvey Movement in the 1920s and 1930s and the Nation of Islam in the 1960s. But none of these xenophobic, essentialist-obsessed groups ever acquired a sustained cross-generational legitimacy and prominence at the core of African American mainstream political leadership and civil society agencies (for example, churches, mutual aid associations, women's organizations, fraternal groups, artisan associations, trade unions, and teachers' and academic associations). I suggest, moreover, that this outcome was partly due to the deep roots in modern African American society of Christian social gospel activism ideas. Black abolitionist clergy in the North propagated social gospel activism ideas that represented a Christian humanitarian ethos, as related by the Wesleyan University historian David Swift in his 1998 book *Black Prophets of Justice: Activist Clergy before the Civil War.*[41]

Thus, I repeat my earlier point that Jonathan Holloway's attempt to attach a superior achievement imprimatur on Harris, Frazier, and Bunche's primal-individualism approach to the evolving twentieth-century African American intelligentsia cannot be supported—it lacks an evidential defense. Equally mistaken is Holloway's caricature formulation of what he views as a kind of *generic intellectual flaw* associated with the Du Boisian black-ethnic commitment leadership orientation—an orientation that broad ranks of the twentieth-century black intelligentsia adhered to in various ways. As Holloway formulates his view of the mainstream black intelligentsia's presumed generic intellectual flaw, he asserts that Harris, Frazier, and Bunche's "commitment to an anti-racialist, class-based agenda . . . proved that black intellectuals and their ideas could not be put into a single box, labeled 'Expert On All Things Black.'"[42]

Here again, Holloway's formulation in support of Harris, Frazier, and Bunche is analytically flawed: from the 1920s onward, talented civil rights activist–oriented black scholars and intellectuals produced superior-quality scholarly works in their academic fields, and those works did not exhibit what Holloway views as a generic intellectual flaw associated with black-ethnic xenophobic essentialism. I have in mind such first-rank African American scholars as Kelly Miller (mathematician and essayist), Carter G. Woodson (historian), Benjamin Mays (theologian), Ira Reid (sociologist), Robert Weaver (economist), Lorenzo Turner (anthropologist), Charles S. Johnson (sociologist), Adelaide Cromwell (sociologist), Irene Diggs (anthropologist), John Aubrey Davis (political scientist), Laurence Foster (anthropologist), William Hastie (law scholar), James Nabrit (law scholar), St. Clair Drake (anthropologist), Doxie Wilkerson (sociologist), Emmett Dorsey (political scientist), Gordon Hancock (sociologist), Horace Mann Bond (sociologist), Charles Hamilton Houston (law scholar), Sterling Brown (literary studies scholar), and George Johnson (law and public policy scholar), to mention just a prominent few.

In short, a sizable cadre of civil rights activist–oriented African American intellectuals produced both high-level and xenophobic-free scholarly studies from the years between the two world wars onward.[43] And they did so without being intellectually and morally entrapped by what Holloway views as the "essentialist mystique." None of them needed what Holloway considers the superior primal-individualism intelligentsia perspective associated with Harris, Frazier, and Bunche to intertwine African American progressivism with high-quality intellectual performance. As I suggested above, the deep normative roots of a Christian social gospel ethos—which has been broadcast in the nooks and crannies of African American culture from the dawn of Emancipation onward—gave the mainstream sector of the evolving twentieth-century African American intelligentsia a virtual immunity against the black-ethnic essentialism mystique.[44]

In general, it can be said that the socioeconomic and institutional attributes that characterize the African American intelligentsia here in the early twenty-first century provide this elite a broad range of resources for a revival of a black-communitarian leadership dynamic. Such a revival would represent the fulfillment of a debt that I believe today's black elite owe to the twentieth-century Du Boisian leadership legacy.

The discourse and analysis that I have presented in this chapter relate how the Du Boisian black-ethnic commitment leadership orientation helped to galvanize the developmental trajectory of the progressive sector of the African American intelligentsia. A sizable part of this chapter also defends the developmental impact of the Du Boisian black-ethnic commitment leadership ethos against critics of the Du Boisian leadership legacy, in particular the Yale University historian Jonathan Holloway.

Finally, what can we say about the character of modern systemic benefits that have accrued to African Americans depending on which segment of the intelligentsia—oriented toward either a black-ethnic commitment ethos or a primal-individualism ethos—held primacy in the post–World War II mature phase of twentieth-century African American society? Let's call this the "systemic benefits" issue.

On the basis of the analytical exegesis on Holloway's discourse that I present in this chapter, it appears that his discourse concludes that, had the twentieth-century African American intelligentsia pursued a primal-individualism leadership orientation, what might be called a high-sophistication intelligentsia leadership dynamic would have been the result in the post–World War II period, which for Holloway would be the desired modern systemic benefit accruing to African American society in its developed or mature post–World War II phase.

But my analytical understanding of the metamorphosis of the twentieth-century African American intelligentsia differs fundamentally from Holloway's. For Holloway, it is the primal-individualism intellectual modalities that would have best defined the overall African American intelligentsia's twentieth-century metamorphosis. From my analytical perspective, however, the ultimate evaluation of the African American intelligentsia should be based on the degree of the aggregate African American society's modern social advancement. My analytical perspective gives very little credence to Holloway's high-sophistication intelligentsia dynamic as a significant systemic benefit accruing to African American society in its mature late twentieth-century phase; instead, it was the black-ethnic commitment leadership orientation that afforded African American society a major systemic benefit during this time period.

This systemic-benefit outcome was achieved because the Du Boisian black-ethnic commitment leadership orientation facilitated what might be called a "black-masses-friendly" identity among the evolving twentieth-century African American intelligentsia. *That identity perspective, in turn, mentally equipped and emboldened the late twentieth-century African American intelligentsia to challenge head on America's racist oligarchy's authoritarian-type interface with African American citizens.* Holloway's high-sophistication intelligentsia identity orientation, on the other hand, translates, I suggest, into an African American intelligentsia leadership dynamic that minimizes the systemic salience of the oligarchic racial realm underlying the oppressed status of black people in the American system.

I suggest, therefore, that when a black-ethnic commitment-oriented African American intelligentsia did in fact evolve as the prominent leadership sector in post–World War II black society, it was reasonable to expect that this sector would mobilize black people against the American racist oligarchy. On the other hand, a high-sophistication, identity-oriented African American intelligentsia that, in Holloway's discourse in *Confronting the Veil,* operated at arm's length vis-à-vis black ethnic-group mobilization in the interwar years was unlikely to challenge America's racist oligarchy in the postwar period.

Accordingly, as related in studies like Barbara Ranby's 2003 book *Ella Baker and the Black Freedom Movement,* it was indeed the black-ethnic commitment-oriented sector of the African American intelligentsia that orchestrated a nationwide civil rights mobilization from the early 1950s onward—a grassroots mobilization of black people that fashioned the militant phase of the Civil Rights movement.[45] Moreover, key progressive groundwork gave organizational muscle to this phase of the Civil Rights movement, for example, the 1950s Montgomery Boycott Movement, the 1960s Freedom Summer and the concomitant launch of the Student Nonviolent Coordinating Committee's voter rights movement led by Robert Moses, John Lewis, and James Lawson, and the Freedom Rides launched by James Farmer's Congress on Racial Equality in May 1961. University of Pennsylvania historian Thomas Sugrue characterizes these progressive building blocks of the Civil Rights movement's militant phase as follows:

> In 1961, CORE sponsored a series of Freedom Rides to desegregate interstate bus transportation in the South. Some of the older protestors—the seasoned veterans of the [Civil Rights] movement such as CORE's James Peck and James Farmer—had come out of the northern [Civil Rights] movement to open up public accommodations. High school and college students, with the aid of Ella Baker, then working for [the Rev. Martin Luther] King and SCLC [Southern Christian Leadership Conference], formed the Student Nonviolent Coordinating Committee and began efforts to organize black voters in the rural Black Belt. In 1962 and 1963, Martin Luther King, Jr., led a series of marches, culminating in the brutal repression of the protests by Birmingham, Alabama, police in April 1963.[46]

It is, I think, a core consensus among the major scholarship produced on the era of the militant Civil Rights movement that its progressive mobilization against America's racist oligarchy—which existed both in the South and North—was absolutely critical to producing the major federal government antisegregation legislation in the mid- and late 1960s (for example, the 1964 Civil Rights Act and the Voting Rights Act of 1965), as well as the general federal public policies that bureaucratically reinforced and institutionalized that legislation. Accordingly, I have argued in this chapter—and indeed, in this book—that the myriad ideological, political, and intellectual strands that gathered under the umbrella of the Du Boisian black-ethnic commitment-oriented intelligentsia were indispensable to the Civil Rights movement's achievements and, thereby, to today's systemically mature African American intelligentsia.

By contrast, I do not believe that an intelligentsia that defined itself along the lines of a primal-individualism intelligentsia orientation would have produced the multilayered progressive activism dynamics that the Civil Rights movement spawned, thereby challenging head on the structural components of America's racist oligarchy. Those structural components were thoroughly anti-democratic, which is to say, they were ideologically white supremacist and committed to state violence and vigilante violence as mechanisms for sustaining America's racist patterns. Accordingly, had an African American intelligentsia defined by a primal-individualism leadership orientation claimed the premier leadership place in late twentieth-century African American society (rather than, as happened, the premier leadership being claimed by an intelligentsia defined by a black-ethnic commitment orientation), I suggest that the militant-phase Civil Rights movement would not have appeared on the American political scene when it did.

Instead, a quite different kind of African American systemic outcome would have occurred. Fashioned by a high-sophistication-oriented African American intelligentsia as understood by Jonathan Holloway, the overall systemic outcome for the late twentieth-century African American society would have been a variant of Booker T. Washington's accommodationist, reconciliation-type African American intelligentsia. In suggesting this hypothetical analysis, I am drawing upon Du Bois' cogent 1903 critique of the accommodationist black leadership that he proffered in *The Souls of Black Folk*.[47] Black men, Du Bois insisted, must vigorously and actively oppose white America's racist oligarchy and never accommodate with it until full-fledged citizenship and human rights for black folks are ensured.

Accordingly, with his candid critique of Booker T. Washington's reconciliation-with-racism outlook, Du Bois in 1903 was delineating the core precepts underlying the black-ethnic commitment leadership orientation. In his formulation of how a fledgling African American intelligentsia's leadership trajectory should interface with the American racist oligarchy during the evolving twentieth century, it appears that Du Bois was echoing aspects of the black leadership orientation articulated forty-six years earlier by the black abolitionist Frederick Douglass. Douglass expounded on a progressive black leadership methodology on numerous occasions, perhaps most notably in an August 1857 address in Canandaigua, New York (on the western branch of the Mohawk River), titled "The Significance of Emancipation in the West Indies." In that portentous speech, Douglass proclaimed to his audience of white and black abolitionists that he wanted to "give you a word of the philosophy of reform." He proceeded thus:

> The whole history of the progress of human liberty shows that all concessions yet made to her august claims, have been born of earnest struggle. . . . If there is no struggle there is no progress. Those who profess to favor freedom and yet deprecate agitation are men who want crops without plowing up the ground, they want rain without thunder and lightning. *This struggle may be a moral one, or it may be a physical one, but it must be a struggle. Power concedes nothing without a demand. It never did and it never will.* . . . If we ever get free from the oppressions and wrongs heaped upon us, we must pay for their removal. We must do this by labor, by suffering, by sacrifice, and if needs be, by our lives and the lives of others.[48]

Thus, in concert with Du Bois' 1903 enunciation of the precepts of a progressive black leadership methodology, the prominent sector of the evolving twentieth-century African American intelligentsia fashioned a broad range of civil society agencies and civil rights organizations that challenged head on the institutional mechanisms and ideologies of America's racist oligarchy. Viewed from our twenty-first-century vantage, it is reasonable to argue that the Du Boisian–inspired leadership trajectory of the twentieth-century black intelligentsia has provided African Americans greater democratic participation rights and egalitarian opportunity than would have the Booker T. Washington reconciliation-with-racism black leadership methodology.[49]

Finally, the overall normative thrust of this book's analysis of the key processes that characterized the transformational dynamics of the twentieth-century African American intelligentsia points toward a possible revival of a Du Boisian–type black-communitarian civic-uplift leadership pattern in contemporary African American society. Of course, whether a viable black-communitarian leadership dynamic will emerge at some point within the twenty-first century remains to be seen. My own analytical pre-dilections suggest to me that there is a good probability that such a leader-ship dynamic will evolve.

Conceptually, such a revival must have at least two sets of facilitating attributes: structural and ideological. The structural attributes relate to the evolution of a fairly broad-based middle-class-type social structure in Afri-can American society as it exited the twentieth century and entered the twenty-first. The ideological attributes relate to the issue of how to fashion a cross-class normative nexus within contemporary African American so-ciety, whereby the nearly two-thirds of today's African Americans who inhabit the middle-class sector develop helping-hand civic-uplift pro-grams to assist social advancement among the 40 percent poor and poor working-class African Americans—those whom Harvard sociologist Wil-liam Julius Wilson labels the "black have-not" sector. I reflect further on this important issue in Chapter 4 of this book.

4

BLACK ELITE PATTERNS IN THE
TWENTY-FIRST CENTURY

W HEN ONE LOOKS BACK across a century to the metamorphosis of the Du Boisian leadership legacy, it is interesting to ponder whether the primarily liberal political contours of today's African American intelligentsia or professional stratum would have prevailed had Booker T. Washington and his masterful leadership survived into the first half of the twentieth century, rather than dying prematurely from a heart attack in 1915. It is arguable that, thanks in large part to the Du Boisian leadership legacy, today's twenty-first-century African American intelligentsia in general embraces liberal ideological and political patterns.

On the basis of both national voting data and attitude surveys, today's African American intelligentsia, or professional stratum, is generally more liberal than its counterparts among Irish Americans, Italian Americans, Jewish Americans, WASP Americans, Hispanic Americans, Asian Americans, and other groups. This, in turn, has contributed to an overall liberal political outlook among African American citizenry in general. These leanings were initially apparent in early studies of black Americans' voting patterns in the North during the 1930s and 1940s, as reported by NAACP official Henry Lee Moon in the pioneering 1948 book *Balance of Power: The Negro Vote*.[1] And following the full-fledged broadening of voting rights for African Americans by the 1965 Voting Rights Act, a variety of studies have reported African Americans' persistent liberal political tendencies, such as those reported in William Nelson and Philip Meranto's 1977 book *Electing Black Mayors: Political Action in the Black Community*.[2]

Liberalism among blacks was especially evident during the 2008 presidential election. For the first time in history, an African American headed the Democratic Party's ticket. Barack Obama, the one-term senator from Illinois, energized the party and rose to the top of the field of candidates, choosing as his running mate the longtime senator from Delaware Joe Biden. An astounding 95 percent of African American voters supported Obama and Biden in their bid for the executive office, compared with 43 percent of white voters, 77 percent of Jewish voters, and 67 percent of Hispanic voters.[3] Furthermore, the liberal Obama-Biden Democratic ticket appealed consistently to African Americans in states with a high electoral-college ranking, as shown in Table 4.1.

Now, in light of the fact that the elite sector and the popular sector of twenty-first-century African American society share similar liberal political views, it is reasonable to suggest that a revitalized black-communitarian leadership dynamic could develop at some point in the near future. As I pointed out in Chapter 2, when I first mentioned the black-communitarian leadership pattern, I was referring to *middle-class and professional-class African Americans' use of their resources to advance overall black civil society development.* In his early intellectual

Table 4.1. Black voters' preference in select states in the 2008 U.S. presidential election (%)

State	Black percentage of voting-age population	Percentage of votes	
		Obama-Biden	McCain-Palin
Alabama	25.0	98	2
Arkansas	15.0	94	4
California	8.0	95	5
Florida	14.0	96	4
Illinois	15.0	96	3
Maryland	29.6	94	6
Michigan	13.8	97	3
Missouri	10.8	93	7
New York	15.9	100	0
North Carolina	21.4	95	5
Ohio	11.3	97	2
Pennsylvania	9.5	95	5
Texas	12.5	98	2
Virginia	19.7	92	8

Source: Data from David Bositis, *Blacks and the 2008 Election* (Washington, DC: Joint Center for Political and Economic Studies, December 2008).

discourse, W. E. B. Du Bois formulates the core attributes of black-communitarian leadership orientation as the desired interface between the Talented Tenth sector of black American society and the Negro masses in the evolving twentieth-century American social system.

Du Bois, of course, did not use the social science term "black communitarian" when describing the generic black leadership nexus with the frightful plight of the socially ravaged early twentieth-century Negro masses. Instead, Du Bois' language was an admixture of clinical and lyrical discourse, a literary writing style he first experimented with in *The Souls of Black Folk* in 1903. In chapter 4, titled "Of the Meaning of Progress," he relates his spiritual quest to reach out to and assist the South's oppressed Negro agrarian masses, whose children he met face-to-face while a Fisk University student and young teacher in rural Tennessee during two summers in 1886 and 1887. "It was a hot morning late in July when the school opened," Du Bois ruminates movingly: "I trembled when I heard the patter of little feet down the dusty road, and saw the growing row of dark solemn faces and bright eager eyes facing me." He continued: "There they sat, nearly thirty of them, on the rough benches, their faces shading from a pale cream to a deep brown, the little feet bare and swinging, the eyes full of expectation . . . and the hands grasping Webster's blue-back spelling book. I loved my school [and for] . . . two summers I lived in this little world."[4]

Here, then, was the kernel of what can be called a black-communitarian leadership ethos dwelling in the fertile mind and soul of a Fisk University student named William Edward Burghardt Du Bois in the late 1880s. The connection he made to those students, I suggest, was also an epiphany moment for Du Bois that eventually shaped the political contours of the evolving twentieth-century Du Boisian leadership dynamic. At the core of that dynamic was, above all else, the goal of intermeshing the accumulated capabilities of the Talented Tenth with the modern development needs of the evolving twentieth-century Negro masses.

Fast-forward to twenty-first-century African American society. Today the sociological and political patterns that characterize African American society differ fundamentally from what Du Bois described in *The Souls of Black Folk* at the dawn of the twentieth century. Thanks in part to the Civil Rights movement's activist challenge to America's racist patterns, myriad federal government policies and bureaucratic practices from 1964 onward—especially the Civil Rights Act of 1964—vanquished legal racist institutions and facilitated important advancement in social mobility for a sizable segment of the African American population.

A substantial middle-class and professional-class sector exists today in African American society, one that can claim educational, occupational, political, and wealth attributes that were totally inconceivable when Du Bois penned his pioneering essay "The Talented Tenth" for the 1903 volume *The Negro Problem.* As Du Bois reported then, in 1900 there were just 1,996 "college-bred Negroes"; today, more than half (55 percent) of African American high school graduates enroll in college (compared with 70 percent of white high school graduates).[5]

Furthermore, according to data from the U.S. Census Bureau's 2002 and 2006 surveys of occupations (shown in Table 4.3), *today some 3,722,000 African Americans hold top-tier white-collar occupations,* or 26 percent of some 14.7 million employed African Americans—even more if the Census Bureau's category of "administrative support and clerical jobs" is included in this calculation. It is this top-tier category of white-collar employed African Americans who constitute the core of the African American middle-class and professional-class sector—referred to as the "black elite sector" in this chapter.

Harvard sociologist Lawrence Bobo presents a five-part classification of today's African American society: "comfortable," "middle class," "new poor," "poor," and "very poor." He characterized the top-tier, "comfortable" rank as follows: "At the very top [of black social structure] are those in the 'comfortable' category, having family incomes that are five times or more the poverty level. The proportion of whites in this upper category exceeded 10 percent in 1960 and rose to nearly 30 percent by 2008. For blacks, the proportion [in the upper category] was less than 5 percent in 1968 but about 12 percent in 2008."[6] Bobo also presents quantified data for what he calls the "middle class" of African American society, as of 2008. This category constituted 8 percent of black American families in 1968 and about 35 percent in 2008. Thus, when Bobo's figures for the "middle-class" and "comfortable-class" categories for African Americans are combined, *some 47 percent of African American families were eligible in 2008 for the sector I label the black elite sector.*

There remains today, however, a sizable weak working-class and poor sector within African American society. This sector ranks very low on the educational, occupational, and income ladder in contemporary

American society and is constrained by multifaceted social crises. In view of the prominence of conservative ideological and political patterns in our twenty-first-century American system (patterns led by the Republican Party and the Tea Party movement), few forces are presently operating in the American polity to help ameliorate the social crises hindering social advancement for the African American poor working-class and poor sectors.[7]

For example, when Newt Gingrich was the leading candidate in polls for the Republican Party presidential nomination by December 2011—garnering 31 percent support among Republicans against 17 percent for Mitt Romney—he pronounced in staunchly right-wing terms a contemptuous view of working-class and poor minority children. At a press conference in Iowa on December 1, 2011, he said that since "poor children in really poor [urban] neighborhoods have no habits of working and have nobody around them who works," such children should be employed as janitors in public schools, cleaning washrooms and toilets. Attitudes such as these held by leading Republican Party politicians like Gingrich make it difficult for the federal government to fashion policies that can assist the amelioration of social crises among the 28 percent of African Americans in the poor sector.[8]

After all, Gingrich's contemptuous attitudes toward poor African Americans reflect persistent anti–African American attitudes among some white Americans, as reported by the Associated Press in October 2012:

Racial attitudes have not improved in the four years since the nation elected its first black president . . . as a slight majority of Americans now express prejudice toward black people. . . . Racial prejudice has risen slightly since 2008 whether those feelings were measured using questions that explicitly asked respondents about racist attitudes, or through an experimental test that measured implicit views toward race without asking questions about that topic directly. *In all, 51 percent of those surveyed expressed explicit racist attitudes toward black people, compared with 48 percent in a similar 2008 survey. When measured by an implicit racial attitudes test, the share with racist sentiments jumped to 56 percent, up from 49 percent during the last presidential election.* . . . Most Americans also expressed racist attitudes toward Hispanics. In an AP survey in 2011, 52 percent of non-Hispanic whites expressed racist attitudes toward Latinos. *That figure rose to 57 percent in the implicit test.*[9]

*   *   *

In the remainder of this chapter, I reflect on whether or not the black middle-class and professional-class sectors here in the twenty-first century are systemically equipped and ideologically predisposed to assist the amelioration of the persistent social crises faced by the poor working-class and poor sectors in African American society. First, I discuss the overall attributes of the twenty-first-century African American social system in an effort to determine whether or not the contemporary black elite sector is likely to assist the African American lower-class sector. Second, I discuss the character of the social crises that restrict the black lower class' viable social advancement. Third, I discuss the emergence of twenty-first-century ideological patterns that have spawned new forms of social and political fissures within African American society.

During the post–Civil Rights movement era from the mid-1970s onward, American society witnessed a broad expansion of both the middle-class and professional-class sectors among African Americans. When America was about to enter World War II in 1940, only 10 percent of blacks belonged to the middle class, while 90 percent were in the poor working-class or poor category. Owing to the combined impact of an expanding national economy in the 1960s and federal policies (fashioned by the Johnson, Nixon, and Ford administrations) that altered—or at least made illegal—racial discrimination in broad areas of American life from the 1970s through the 1980s, the African American middle-class and professional-class sectors grew significantly.

Overall data on this social structure transformation among African Americans are provided by University of South Carolina sociologist Andrew Billingsley (Table 4.2).[10] Looking at the late-1980s data, Billingsley classifies 8 percent of African American families or households as "upper class" and 27 percent as "middle class." In the "working-class" category, which Billingsley divides into two segments, the higher-ranked "working-class nonpoor" describes 34 percent of African American households of this period, while the low-ranked category "working-class poor" describes 14 percent of total black households. Finally, Billingsley's quantitative classification of the "underclass poor," which amounted to 14 percent of African American families at the start of the 1970s (some 716,000 households), skyrocketed to 30 percent by the late 1980s (some 2,142,000 households).

Thus, this social-mobility pattern among African American families during the post–Civil Rights movement period reflected a rather contra-

Table 4.2. Social class structure of African American households, 1969–1986

Class category	1969		1983		1986	
	Number of families	Percent	Number of families	Percent	Number of families	Percent
Upper class	143,000	3	267,000	4	624,000	9
Middle class	1,100,000	25	1,500,000	23	1,900,000	27
Working-class nonpoor	2,100,000	44	2,400,000	36	2,420,000	34
Working-class poor	688,000	14	963,000	14	—	—
Underclass poor	716,000	14	1,500,000	23	2,142,000	30

Source: Data from Andrew Billingsley, "Understanding African American Family Diversity," in Lee A. Daniels, ed., *State of Black America 1990* (New York: National Urban League, 1990).

dictory development. Whereas that period witnessed a positive social-mobility pattern between 1969 and the mid-1980s among middle-class and upper-class households (they expanded from 28 percent to 36 percent), the poorest social class sector (popularly dubbed the "underclass") also expanded. Thus, whereas the underclass constituted 14 percent of African American households at the start of the 1970s, *this occupationally disheveled sector exploded to 23 percent (1,500,000 families) by the early 1980s and to 30 percent (2,142,000 families) by the late 1980s.*

In light of what might be called an asymmetrical African American social-mobility dynamic in the 1970s and 1980s, it is analytically useful to translate Billingsley's class categories into two rankings: the black mobile stratum, comprising Billingsley's upper class, middle class, and working-class nonpoor categories, and the black static stratum, comprising Billingsley's working-class poor and underclass categories. Based on data in Table 4.2, by the late 1980s some 3.2 million, or about 30 percent, of African American households were in the black static stratum, and around five million, or just over two-thirds of all African American households, were in the black mobile stratum.

Fortunately for the ranks of the black mobile stratum, the 1990s and the early 2000s witnessed a steady expansion of income and overall wealth in upper-class and middle-class African American households. This expansion is partly demonstrated by data in Table 4.3. By 2006, nearly fifteen million African Americans (out of thirty-two million total)

Table 4.3   White-collar occupations* held by black Americans in 2006

Measure	Executive/ administrative managerial	Professional	Technical	Sales	Administrative support/clerical
Number	1,430,000	1,853,000	439,000	1,359,000	2,369,000
Percent employed	(10%)	(13%)	(3%)	(9.2%)	(16%)

Source: Data from U.S. Census Bureau, *Occupation Survey* (Washington, DC: U.S. Department of Commerce) for 2006.

Percent employment reflects average percentage of total black employment (14,725,000 in 2006).

*The list of occupations is derived from the above U.S. Census Bureau survey.

were employed, of whom an overall 6.5 million held what the U.S. Census Bureau surveys characterize as "white-collar workers."

The top-tier 3.7 million white-collar workers among African Americans constituted one-fourth of the total fifteen million employed African Americans by 2006. A valuable source on the wide variety of African American individuals holding these white-collar jobs is the monthly magazine *Black Enterprise*, especially its section "On the Move." In the June 2011 issue, among the individuals featured in this section were Karen McDowell, a group account director at Burrell Communications in Chicago; Dennis Walcott, New York City public schools chancellor; Ronald Stroman, deputy postmaster general for the U.S. Postal Service; and William Kornegay Jr., vice president of supply management for Hilton Worldwide. This same issue of *Black Enterprise* also contains its "39th Annual Report on Black Business," which lists the owners and business biographies of the top one hundred black-owned firms in four business categories: industrial/service firms (which include food/hotel services), automobile dealers, advertising agencies, and financial services. The financial services were, in 2010, the most financially successful black-owned businesses, with some $114.5 billion in financial assets under management.[11]

Moreover, at the apex of the new growth in the ranks of white-collar occupations among African Americans in the early 2000s has been an expanding category of mobile-stratum individuals who hold top-tier executive posts in major corporations. Table 4.4 shows some of these executives, in such corporations as Xerox, IBM, Pitney Bowes, and Boeing Defense Systems.

Table 4.4. Black executives in major corporations in 2005

Name	Position held	Corporation
Rodney Adkin	Vice president, development	IBM Systems Technology
Quincy Allen	President, production systems	Xerox Corp.
Paget Alves	President, Sprint business solutions	Sprint Corp.
James Andrade	Vice president, research and development	Kraft Foods, Inc.
James Bell	Chief financial officer	Boeing Corp.
Thomas Brown	Senior vice president, global purchasing	Ford Motor Corp.
Ursula Burns	President, business group operations	Xerox Corp.
Norma Clayton	Vice president, supply management	Boeing Defense Systems
William Cooksey	Plant manager	General Motors Co.
Greg Daniels	Senior vice president, U.S. manufacturing	Nissan North America
Erroll Davis Jr.	Chairman/chief executive	Alliant Energy Corp.
Dallas Delaney	Global operations manager	Abbott Corp.
W. H. Easter	Chief executive officer	Duke Energy Services
Byron Green	Vice president, truck assembly operation	Daimler Chrysler Co.
Frederick Gregory	Deputy administrator	NASA
Arthur Harper	Chief executive officer	GE Equipment Service
Wyllstyne Hill	Vice president, missile systems	Raytheon Corp.
Anthony James	Chief executive officer	Savannah Electric
Renetta McCann	Chief executive officer	Starcom America
Patricia Newby	President	Xetton
General Lloyd Newton	Executive vice president	Pratt & Whitney Co.
Dan Parker	Chief executive officer	Energy New Orleans
Vallerie Parrish-Porter	Vice president, enterprise service	Sprint Corp.
Desiree Rodgers	President and chief marketing officer	People's Gas Corp.
Cathy Ross	Chief financial officer	FedEx Corp.
Barbara Sanders	Director, engineering operations	Delphi Thermal
Albert Tervalon	Director, glass operation	Visteon Corp.
Lydia Thomas	President and chief executive officer	GE Consumer and Industrial
Belinda Watkins	Vice president, network computing	FedEx Corp.
Edward Welburn Jr.	Vice president, design	General Motors Co.
George Williams	Vice president, operations	Grand Gulf Energy
Keith Williamson	President, capital services	Pitney Bowes Inc.
Jacqueline Woods	Vice president, global licensing	Oracle Corp.
Alfred Zollar	General manager, Tivoli software	IBM Corp.

Sources: Data from *Black Enterprise* (February 2005); *U.S. Black Engineer and Information Technology* (2005).

Notable is the number of female executives: eleven out of a total of twenty-four listed in Table 4.4. One prominent top-tier black female executive was Renetta McCann, CEO of Starcom Corporation, a major player in the hotel industry. Another was Ursula Burns, president of Business Group Operations at Xerox in 2005; in 2009 she was elevated to CEO there, becoming the first African American woman named as CEO of a Fortune 500 corporation. The significant representation of black females in top-tier positions in major corporations by 2005 reflects the important U.S. Census Bureau data, which reveal that by 2002 some 11 percent of 7.9 million employed black females (869,000) held white-collar occupations labeled "executive-administrative-managerial" jobs, compared with 8.7 percent of 6.7 million employed black males (594,000) in the same white-collar category.[12]

William Julius Wilson offers an interesting explanation for the sizable representation of black females among African Americans in top positions at major corporations. In a 2011 article in the journal *Daedalus,* he revisits his analysis of African American class patterns that he first made famous in his 1978 book *The Declining Significance of Race:*

> [Black] . . . males have fallen behind females on a number of socioeconomic indicators: employment rates, high school completion rates, and average income. . . . Black women have also far outpaced black men in college completion in recent years, [though] . . . the gender gap in college degree attainment is increasing across all racial groups. . . . *That gap [among blacks] has widened steadily over the past twenty-five years.* In 1979, for every 100 bachelor's degrees earned by black men, 144 were earned by black women. In 2006–2007, for every 100 bachelor's degrees conferred on black men, 196 were conferred on black women—nearly a two-to-one ratio. . . . *The gap widens higher up the educational ladder. For every 100 master's degrees and 100 doctorates earned by black men, black women earned 255 and 193, respectively.*[13]

Furthermore, in order to illustrate more substantively the expanding social-mobility differentials between those Wilson dubs the "haves" and "have-nots" in early twenty-first-century African American society, he presents data shown in Table 4.5. As Wilson explains in a summary observation on these data, between 1975 and 2007, "the family income gap between poorer and better-off African Americans continued to widen." Thus, by 2005, the average income of black families in the fourth quintile ($61,407) was nearly double the average income of families in the middle

Table 4.5. Average income of black families by income percentile, 1975–2007

Income percentile	1975 ($)	1985 ($)	1995 ($)	2005 ($)	2007 ($)	Change ($)
Lowest quintile	8,939	7,284	7,463	7,784	8,143	−796
Second quintile	18,533	17,833	20,073	22,085	23,384	4,851
Middle quintile	30,650	30,832	35,022	35,842	40,278	9,628
Fourth quintile	46,095	49,356	55,408	61,407	64,573	18,478
Highest quintile	78,031	90,902	111,767	129,002	132,565	54,534
Top 5 percent	106,908	131,672	183,471	212,818	220,916	114,008

Source: Data from William Julius Wilson, "The Declining Significance of Race: Revisited and Revised," *Daedalus: Journal of the American Academy of Arts and Sciences* (Spring 2011): 64.

quintile ($35,842), and the average income of families in the highest quintile ($129,002) was more than double that of families in the fourth quintile. Inasmuch as the fourth-quintile black families were by 2005 solidly middle class in social rank, their income dwarfed that of families in the middle quintile ($35,842), the second quintile ($22,085), and the lowest quintile ($7,784). Wilson's analysis of today's economic disparities between "poorer and better-off African American families" suggests that *those disparities show no sign of ebbing in the near future.*

Although Wilson's analysis of African American family income patterns appears quite pessimistic here in the early twenty-first century, data on the comparative income and wealth patterns between black and white Americans suggest an equally pessimistic state of affairs. As reported by Brandeis University sociologist Thomas Shapiro in his 2004 book *The Hidden Cost of Being African American:* "The black-white earnings gap . . . has remained relatively stable since [the 1970s]. . . . The average black family earned 55 cents for every dollar earned by the average white family in 1989; by 2000 it reached an all-time high of 64 cents on the dollar. For black men working full-time, the gains are more impressive, as their wages reached 67 percent of those of fully employed white men, up from 62 percent in 1989 and only 50 percent in 1960."[14]

Shapiro also discusses the overall wealth gap between white and black Americans during the late twentieth century and early twenty-first century, and his findings are equally pessimistic regarding African Americans' wealth status: "The average African American family holds ten cents of wealth for every dollar that whites possess," says Shapiro. He continues: "Black and white professionals in the same occupation earning the same salary typically move through life with significantly unequal housing, residential, and educational prospects, which means that their children are not really on the same playing field."[15]

Furthermore, the data on both the income gap and the overall wealth gap between white American and black American families for 2011, reported by Economic Policy Institute vice president Ross Eisenbrey in early 2013, are as follows:

- In January 1966, the ratio of black median family income to white median family income was 60%. Forty-five years later, in January 2011, the ratio was virtually unchanged: 63%.
- The ratio of median household wealth among blacks and whites has worsened over the past three decades, falling from a tiny 6.3% in 1983 to an even tinier 5.0% in 2010. Even in absolute terms, median black household wealth is less today than in 1983.
- The home-ownership rate for black families was 45% in 2011, essentially unchanged since 1975, the first year for which we have racial data.
- And by some measures, residential segregation is no less today than it was in 1950.[16]

What the foregoing data on a persistent income-gap and wealth-gap pattern between white and black American families extending back to 1966 tell us is that, despite these income and wealth differentials, the occupation growth pattern in the post–Civil Rights movement era has been sizable enough to include an important segment of African American citizens, as documented by U.S. Census Bureau occupation surveys in 2002 and 2006 (see Table 4.3). As mentioned above, nearly 7 million white-collar jobs were acquired by African Americans by the first decade of the twenty-first century. This development, in turn, has qualitatively strengthened the social and professional capabilities of the black elite sector in African American society.

However, in light of the advanced social-class and professional capabilities of today's black elite sector, does this mean that this sector will initiate new endeavors to revitalize new variants of the Du Boisian black-communitarian social-uplift leadership pattern in order to help ameliorate persistent social crises among the poor sector of today's African American society? I have a somewhat ambivalent feeling about this query. Why?

Because two coexisting negative black systemic dynamics are prevalent within today's African American society that might make problematic the launching of new black-communitarian social-uplift leadership patterns.

The first such negative dynamic relates to the plethora of social crises that presently plague what William Julius Wilson aptly dubs the have-not sector in contemporary African American society. Brandeis University social historian Jacqueline Jones offers a depressing characterization of the weak socioeconomic status of the African American have-nots by the mid-1990s:

> From a variety of social indicators came proof that the destruction [through federal policies] of the legal basis of discrimination was unequal to the tasks of erasing or reversing the effects of generations-old systems of racial oppression. [Thus,] of all black female-headed households, more than half qualified as poor (compared to 16 percent of white children). Although blacks represented 12 percent of the total population, they constituted about two-fifths of all recipients of Aid to Families with Dependent Children. . . . Black unemployment rates were consistently two or two and a half times greater than the rates for whites, and nationwide, three out of ten of all "discouraged" workers were black. Among wage-earning household heads [in total black employed of 15 million] with less than a high school education, almost 40 percent of fully employed black women, and 24 percent of fully employed black men, lived beneath economic self-sufficiency.[17]

The second negative black systemic dynamic relates to the growth of conservative-leaning ideological fissures among African Americans. These fissures reflect, I think, the social-class fault line that began to appear between the African American have and have-not sectors during the post–Civil Rights movement period. I discuss this second set of negative dynamics in the last part of the chapter.

Although the post–Civil Rights movement period from the mid-1970s onward witnessed significant social-class advances for middle-class and professional-class African Americans, that period also witnessed downward-mobility patterns among African Americans. By the early 1990s, these downward-mobility patterns began to calcify, growing into multilayered social crises afflicting a sizable segment of African American society. This category of African Americans constituted a combined segment of poor working-class and poor families, classified here as the black static stratum. Thus, by 2010, this stratum had increased to about 40 percent of African American households, owing to the impact of the Great Recession that commenced in 2007.[18] Clearly, it is a significant crisis situation for any American ethnic community when two-fifths of its households have either poor working class or poor underclass social status.

Accordingly, here in the early decades of the twenty-first century, around ten million African Americans find themselves in dire straits, devastated by tenacious social crises: joblessness, fragile families, unwed motherhood/fatherhood, internecine "black-on-black" violence in inner-city neighborhoods, high incarceration rates, and, last but not least, poor school performance. At a Harvard School of Education seminar in November 2007, education scholar John Merrow presented a thoroughly depressing characterization of the school performance crisis among poor working-class and poor black youth: "The achievement gap in American K–12 schools is well-documented, and is characterized by racial and class differences," he explained. "By the end of fourth grade, black, Latino, and poor students of all races are two years behind their wealthier (and mostly white) peers in reading and math scores. By 12th grade, that gap has widened by four years. By age 17, only one in 50 black and Latino students can read and comprehend something like the science section of a newspaper. For whites, the comparable rate is one in 12."[19] Poor school performance among today's poor African American youth is particularly onerous, given that it is a crucial strand in a persistent web of black social crises.

In a 2006 survey, the Kaiser Family Foundation identified a host of crises plaguing the static stratum in today's African American society:

1. More than half of 5.6 million black boys in America live in fatherless households, of which 40 percent are at poverty level.
2. Homicide-related violence affects black males six times more often than white males. Black males in the 14–24 age group are involved in 25 percent of the nation's homicides.
3. Incarceration rates as of 2006 indicate that one-third of black males born in 2006 will experience imprisonment.
4. Death from AIDS affects black males nine times more than white males.
5. The 62.9-year life expectancy for black males is six years less than that of white males.[20]

A year later, Marian Wright Edelman, director of the Children's Defense Fund, identified another strand of the destructive web of social crises among the poor working-class and poor sectors of twenty-first-century African American life: the hip-hop entertainment industry, which Edelman accused of damaging the traditional function of African American civil society agencies to provide civic and ethical uplift to black communities. As Edelman puts it:

> Regrettably, somewhere in the last twenty to twenty-five years, many of our young [black] people have been crowded into a cultural corner down a dark alley where violence, hedonism, misogyny and materialism are celebrated. Gangsta rap songs and videos in which women are referred to as bitches . . . and hoes assault our children constantly, regardless of whether they live in the inner city or the suburbs. *Rappers who dish up this form of music glamorize lives riddled with gun violence, drug dealing, bling, Bentleys and harems of mindless female sex toys.*[21]

Thus, as the reality of these societal crises gained wide recognition in African American society from the last two decades of the twentieth century onward, a variety of what can be called class and attitudinal fissures surfaced among African Americans. By the late 1970s, an early manifestation of such fissures was the phenomenon of black middle-class flight from inner-city African American neighborhoods, discussed in Chapter 2. As the twenty-first century ensued, class and attitudinal fissures reached such a broad scale within African American society that major research organizations began to study them. In 2007, the prominent Pew Research Center based in Philadelphia and Washington, D.C., published a major survey of African American ethnic-group attitudes that contributed enormously to our sociological understanding of African American class and attitudinal fissures. The subtitle of the 2007 Pew report bluntly underscored its findings: *Blacks See Growing Values Gap between Poor and Middle Class.*[22]

When viewed in the historical context of the Du Boisian leadership legacy's influence on the ideological and political character of the twentieth-century African American intelligentsia (some key dimensions of which are probed in Chapters 2 and 3), the appearance of class and attitudinal fissures in African American society from the 1980s to today bring to light an important dilemma for the intelligentsia. A basic reason behind this dilemma is, of course, plain enough: it stems from a core element in the Du Boisian leadership legacy—the broad influence of the black-ethnic commitment leadership orientation. Inasmuch as by the 1940s a sizable segment of the twentieth-century black intelligentsia was influenced by a Du Boisian black-ethnic commitment leadership perspective—a pattern that was further strengthened by the militant phase of the postwar Civil Rights movement—the appearance of class-based attitudinal fissures in African American society by the 1980s onward was, shall we say, disconcerting.[23]

Considering the numerous black middle-class and professional-class individuals who imbibed the ideological and political precepts that defined the Du Boisian leadership legacy during the evolving twentieth-century African American social system, it might be reasonable to expect a sizable segment of the twenty-first-century black intelligentsia to sustain a viable sociopolitical nexus with the poor working-class and poor African American sectors. Of course, when I say "reasonable," I am making an observation informed by a liberal ideological outlook. Be that as it may, what is fascinating about the 2007 Pew survey findings is that they clearly show that a sizable segment of the black middle-class and professional-class sectors exhibits some degree of ideological and cultural antipathy toward the poor working-class and poor sectors of African American society.

In the 2007 Pew survey, two sets of questions were posed to a nationwide sample of 1,007 African Americans. One set of questions focused on the degree to which twenty-first-century African Americans "shared values with other African Americans." A second set queried the degree to which they viewed themselves as a coherent ethnic group or, to use the survey's wording, "as a single race." The responses to these two sets of queries are shown in Table 4.6. The Pew Research Center commented on the responses as follows: "By a ratio of two-to-one [61 percent to 31 percent] blacks say that the values of poor and middle-class blacks have grown more dissimilar over the past decade. [And] a sizable minority of African Americans (37 percent) agrees with the idea that blacks today can no longer be thought of as a single race because the black community today is so diverse."[24]

On one analytical level, the findings of the 2007 Pew survey suggest that the quest for a twenty-first-century version of the Du Boisian black-communitarian leadership pattern may face a variety of obstacles in the

Table 4.6. Pew survey of African American attitudes and values, 2007 (%)

Are blacks better off?	Will blacks be better off in the future?	Are values of middle class and poor more similar/ different?	Are blacks a single race?
Better 20	Better 44	More similar 31	Single race 63
Worse 29	Worse 21	More different 61	No single race 37
Same 49	Same 31	No change 2	
Don't know 2	Don't know 4	Don't know 6	

Source: Data from Pew Research Center, *Optimism about Black Progress Declines: Blacks See Growing Values Gap between Poor and Middle Class,* Pew Research Sociographic and Demographic Trends Report (Washington, DC: Pew Research Center, 2007).

years ahead. For example, the survey clearly indicates that aspects of American conservative ideologies have influenced the attitudes of the black middle-class and professional-class sectors much more than they did several generations ago.

This is the case, I think, regarding the American conservative predilection that might be dubbed an "I'm-alright-Jack" conservatism—a vintage American conservative mantra that celebrates the *bourgeois self-serving ethos.* As shown in Table 4.7, the Pew survey suggests that this outlook has become more prevalent among the African American middle-class and professional-class sectors: "A narrow majority of blacks (53%) believe that blacks who have not gotten ahead in life are mainly responsible for their own situation." I interpret this finding as *supportive of I'm-alright-Jack conservatism,* partly because African Americans in this 53 percent majority are apparently comfortable in their newly acquired social status in American society. Many of these individuals are now presumably satisfied that the viciously dispiriting, pariah, and restrictive aspects of American society's racist practices have now dissipated. In this connection, however, the critical view of this issue proffered in the late Harvard Law School scholar Derrick Bell's 1992 book *Faces at the Bottom of the Well* warrants mentioning. Bell's discourse suggests that our American civilization is dependent, in some generic psychocultural manner, upon a white supremacist defining ethos. Hence, our society faces a persistent cross-generational struggle to contain and hopefully vanquish this generic cultural flaw.[25]

Table 4.7. Pew survey of attitudes about black mobility problems, 2007 (%)

Reasons for mobility problems	Blacks' response	Whites' response	Hispanics' response
Racial discrimination	30	15	24
Blacks responsible for their own mobility problems	53	71	59
Neither or both	14	9	8
Don't know	3	6	9

Source: Data from Pew Research Center, *Optimism about Black Progress Declines: Blacks See Growing Values Gap between Poor and Middle Class* (Washington, DC: Pew Research Center, 2007).

Note: Percentages in the "Whites' response" column do not total 100 due to rounding.

Compared with some four generations ago when Jim Crow practices polluted virtually every corner of American life, today's American society, in relation to black folks, has changed for the better—not perfectly or adequately, but it has improved. Indeed, our society today enables more African Americans than ever before to feel mentally and spiritually free from centuries-old tenacious racism, thereby viewing their life chances (and those of their children) as dependent upon their own capabilities. Hence, today a sizable segment of African Americans can and do embrace some aspects of the I'm-alright-Jack conservative orientation.

This embrace also translates into becoming Republican Party voters: about 5 percent of African Americans did in fact vote for the Republican McCain-Palin ticket in the 2008 presidential election, and 7 percent voted for the Romney-Ryan ticket in 2012. It should also be mentioned that there is an interlocking ideological chemistry, so to speak, between the belief that today African Americans' mobility problems are self-induced (held by 53 percent of African Americans in the 2007 Pew survey) and the belief that "the values of poor and middle-class blacks have grown more dissimilar over the past decade" (held by 60 percent of African Americans in the Pew survey). I say this for a very important reason: insofar as there is a relationship between the I'm-alright-Jack conservative outlook, on the one hand, and the fact that some 53 percent of today's African Americans no longer view discrimination as an obstacle to black social mobility, on the other, this situation constitutes what might be viewed as a paradox in the post–Civil Rights movement era.

As I remarked earlier in this chapter, today's twenty-first century African American intelligentsia is, in general, characterized by liberal ideological and political patterns, owing significantly to the Du Boisian leadership legacy. Accordingly, based on my understanding of the evolving twentieth-century African American intelligentsia, I believe that today's black elite sector—especially its liberal wing—has a moral obligation to ensure the advancement of a core goal of African Americans' liberal leadership patterns.

That core goal (with deep roots in progressive black leadership traditions—the abolitionist tradition, the social gospel-activist black church tradition, the civil rights activist tradition) is this: *There can be no morally definitive equalitarian sociopolitical advancement for black folks in general until the poor sectors among African Americans are provided a "fair opportunity" by our American system to mount the rungs on America's social-mobility ladder.*

A keen perspective on this failure of our American system thus far to facilitate morally definitive equalitarian assistance in this regard was recently delineated by *New York Times* economics columnist Eduardo Porter. Porter uses recent data from the Organization for Economic Cooperation and Development (OECD) to critique the American system's social-mobility assistance to the poor sector of Americans, of which African Americans are a sizable part:

> For all the riches we have amassed [as a nation] . . . we suffer from some of the worst social ills known to the industrialized world. It is not just that income inequality is the most acute of any industrialized country. More American children die before reaching age 19 than in any other rich country in the O.E.C.D. More live in poverty. Many more are obese. . . . We understand the importance of early childhood development. Yet our public spending on early childhood is the most meager among advanced nations. We value education. Yet our rate of enrolling 3- to 5-year-olds in preschool programs is among the lowest among advanced nations. . . . A particularly telling statistic speaks of how we deal with social dysfunction: there are 743 Americans in jail for every 100,000. That's more than in any other country in the world, according to the International Center for Prison Studies. . . . [T]hough we seem to suffer more than our fair share of social ills, by the O.E.C.D.'s calculations our public spending to address them is smaller as a share of the economy than in any other country in the developed world.[26]

Although I have already discussed the findings of the 2007 Pew survey of black attitudes that relate to new patterns of conservative-skewed fissures within African American society, that survey also produced data on the persistence of liberal ideological patterns within African American life. These findings might be viewed as countervailing findings to the growing number of African Americans who espouse I'm-alright-Jack conservatism. These countervailing findings reveal that, while an important segment of today's middle-class and professional-class African Americans espouse the I'm-alright-Jack conservative mantra, *a sizable segment of middle-class and professional-class African Americans nevertheless remain committed to liberal black leadership patterns.*

Yet, according to the 2007 Pew survey, some 37 percent of African Americans "agree with the idea that blacks today can no longer be thought of as a single race because the black community today is so diverse." But a countervailing finding emerged as well in the Pew survey: "A majority of 53% disagrees, endorsing instead the view that 'blacks can still be thought of as a single race because they have so much in common.' "[27]

A second important finding in the survey is the two-to-one belief among African Americans (61 percent to 31 percent) that "the values of poor and middle-class blacks have grown more dissimilar over the past decade." The countervailing finding regarding this so-called values gap is that a sizable majority of African Americans nevertheless believe in the existence of generalized shared black ethnic values. The Pew survey describes the apparent contradiction in this finding as follows: "Even though many blacks believe there is a growing values divide within the black community, most blacks still see at least some measure of [black ethnic] solidarity in values shared by blacks. *A majority (65%) says middle-class blacks and poor blacks share at least some values in common, with nearly a quarter (23%) saying they share a lot in common.*"[28]

Based on answers to the question of whether or not political affiliation regarding liberalism and conservatism in American society influences African American attitudes toward the "values gap" issue, a third "countervailing finding" emerged. In general, the Pew survey found that African Americans *who identify as liberals* are more inclined to proclaim that shared values exist among middle-class and poor African Americans. As the survey puts it: "There are also political differences on this [shared values] question. Black liberal Democrats are fifteen percentage points more likely than political Independents (74% compared with 59%) to say middle-class and poor blacks have values in common."[29] The rather strong inclination among liberal middle-class African Americans to believe that ethnic-group values are shared by middle-class and poor black folks, was also uncovered in 1990s surveys by the University of Chicago political scientist Michael Dawson.[30]

A fourth important countervailing finding in the Pew survey informs us that although an overall 61 percent of African Americans agree that "values of poor and middle-class blacks have grown more dissimilar over the past decade," *persistent belief in shared values among poor and middle-class blacks is strongest among the best-educated sector of African Americans*. This countervailing finding is revealed by data shown in Table 4.8. For example, belief in shared values among poor and middle-class blacks is proclaimed by 70 percent of African Americans with some college education and by 78 percent of African Americans who are college graduates.

It is also important to mention that a predominantly favorable attitude among African Americans toward the existence of shared values among poor and middle-class blacks was prevalent across the major geographical regions in the country: in the South, where the largest segment of African Americans live, 63 percent say "a lot or some shared values"; in the West, home to the smallest segment of African Americans, it is 65 percent; and percentages in the East and Midwest, where the second largest segment of African Americans reside, are 68 percent and 66 percent, respectively.

Finally, these positive attitudes toward the existence of cross-class shared values prevailing among African Americans in all geographical regions were reinforced by data reported in a New American Media survey in September 2007. This survey found that *67 percent of African Americans say that most of their friends are of the same race and ethnicity*. Interestingly enough, this high level of intrarace or intraethnic friendship patterns among African Americans in 2007 compared with similarly high levels (73 percent) of intraethnic friendship patterns among Hispanic Americans.[31]

Now inasmuch as a 2007 Pew Research Center survey revealed that what can be called the ideological terrain among African Americans exhibited a weakening coherence regarding shared ethnic group values (with 61 percent of African Americans responding favorably to the statement "[the] values of poor and middle-class blacks have grown more dissimilar over the past decade"), it is reasonable to infer that

Table 4.8. Pew survey of cross-class shared values among blacks, 2007 (%)

Category	Share several or some values	Share few or no values
All African Americans	65	31
Gender		
Males	66	31
Females	64	31
Age (years)		
18–29	68	29
30–49	66	32
50–64	68	29
65+	50	38
Education		
College graduate	78	19
Some college	70	28
High school or less	58	37
Income		
$100,000+	66	27
$50,000–99,000	78	19
$30,000–49,000	67	32
Less than $30,000	57	39
Region		
East	68	26
Midwest	66	30
South	63	33
West	65	34

Source: Data from Pew Research Center, *Optimism about Black Progress Declines: Blacks See Growing Values Gap between Poor and Middle Class,* Pew Research Sociographic and Demographic Trends Report (Washington, DC: Pew Research Center, 2007).

during the post–Civil Rights movement era, an opportunity for conservative political mobilization—including shifting black voters' preference from the Democratic Party to the Republican Party—has been available among some African American voters. Accordingly, starting in the early 1980s during the first Reagan Republican administration and continuing through the remainder of the twentieth century, a small cadre of conservative African American intellectuals mounted a conservative ideological and political mobilization among African Americans. As I discussed in Chapter 3, William Braithwaite and George Schuyler were leading examples of evolving twentieth-century black intellectuals who embraced perspectives more typically found among the mainstream white American conservative intelligentsia. As such, Braithwaite and Schuyler stood out as exceptional figures, because the vast majority of their black intellectual peers inhabited the liberal and progressive side of the American political spectrum. By the mid-1920s, Braithwaite had surfaced as a rather austere conservative black intellectual (chastising black intellectuals for writing as "Negro writers"). Schuyler, on the other hand, initially functioned as a liberal intellectual in concert with the mainstream liberal-oriented black intelligentsia. This was Schuyler's intellectual modus operandi from the 1930s into the 1940s, and he did not morph into a full-fledged conservative intellectual until the early post–World War II years, during the 1950s into the 1960s.

However, neither Braithwaite, during the intrawar period, nor Schuyler, in the postwar years, attempted to amass anything comparable to a following of conservative black intellectuals. In fact, although Schuyler sat on the editorial board of William Buckley's *National Review,* he did not attempt to use his relationship with that influential mainstream conservative journal to mobilize a conservative following among the black intelligentsia. Why the reticence?

No doubt, part of the reason for this was the broad sway of liberalism prevalent among the black intelligentsia during the 1950s and 1960s—the decades when the African American Civil Rights movement was ascendant. Another reason was related to the overall liberal ideological and political character of African Americans generally by the 1930s. Owing to Franklin Delano Roosevelt's hegemony in the Democratic Party from the late 1930s until his death in 1945, the black-voter bloc underwent a veritable revolution by scuttling its long-standing electoral fidelity to the Republican Party—popularly called "the party of Lincoln" among black Americans. It was during the 1936 presidential election that the black-voter bloc gave a majority of its votes to Roosevelt, thus ensuring his second term as president. This was an earth-shattering electoral transformation, given the fact that black voters, extending back to the Reconstruction era, had consistently supported Republican Party presidential candidates.[32]

Moreover, the black-voter bloc's metamorphosis into a Democratic-leaning bloc persisted through the remainder of the twentieth century, a development that was influenced very little by a slow but steady move among white voters in the opposite direction, from the Democratic

Party to the Republican Party. The consolidation of white voters' preference for Republicans occurred during the two-term presidency of Ronald Reagan (1981–1989); it was also during Reagan's presidency that,
for the first time since the 1920s, the black intelligentsia experienced the
emergence of a cadre of conservative intellectuals.

While this network of conservative black intellectuals was gaining
influence among white conservatives during the 1980s and 1990s, the
liberal ideological and voting pattern that had begun among African
American voters in the late 1930s—in favor of Democrats—remained
intact. For example, during the nearly twenty-five years of Republican
dominance in presidential elections, between 1980 and 2004 (Reagan
won in 1980 and 1984, George H. Bush in 1988, and George W. Bush in
2000 and 2004), the successful Republican candidate gained between
10 and 20 percent of African American voters. Furthermore, polls mea-
suring party identification patterns among voters during the 1990s
showed that African American voters still registered the strongest identification with the Democratic Party: 78 percent favored the Democrats,
compared with 54 percent of Hispanic voters and only 34 percent of
white voters. Similarly, while some 70 percent of white Americans identified themselves as conservatives, only 35 percent of African Americans
identified themselves as such.

Thus, the emergence of a network of conservative black intelligentsia
personalities during the 1980s and 1990s occurred *despite* a rather
prominent liberal ideological and political pattern among African Americans generally. This meant that the network of conservative black political figures in the 1980s and 1990s was not connected to traditional
African American civil society agencies, such as churches, fraternal and
sororal associations, professional and business organizations, major
black colleges like Howard University and Hampton University, and especially not to civil rights organizations. This meant also that these new
black conservatives of the 1980s and 1990s had to create an institutional network for mediating their conservative discourse and activism
that was external—not internal—to African American society.

Furthermore, this "external-internal dilemma" exerted a significant
influence on both the kind of African American persons who joined the
conservative black intelligentsia networks and the character of black
conservatives' surrounding political milieu. Accordingly, the black intelligentsia personalities who joined ranks with white conservatives during

the last two decades of the twentieth century were mainly members of that first group of African American scholars appointed to the faculties of white colleges and universities. Prominent among them were Thomas Sowell (an economist at Stanford University), Shelby Steele (an English studies scholar at California State University), Walter Williams (an economist at George Mason University), Alan Keyes (a political philosophy scholar at the University of Maryland), Glenn Loury (an economist first at Harvard University and later at Boston University), Anne Wortham (a sociologist at the University of Missouri), Stephen Carter (a law scholar at Yale University), Randall Kennedy (a law scholar at Harvard University), and Eileen Gardner (a psychologist at the Heritage Foundation, a leading conservative research foundation). Several other African American academics joined the core cadre of conservative black intelligentsia by the late 1990s and early 2000s, including John McWhorter, a linguist and literary studies scholar at the Manhattan Institute, a conservative research foundation, and Carol Swain, a political science scholar at Vanderbilt University. As time progressed, several of the original cadre of black conservative academics—Stephen Carter, Randall Kennedy, and Glenn Loury, to name a prominent few—moved away from mainstream conservative networks and fashioned variants of an independent liberalism outlook for themselves.[33] This suggests that, in recent years, the top-tier ranks of conservative black intellectuals have been quite unstable.

Although the actual number of conservative black intelligentsia figures from the 1980s onward was small, their ideological and political discourse nevertheless acquired a nationwide market and visibility. How was this possible? *Because the small cadre of conservative black intellectuals was co-opted by an array of influential, well-endowed white conservative institutions and networks.*[34] Those mainstream white conservative networks—among them research centers like the Heritage Foundation, the American Enterprise Institute, the Manhattan Institute, and the Hoover Institution at Stanford University—gained financial support from wealthy right-wing institutions like the Lynde and Harry Bradley Foundation, the Richardson Mellon Scaife Foundation, and the John M. Olin Foundation.

These financial resources provided conservative black intellectuals like Shelby Steele, Thomas Sowell, Walter Williams, Alan Keyes, and Glenn Loury significant backing that facilitated the publication of books, reports, and articles. The wide circulation of both intellectual journals and popular magazines controlled by American conservative organizations (among them the *National Review,* the *Public Interest,* the *New Republic,* the Hoover Institution's *Policy Review,* the *Wall Street Journal,* the *San Francisco Chronicle,* the *Washington Times,* New Hampshire's *Union Leader,* and the *New York Post*) afforded these conservative black intellectuals the widest possible exposure for their conservative discourse. Perhaps the conservative writings of Shelby Steele, who began his career in the 1970s as a literary studies teacher at California State University, offer a broad-gauged understanding of the core theoretical and ideological precepts that have guided the political discourse of conservative black intelligentsia figures since the 1980s.

Before I discuss one of Steele's major works, however, it should be mentioned that the writings of virtually all the top-tier conservative black intelligentsia figures—Steele, Sowell, Keyes, Williams, Wortham, Carter, Loury, McWhorter—in conjunction with the writings of conservative white political pundits, ignore a quite incredible fact about twentieth-century American conservatism: *most white American conservative leadership figures and groups have never challenged America's racist oligarchy in a manner that encouraged that oligarchy to alter its behavior to facilitate, even slightly, the egalitarian sociopolitical advancement of black folks.* During the long historical period from the federal government's betrayal of Reconstruction by the late 1870s to the enactment of the first major twentieth-century federal civil rights legislation in the form of the Civil Rights Act of 1964, the leadership groups of mainstream American conservatism offered no significant support toward the democratic goal of ending racism in American life and thus that racism's massive injuries to black people.

Indeed, this generic moral failure of mainstream American conservatism represented a stunning conundrum: the leadership of America's prominent conservative groups often trumpeted "freedom movements" in far-flung places around the world—Europe, Asia, Latin America. Throughout late nineteenth century and into the first sixty years of the twentieth century, the agencies and leadership of mainstream American conservatism rejected a proactive conservatism methodology vis-à-vis the racist-riddled plight of black folks. By "proactive conservatism," I mean one that entertained some degree of humanitarian ethos that could propel American conservatism toward surmounting its core reactionary posture toward African American citizens.

Be that as it may, although small in number, the cadre of black conservatives that emerged during the late twentieth century has been incredibly prolific. Since his arrival among black conservative ranks in the early 1980s, Shelby Steele has been one of the most productive of this group. In general, Steele's writings have focused a kind of "blaming-the-victim" discourse that he uses to explain how and why African Americans have lagged behind their white counterparts in overall socioeconomic advancement in American life during the post–Civil Rights movement era. Interestingly enough, this blaming-the-victim discourse theme has been picked up by other conservative black intellectuals, especially by the oldest member of the conservative black intellectuals, Thomas Sowell, and his protégé in the field of economics, Walter Williams.

Steele initially delineated his conservative discourse theme in his 1990 book *The Content of Our Character*. Steele's conservative ideological perspective regarding the black-white social development gap revolved around a blaming-the-victim analytical proposition. First, Steele and other conservative black analysts (e.g., Sowell, Wortham, Williams, Carter, Loury) have argued that federal court decisions and congressional legislation outlawing segregation in public institutions created a "color-blind" society in terms of overall African American social mobility. Therefore, Steele and his conservative circle reasoned that the historically rooted perception that racism restricted African Americans' status in American life had lost its veracity, which in turn means that African Americans' persistent belief of having been systemically victimized by American racism would be counterproductive to their quest for parity of social status in American society.

In his second argument, which specifically countered the "victim-of-racism" group perception among African Americans, Steele criticized one of the several federal government public policies that sought to facilitate what might be called a government-assisted social advancement for African American citizens: the affirmative action policies. For Steele and his conservative black intellectual peers, such policies violated the merit-based social mobility practices so widely touted in American mainstream society. Affirmative action policies would eventually devalue the real achievement of successful African Americans, Steele argues in *The Content of Our Character*. Why? Because white Americans would ask, "Did they make it by themselves or because of affirmative action?"[35] Interestingly enough, when writing *The Content of Our Character*, Shelby

Steele was clearly lacking in a serious knowledge of the sizable historical and social science literature showing the role of government affirmative action–type public policies that facilitated modern social mobility for large segments of white American groups.[36] Thus, Steele's and other black conservative intellectuals' critiques of affirmative action policies that have assisted African Americans' social mobility are uninformed.

Strange as it might seem to African American intellectuals on the liberal side of the ideological spectrum, Steele supports his views on affirmative action with references to the discourse of the Reverend Martin Luther King Jr. In fact, the title of his book, *The Content of Our Character,* comes from a section of King's famous speech delivered during the historic March on Washington in 1963. Of course, the extensive literature that has parsed King's celebrated speech arrives at a fundamentally different conclusion from Steele's. Contrary to most other interpretations, Steele claims that King's discourse against America's racist practices did not include "government pump-priming advancement" policies like affirmative action. As University of California political scientist Charles Henry remarked on this issue in his 2011 book *The Obama Phenomenon:* "Ironically, the . . . Black neoconservative leadership based its call for 'color-blindness' on Martin Luther King. . . . By embracing King as one of their own, Black neoconservatives declared that the playing field was level and the era of identity politics and victimhood had passed. Those that had not achieved an adequate quality of life [social advancement] were obviously deficient in intelligence or morals or culture, and a host of code words replaced race to describe them."[37]

Although Steele unapologetically co-opted for conservative purposes King's words regarding racist American society's need to recognize the human character of its African American citizens, it was patently clear that, as Henry observed, this was a disingenuous intellectual procedure. Much of the discourse in Steele's *The Content of Our Character* revolves around his manipulation of Martin Luther King's words. One of Steele's famous arguments against the continuation of civil rights activism by African Americans during America's color-blind society era is that this ethnic-group pattern ultimately became culturally and politically dysfunctional.

In Steele's analytical perspective—premised on the idea of a "color-blind society"—African Americans suffer not from American racism but from what Steele calls a self-imposed "enemy memory." Accordingly, Steele says that this "dangerously powerful [enemy] memory . . . can pull us [blacks] into warlike defensiveness at a time when there is more opportunity for development [mobility] than ever before."[38]

When Steele initially characterizes African Americans as possessing an enemy-memory malady or neurosis, he asserts this with a black-people dismissive air: "I can think of no group with a more powerful collective memory of its enemy than black Americans." This statement is both intellectually and historically bizarre—and it calls into question Steele's own rather poor memory of modern European and American history.

In characterizing African Americans thus, Steele conveniently ignores, for example, the Irish American enemy-memory pattern vis-à-vis centuries-old British oppression in Ireland, exhibited prominently throughout the twentieth century in the anti-British violent acts of the Irish American–assisted Irish Republican Army. Steele also conveniently ignores the Armenian American enemy-memory pattern in response to Turkey's early twentieth-century genocide against Armenians. And, finally, Steele ignores the Jewish American enemy-memory pattern in response to a long history of European pogrom-riddled oppression of European Jews, not to mention the hideous anti-Semitic genocidal crimes of Nazi Germany—an enemy-memory pattern rightly kept alive through Jewish organizations worldwide.

From my analytical perspective, Shelby Steele's enemy-memory proposition seems a kind of rhetorical ruse used to cloak his deep antipathy toward black Americans' civil rights activism. Through his enemy-memory proposition, Steele fashions a blaming-the-victim discourse in which he lays the blame for African Americans' weak social mobility position relative to white Americans at the feet of African Americans themselves. *Thus, Steele's argument absolves white Americans and our country's racist patterns of responsibility for the challenges faced by African Americans regarding their mobility quest in contemporary American society.*

Furthermore, Steele indicts what he views as a kind of mental proclivity among African Americans to attribute the causes of deficiencies in their status to oppressive racist realities of the past. One such example he refers to involves the interpretation of anti–affirmative action decisions by the U.S. Supreme Court as merely a continuance of past white-supremacist values in American culture. For Steele, however, the rise of what he considers a "color-blind" American society by the 1980s represented the death knell for white-supremacist values of the past. So viewed through Steele's analytical lens, this meant that African Americans' continuance of their civil rights activism was no longer necessary and was therefore irrational.

However, if, alas, we fast-forward Steele's color-blind society mantra to 2012, we have news for him: an Associated Press Poll reported in October 2012 informed Americans that "racial attitudes have not improved in the four years since the nation elected its first black president. . . . In all, 51 percent of those surveyed expressed explicit racist attitudes toward black people, compared to 48 percent in a similar 2008 [Associated Press] survey. . . . In an AP survey in 2011, 52 percent of non-Hispanic whites expressed racist attitudes toward Latinos."[39]

Viewed from a strategic perspective, I suggest that Steele's formulation of a black conservative critique of African Americans' civil rights activism patterns during the "color-blind society" era in American life was a shrewd maneuver, which became an ideological mantra for many conservative black intellectuals. This mantra, in turn, attracted broad support among conservative white groups for Steele and his circle of black conservatives—support in the form of major financial and institutional resources. Here's how Steele initially formulated his color-blind society proposition: "There is today, despite America's residual racism, an enormous range of opportunity open to blacks in this society."[40]

If truth be told, however, Shelby Steele's color-blind discourse proved shallow when tested against empirical evidence. In their writings, neither Steele nor any of his black conservative colleagues weighed the extensive evidence of typical racist practices against African Americans that persisted throughout the 1980s onward—practices like being charged more than white Americans when purchasing an automobile, or being denied a job one-third of the time during undercover tests where blacks and whites with equal qualifications were applying for the same job.

Perhaps the racist practices particularly damaging to African Americans throughout the 1980s and since were discrimination in housing markets and residential choice, and thereby also in job market opportunities—a discriminatory pattern that persists into the early twenty-first century. As

University of Chicago sociologist Douglas Massey—a major scholar in the field of housing discrimination—has remarked on this issue: "Extreme levels of racial segregation have serious negative consequences for black households struggling to escape poverty, since residential mobility is a major avenue of social mobility." Furthermore, Massey referred to a National Academy of Sciences study of housing discrimination patterns in sixteen metropolitan areas with the largest African American populations, based on the 1980 census. The study uncovered that, using a segregation index on a scale of 0 to 100, the black average segregation index was 80 and that "it would take about 60 years for the Black-White index to fall to the [segregation index] currently observed for Hispanic-Americans and Asian-Americans."[41]

Furthermore, Massey's study of housing segregation patterns during the late twentieth century found that in ten of America's major metropolitan areas, African Americans were massively segregated—a pattern Massey calls "hypersegregation." In those same metropolitan areas—Baltimore, Chicago, Cleveland, Detroit, Gary, Indiana, Los Angeles, Milwaukee, Newark, New Jersey, Philadelphia, and St. Louis—Hispanic Americans did not experience hypersegregation. Indeed, middle-class African Americans earning more than $50,000 per year were more discriminated against than Hispanic Americans earning under $25,000.

Finally, a core conceptual element in quite strained "color blind society" discourse is that America's liberal public policy intervention to compensate African Americans for injurious racist practices is unwarranted. Such intervention, Steele insists, would violate the individualism ethos underlying the American system, on the one hand, and would reflect white guilt regarding America's racism legacy, on the other. As Steele puts it: "Suffering cannot be repaid. Blacks cannot be repaid for the injustice done to the race, but we can be corrupted by society's guilty gestures of repayment. Affirmative action is such a gesture."[42]

This, I think, is a strange argument, and I might add that it is intellectually mischievous as well. What, after all, is intrinsically wrong with the role of guilt in aiding individuals, groups, and even nations to atone or correct injury done undemocratically to others in our modern civilization? After all, the judicious application of a guilt-redemption ethos, so to speak, has played a long-standing role in advancing Christian humanitarian patterns in Western civilization. Indeed, it was precisely such a guilt-redemption ethos that informed the historic antislavery movement itself, initially in England and later in the United States.[43]

One last and rather intriguing ideological formulation by conservative black intellectuals in the post–Civil Rights era remains to be discussed. The formulation I have in mind was articulated by the law scholar Stephen Carter in his 1992 book *Reflections of an Affirmative Action Baby*. In his book, Carter offers a rather novel explanation for why a cadre of conservative black intellectuals appeared during the early phase of the post–Civil Rights movement era. During the early phase, explains Carter, this small group of intellectuals was shut out of the mainstream liberal African American intelligentsia; they were not welcomed into the ranks of mainstream black intelligentsia organizations like the National Urban League, the NAACP, and the Southern Christian Leadership Conference. In response, Carter argues, those he views as ostracized black conservatives, such as Thomas Sowell, Anne Wortham, Walter Williams, Shelby Steele, Glenn Loury, and others, sought *refuge* in white conservative networks.

In so doing, says Carter, the conservative black intellectuals evolved into what he calls "black dissenters." In Carter's discourse, the term "black dissenters" is politically tendentious, as he uses it to create a heroic egalitarian image of conservative black intellectuals, so to speak. However, I suggest that Carter's term is a faux-heroic characterization of these black conservatives. Carter's characterization of these conservative intellectuals as black dissenters will strike most serious analysts of the dynamics of dissent in American history as quite curious indeed.[44]

Carter fashions his discussion by way of a rather strange comparison between his conservative black dissenters, on the one hand, and those activist intellectuals among the twentieth-century African American intelligentsia whom I would characterize as authentic black dissenters, on the other—such as Du Bois, Anna Julia Cooper, Ida Wells-Barnett, Paul Robeson, A. Philip Randolph, Benjamin Davis, Fanny Lou Hamer, John Lewis, and Martin Luther King Jr. Nevertheless, in his quest for a heroic characterization of conservative black intellectuals, Carter convolutedly conflates his black dissenters with authentic black dissenters. As Carter puts it: "Looking at the deep rift between the [conservative] black dissenters and the mainstream [African American intellectuals], I cannot help but think back on the Niagara Movement, a forerunner of the NAACP, organized in 1905 by Du Bois and other opponents of Booker T. Washington in order to provide a platform for their dissenting ideas and a base for their burgeoning efforts to thwart Washington's ascendancy."[45]

The foregoing I think is convoluted indeed. So I suggest that it is only through an extraordinary stretch of his analytical imagination that Carter can pretend to equate those he calls conservative black dissenters with those I call authentic black dissenters. I believe that Carter's argument, therefore, is mistaken. There is a consensus among historical scholars of twentieth-century African American history that Du Bois, Monroe Trotter, Ida Wells-Barnett, Bishop Reverdy Ransom, Martin Luther King Jr., and numerous other proponents of civil rights activism were truly authentic black dissenters. Above all, they carried out a *genuine political struggle against the very grain of the authoritarian racist oligarchy at the core of the evolving twentieth-century American society, as well as against the accommodationist black leadership methodology of Booker T. Washington.*[46] By contrast, those whom Carter refers to as conservative black dissenters—Shelby Steele, Thomas Sowell, Walter Williams, Glenn Loury, Alan Keyes—can be called "dissenters" only in a rhetorical. ritualistic sense.

Put another way, Carter confuses two different genres of oppositionary leadership figures in twentieth-century African American society: activist dissenters and ritualistic dissenters, let's call them. The former seek to mobilize or activate popular forces (the weak, the excluded, the oppressed) against privilege, greed, and the racist-oligarchy practices in America's democratic processes. The latter, on the other hand, are practitioners of ritualistic dissent and, thereby, perpetrate mainly political obfuscation—manipulating the authentic dissenter tradition for establishmentarian purposes.

Accordingly, this faux-opposition pose of Carter's conservative black dissenters is little more than a clever rhetorical ruse, behind which a small cadre of conservative black intelligentsia personalities have constructed a national platform within mainstream American conservative networks. At the same time, however, the conservative black intellectuals have inhabited a rather anomalous status within the overall African American intelligentsia. Above all, they do not have what might be called an operational constituency among African Americans—an ethnic-bloc operational constituency that is comparable, say, to the operational constituency that enables neoconservative Jewish American intellectuals to interconnect with mainstream Jewish Americans.

Earlier in this chapter, I asked whether or not it is reasonable to view the early twenty-first century black elite sector as possessing the systemic capabilities, as well as the ideological orientation, that might enable it to help ameliorate some of the social crises plaguing poor working-class and poor African Americans. The analysis presented in this chapter suggests that today's black elite sector does indeed claim a new range of systemic capabilities and, moreover, that those capabilities are intertwined with sufficient liberal patterns among today's black elite sector. Thus, it seems reasonable to suggest that the prospects for a new era of black-communitarian leadership patterns in twenty-first-century African American society are quite good.

There remains, however, what might be called the "operational" issue— whether the resource-capable and ideologically liberal twenty-first-century black elite sector is willing to fashion significant "black-folks helping-hand" strategies. The ultimate goal of such strategies would be to constitute a full-fledged black-communitarian civic-uplift leadership process, whereby broad sections of African American civil society agencies— churches, women's associations, fraternal associations, teachers' and academic associations, business groups, entertainment groups, and so forth—*assume a broad obligation to facilitate the social uplift of poor working-class and poor African Americans.*

In operational terms, such an African American civic-uplift revitalization might be based on a variety of intermediate social-uplift transformations. Associated Press reporter Jesse Washington wrote a fascinating article on such transformations published in November 2010 in the *Boston Globe*. The article relates the difficult sociological dimensions surrounding "intermediate social-uplift transformations," inasmuch as this process entails ameliorating deep-seated societal disorders among the working-class and poor African American sector:

> One recent day at Dr. Natalie Carroll's OB-GYN practice [in Houston], located inside a low-income apartment complex between a gas station and a freeway, 12 pregnant black women come for consultations. Some bring children or their mothers. Only one brings a husband.... Dr. Carroll

spends time talking to the mothers about why they need to get married. . . . As the issue of black unwed parenthood inches into public discourse [70 percent of black children are born to unwed mothers], Dr. Carroll is among the few speaking boldly about it. And as a black woman who has brought thousands of babies into the world, who has sacrificed income to serve Houston's poor, Carroll is among the few whom black women actually listen to.[47]

There is no doubt that in the long run, any significant advancement in social mobility for today's crisis-plagued African American sector will require the assistance of federal government policies. After all, as *Washington Post* columnist Eugene Robinson observes in his 2010 book *Disintegration: The Splintering of Black America,* the term "abandoned blacks" aptly describes poor working-class and poor African Americans. He also comments—rightly, I think—on an appropriate public policy response required to address the plight of this African American sector: "What is needed is a kind of Marshall Plan for the 'Abandoned'—a massive intervention in education, public safety, health, and other aspects of life, with the aim of being able to arrest the downward spiral."[48]

I close this chapter with the observation that something like blackfolks' helping-hand strategies—such as the one practiced by Dr. Natalie Carroll in Houston—can be today a logical extension of what I have probed throughout this book under the conceptual formulation of the Du Boisian black-communitarian leadership ethos. Today's twenty-first-century variant of Du Bois' Talented Tenth—the mature-phase African American elite sector—has the resource capabilities and overall liberal leanings that could enable it to launch a new black-communitarian leadership pattern. A twenty-first-century black-communitarian leadership dynamic could galvanize a broad swath of the African American middle-class and professional-class sectors in order to help ameliorate the social crises plaguing the African American poor sector.[49] Indeed, as *New York Times* columnist Bob Herbert made graphically clear in his column titled "This Raging Fire," the social crises plaguing the African American poor sector are both elephantine and tenacious:

We know by now . . . that the situation is grave. We know that more than a third of black children live in poverty; that more than 70% are born to unwed mothers; that by the time they reach their mid-30s, a majority of black men without a high school diploma has spent time in prison. *We know all this, but no one seems to know how to turn things around. No one has been able to stop this steady plunge of young black Americans into a socioeconomic abyss. . . .*

The terrible economic downturn [since 2007] has made it more difficult than ever to douse this raging fire that is consuming the life prospects of so many young blacks, and the growing sentiment in Washington is to do even less to help any Americans in need.[50]

My concluding thought regarding today's African American leadership organizations' ameliorating what Herbert aptly dubs "this raging fire" consuming the African American poor sector, is this: these organizations— the NAACP, National Urban League, Children's Defense Fund, National Council of Negro Women, the National Bar Association, the National Medical Association, the African Methodist Episcopal Church, the National Baptist Convention, the Black Pentecostal churches, and others— might fashion a two-tier civic-uplift African American leadership strategy. This twenty-first-century leadership strategy could, on the one hand, continue the long-standing task of challenging persistent racist patterns in American life while, on the other hand, mobilizing the new systemic resources available to today's African American elite to help ameliorate the social crises constraining the life prospects of two-fifths of African American families.

It should be noted, finally, that in pursuit of an African American twenty-first-century civic-uplift leadership strategy, today's African American elite sector has a special leadership attribute that no previous generation of elite-level African Americans possessed: *it claims within its ranks a full-fledged African American political class.* At its base, this African American political class comprises some ten thousand black elected officeholders nationwide, in cities, counties, and state legislatures. At its top tier, today's African American political class comprises forty-three federal officeholders in the U.S. Congress and a sizable number of top- and middle-tier federal administrators, policy makers, and technicians.[51] Among those top-tier African American administrators and policy makers are personalities like Rob Nabors, who is the first ever African American to be the White House legislative affairs director,[52] and personalities like Jeh Johnson, the first ever African American chief legal counsel at the Department of Defense. Johnson, by the way, is the grandson of the prominent African American sociologist Charles S. Johnson, who founded Fisk University's Institute of Race Relations in the 1930s and was president of Fisk University in the late 1940s through the 1950s.

Above all, of course, at the apex of today's African American political class is an African American president of the United States, Barack Obama, who was elected to a first term in 2008 and a second term in 2012.[53] In an extended editorial commentary in the *New York Times* a week before the 2012 presidential election, the editors presented the following defense for the election of Obama to a second term:

> President Obama has shown a firm commitment to using government to help foster growth. He has formed sensible budget policies that are not dedicated to protecting the powerful, and has worked to save the social safety net to protect the powerless. Mr. Obama has impressive achievements despite the implacable wall of refusal erected by Congressional Republicans so intent on stopping him that they risked pushing the nation into depression, held its credit rating hostage, and hobbled economic recovery. . . . In the poisonous atmosphere of this [electoral] campaign, it may be easy to overlook Mr. Obama's many important achievements, including carrying out the economic stimulus, saving the automobile industry, improving fuel efficiency standards, and making two very fine Supreme Court appointments.
>
> Mr. Obama has achieved the most sweeping health care reforms since the passage of Medicare and Medicaid in 1965. The reform law takes a big step toward universal health coverage, a final piece of the social contract. It was astonishing that Mr. Obama and the Democrats in Congress were able to get a bill past the Republican opposition. . . . Mr. Obama prevented another Great Depression. The economy was cratering when he took office in January 2009. By June it was growing, and has been ever since.[54]

The article goes on to mention Obama's $840 billion stimulus bill, billions spent to help Americans through the crisis, and administrative policies to help restore voting rights and decriminalize undocumented workers. Although various progressive groups and political pundits critiqued Obama and his administration for not producing enough policies on behalf of the socioeconomic needs of working-class and poor African Americans, the foregoing *New York Times* editorial supporting President Obama's second-term election suggests, rightly I think, that many of the progressives' criticisms are not warranted. One of those criticisms emanated from Frederick Harris, a progressive African American political scientist at Columbia University's Institute for Research in African

American Studies, whose opinion piece in the *New York Times* a week before the November 6 election lambasted the African American professional class for "giving President Obama a pass," so speak. Harris summarized his criticism in what I thought were unfortunately dismissive terms:

> For those who had seen in President Obama's [2008] election the culmination of four centuries of black hopes and aspirations and the realization of the Rev. Martin Luther King Jr.'s vision of a "beloved community," the last four years must be reckoned a disappointment. Whether it ends in 2013 or 2017, the Obama presidency has already marked the decline, rather than pinnacle, of a political vision centered on challenging racial inequality. The tragedy is that black elites—from intellectuals and civil rights leaders to politicians and clergy members—have acquiesced to this decline, seeing it as the necessary price and satisfaction of having a black family in the White House.[55]

As it happened, the foregoing type of criticism of Obama's administration by progressive groups and pundits—a criticism I disagree with—did not deter the vast majority of African American voters from voting on November 6, 2012, to reelect to a second term the first African American president of the United States. Most African American voters are, I suggest, guided by a pragmatic political hard-headedness that some leftist analysts seemingly lack.

African Americans voted 93 percent in favor of the Obama-Biden Democratic ticket in 2012, and 53 percent of all voters supported the Democratic ticket, thereby giving the Obama-Biden ticket a 5 million vote advantage over the Romney-Ryan ticket. This amounted to a momentous electoral achievement, in light of the many billions of dollars in conservative corporate "Super Pac" funds arrayed against the Obama-Biden ticket. The Obama-Biden ticket gained a decisive 332 Electoral College victory as well.[56]

This reelection victory will help checkmate the broad right-wing endeavor to weaken overall liberal American governance that a Tea Party–harassed Republican Party appears to have at the top of its political agenda. Postelection analyses suggest that a new Democratic Party electoral alliance produced this outcome. That alliance contained important support by African American voters, Asian American voters, Hispanic American voters, Jewish American voters, the white liberal voter bloc, and the women's voter bloc. Compared with African American voter support for the Obama-Biden ticket of 93 percent, the Asian American voter support was 73 percent; Hispanic voters, 71 percent; Jewish voters, 69 percent; and women voters, 55 percent. In this connection, the quite shrewd reflections on the systemic meaning of the second-term reelection of Obama by *Nation* magazine's political columnist William Greider warrant mention here:

> The 2012 election was a crucial watershed in the life of the nation. Obama's re-election is in some ways even more significant than his initial triumph in 2008. If he had lost, historian Lawrence Goldwyn pointed out to me, it would have been taken many years—probably many decades—before either major party dared to nominate a person of color for president again. Black Americans understood this, probably better than most of us white folks. So did Latinos, Asians and a whole bunch of other "minority" voters. African-Americans might have had quarrels or disappointments with Obama, but they understood the historic stakes in winning a second term for him. *Otherwise, he would have been dismissed as a fluke.* Whatever else he accomplishes or fails to accomplish in his second term, *Obama will be forever remembered as the president who opened America to a different future—more promising and fulfilling, more just and democratic, than ever before.*[57]

Furthermore, the 2012 election of Obama to a second term will, I think, have a special political-systemic impact on the overall leadership capability of the twenty-first-century African American intelligentsia. I need hardly mention that the combined membership of today's African American professional class sector eclipses the nascent membership of the African American professionals for whom the young scholar Du Bois first wrote the term "Talented Tenth" in 1903. As Du Bois informed the American public in 1903, the U.S. Census Bureau in 1900 recorded a miniscule 1,996 college-educated African Americans for the academic year 1899–1900. Forward to 103 years later: the 2006 U.S. Census Bureau recorded 3.5 million African Americans holding top-tier "white-collar jobs," among a total of 15 million African Americans employed.

From our vantage in the first decades of the twenty-first century, one thing can be said with full confidence regarding the overall contemporary status of the African American middle-class and professional-class sectors, relative to where those sectors stood at the dawn of the twentieth century: times have changed and, in many regards, changed for the better.

Meanwhile, I further suggest that this book's probe of over a hundred years of the African American intelligentsia's development indicates that it might, in time, fulfill what might be called a "Du Boisian moral leadership obligation." From today's vantage, that moral leadership obligation is, I think, plain and clear: *to facilitate, at relative parity with American society in general, the social and civic advancement of today's African American poor sector*—the "Negro masses," as Du Bois labeled this sector in his 1903 classic tome *The Souls Black Folk*.

APPENDIX

NOTES

ANALYTICAL BIBLIOGRAPHY

ACKNOWLEDGMENTS

INDEX

APPENDIX

Class Attributes of Elite Strata

Based on data in Richard Bardolph, *The Negro Vanguard* (New York: Rinehart, 1959). See also Tables 1.2 and 1.3.

Table A.1. Class attributes of Bardolph's "Out-of-Bondage Black Elite, 1865–1900" (n = 28)

Name	Home region	Family background	Skin color	Educational background	Occupation
C. C. Antoine	South	White planter	Light	Mission school	Grocer
Ebenezer Bennett	North	—	Light	College	Teacher
Richard Boyd	South	White planter	Light	Mission school	Clergy
Blanche K. Bruce	South	White planter	Light	College (Oberlin)	Reconstruction-era politician
Richard Cain	North	—	Dark	College (Wilberforce)	A.M.E. bishop
Francis Cardoza	South	White professional	Light	College (Glasgow Univ.)	Reconstruction-era politician
Archibald Carey	South	Clergy (A.M.E.)	Light	College (Wilberforce)	A.M.E. bishop
Henry Cheatham	South	White planter	Light	College (Shaw Univ.)	Reconstruction-era politician
Robert DeLarge	South	White planter	Light	Mission school	Reconstruction-era politician
Robert Elliott	North	Domestic servants	Dark	High school	Reconstruction-era politician
T. Thomas Fortune	South	White planter	Light	College (Howard Univ.)	Newspaper owner
Jonathan Gibbs	South	—	Light	College (Dartmouth)	Clergy (Presbyterian)
Archibald Grimké	South	White planter	Light	College (Lincoln Univ.)	Lawyer
Francis Grimké	South	White planter	Light	College (Lincoln Univ.)	Clergy

Name	Region	Parents' occupation	Skin color	Education	Career
William Heard	South	Artisan (wheelwright)	Light	College (Univ. of South Carolina)	Clergy (A.M.E.)
James Jones	South	Artisans	Light	Mission school	Tailor
Isaac Lane	South	Field hands	Dark	Mission school	C.M.E. bishop
John Langston	South	White planter	Light	College	Reconstruction-era politician
Thomas Miller	South	White planter	Light	High school	Reconstruction-era politician
Daniel Payne	South	Field hands	Dark	College	Clergy (A.M.E.), college president
Joseph Price	South	Artisans	Dark	Mission school	Clergy (A.M.E.), college president
Joseph Rainey	South	Barber	Light	Mission school	Reconstruction-era politician
James Rapier	South	White planter	Light	Mission school	Lawyer, Reconstruction-era politician
Hiram Revels	South	Farmers	Light	College (Knox)	Reconstruction-era politician
Henry McNeal Turner	South	Field hands (Freeborn)	Dark	Mission school	A.M.E. bishop
Booker T. Washington	South	White planter	Brown	College (Hampton Institute)	College president
Albery Whitman	South	Field hands	Light	College (Wilberforce)	A.M.E. clergy, poet
James Wormley	South	Domestic servants	Light	Mission school	Hotelier (Washington, DC)

Source: Data from Richard Bardolph, *The Negro Vanguard* (New York: Rinehart, 1959), chap. 1.
Note: "A.M.E." is the abbreviation for African Methodist Episcopal; "C.M.E." is the abbreviation for Colored Methodist Episcopal.

Table A.2. Class attributes of Bardolph's "Black Educator Elite, 1920s–1940s" (n = 39)

Name	Home region	Family background	Skin color	Occupation*
Mary McLeod Bethune	South	Domestic servants	Dark	College president
Horace Mann Bond	South	Clergy (Presbyterian)	Brown	College president
J. Max Bond	South	Clergy (Presbyterian)	Brown	College president
Maudelle Bousfeld	North	Teacher	Light	High school principal
Benjamin Brawley	North	Laundress	Light	College president
Charlotte H. Brown	South	Laundress	Light	College president
Ralph Bunche	West	Barber	Light	Academic, diplomat
Ambrose Caliver	South	Coal miner	Dark	College dean
Allison Davis	North	Farmer and clerk	Light	Academic (anthropologist)
Arthur Davis	South	Teacher	Light	Academic (English)
John W. Davis	South	Domestics	Light	College president
Matthew Dogon	South	Barber	Light	College president
St. Clair Drake	North	Clergy (A.M.E.)	Brown	Academic (anthropologist)
W. E. B. Du Bois	North	Barber/clergy	Light	Academic (sociologist)
John Hope Franklin	West	Lawyer	Dark	Academic (historian)
E. Franklin Frazier	North	Bank messenger	Brown	Academic (sociologist)
William J. Hale	South	White professional	Light	College president
C. V. Abram Harris	South	Butcher	Brown	Academic (economist)
Joseph Holley	South	Sharecropper	Light	College president
Dwight Holmes	South	Clergy	Light	College president
John Hope	South	White merchant	Light	College president
Benjamin Hubert	South	Farmer	Brown	College president
Henry A. Hunt	South	White professional	Light	College president

Name	Region	Father's occupation	Color	Role
Martin Jenkins	South	Artisan	Light	College president
Mordecai Johnson	South	Factory laborer and clergy	Light	College president
David Jones	South	Saloon keeper	Light	College president
Lawrence Jones	South	Hotel porter	Brown	College president
Rayford Logan	South	Butler	Light	Academic (historian)
Benjamin Mays	South	Field hands	Dark	College president
Kelly Miller	South	Field hands	Dark	Academic (mathematician)
Robert Moton	South	Plantation foreman	Dark	College president
Frederick Patterson	South	Teacher	Light	College president
Saunders Redding	South	Teacher	Brown	Academic (literary studies)
Ira D. Reid	South	Clergy	Brown	Academic (sociologist)
Merze Tate	North	Farmer	Brown	Academic (political scientist)
Charles Thompson	South	Business	Light	College dean
Lorenzo Turner	South	Domestic servants	Brown	Academic (linguist)
Carter G. Woodson	South	Farmer	Brown	Academic (historian)
R. R. Wright Sr.	South	Field hands	Brown	College president

Source: Data from Richard Bardolph, *The Negro Vanguard* (New York: Rinehart, 1959), chaps. 2 and 3.

Note: "A.M.E." is the abbreviation for African Methodist Episcopal.

*Educators listed as "college president" headed up the following institutions: Mary McLeod Bethune, Bethune-Cookman College; Horace Mann Bond, Fort Valley State/Lincoln University; J. Max Bond, University of Liberia; Benjamin Brawley, Morehouse College; Charlotte Brown, Palmer Memorial Institute; John W. Davis, West Virginia State University; Matthew Dogon, Wiley State College; William Hale, Tennessee Agriculture and Industrial College; Joseph Holley, Fort Valley State; Dwight Holmes, Morgan State College; John Hope, Atlanta University; Benjamin Hubert, Georgia State College; Henry Hunt, Fort Valley State; Martin Jenkins, Morgan State College; Mordecai Johnson, Howard University; David Jones, Bennett College; Lawrence Jones, Tougaloo College; Benjamin Mays, Morehouse College; Robert Moton, Tuskegee Institute; Frederick Patterson, Tuskegee Institute; and R. R. Wright Sr., Georgia State Industrial College for Colored Youth, now called Savannah State University.

Table A.3. Class attributes of Bardolph's "Black Creative and Media Elite, 1920s–1940s" (n = 20)

Name	Home region	Family background	Skin color	Educational background	Occupation
Robert Abbott	South	Teacher/clergy	Dark	College	Newspaper founder (*Chicago Defender*)
Claude Barnett	South	Lawyer	Brown	College (Tuskegee Institute)	News agency
Arna Bontemps	West	Teacher	Light	College (Hampton Institute)	Academic (literary studies)
William Braithwaite	North	Medical assistant	Light	High school	Academic (literary studies)
Sterling Brown	North	Academics	Light	College (Williams College)	Academic (literary studies)
Harry Burleigh	North	Laundress	Dark	Conservatory	Soloist/composer
Countee Cullen	North	Domestic servants (adopted by whites)	Dark	College (New York Univ.)	Writer/poet
Wendell Dabney	South	Waiter/jockey	Light	College (Oberlin)	Newspaper founder (*Cincinnati Union*)

Name	Region	Parent occupation	Complexion	Education	Profession
William Dawson	South	Laborer	Dark	Conservatory	Composer
Roscoe Dunjee	South	—	Light	College	Newspaper founder (*Oklahoma Black Dispatch*)
Angelina Grimké	North	Lawyer	Light	College	Playwright
Roland Hayes	North	Domestic servants	Dark	Conservatory	Soloist
Langston Hughes	South	Teacher	Light	College (Lincoln Univ.)	Writer/poet
Zora Neale Hurston	South	Field hands	Brown	College (Barnard College)	Writer/novelist
Fred Moore	South	Farmer	Dark	High school	Newspaper founder (*New York Age*)
Paul Robeson	North	Clergy	Dark	College (Rutgers Univ.)	Soloist/actor
George Schuyler	North	Laundress	Dark	Grammar school	Journalist
Monroe Trotter	North	Government clerk	Light	College (Harvard Univ.)	Newspaper founder (*Boston Guardian*)
Robert Vann	South	Sharecropper	Dark	College	Newspaper founder (*Pittsburgh Courier*)
Ida Wells-Barnett	North	Laborer	Dark	College	Journalist

Source: Data from Richard Bardolph, *The Negro Vanguard* (New York: Rinehart, 1959), chaps. 2 and 3.

NOTES

Prologue

1. See Martin Kilson, "The Afro-Americanization of Lincoln University: Horace Mann Bond's Legacy, 1945–1957," *A.M.E. Church Review* (April–June 2007): 76–91.

2. See Horace Mann Bond, *Negro Education in Alabama: A Study in Cotton and Steel* (Washington, DC: Associated Publishers, 1939). Associated Publishers was the publication arm of the Association for the Study of Negro Life and History, which Carter G. Woodson founded in 1915. Woodson was the second African American to earn a Ph.D. from Harvard, which he did in 1912. In 1916 he founded the *Journal of Negro History*.

3. See Horace Mann Bond, *The Education of the Negro in the American Social Order* (New York: Prentice Hall, 1934). Thirty years later, Bond completed a study for the U.S. Department of Education that probed the sociodemographic background of African American scholars who, like himself, were born toward the end of the Emancipation era and during the first decade of the twentieth century. That study was published in 1969, three years before Bond died: *Black American Scholars: A Study of Their Beginnings* (Detroit: Balamp Publishing, 1969). During Bond's twelve-year presidency at Lincoln University (1945–1957), he researched in the university's archives on the history of Lincoln University, which was the first higher education institution established for black youth. That research was published as *Education for Freedom: A History of Lincoln University, Pennsylvania* (Princeton, NJ: Princeton University Press, 1976). This is a nearly seven-hundred-page case study of how the first three generations of college-educated black Americans—from the 1870s to the 1940s—were provided a top-tier classical education, which included required courses in Greek and Latin.

4. The figures on literacy and college education are from Monroe N. Work, *The Negro Year Book: An Annual Encyclopedia of the Negro, 1931–1932* (Tuskegee, AL: Negro Yearbook Publishing, 1932), 20; and Charles S. Johnson, *The Negro College Graduate* (Chapel Hill: University of North Carolina Press, 1938).

5. See John DeSantis, "North Carolina City Confronts Its Past in Report on White Vigilantes," *New York Times,* December 19, 2005.

6. John W. Blassingame and John R. McKivigan, eds., *The Frederick Douglass Papers,* ser. 1, *Speeches, Debates, and Interviews,* vol. 4, *1864–1880* (New Haven, CT: Yale University Press, 1991), 442.

7. For a cogent overview of the social gospel Christian discourse and its application among African Methodist churches since the late nineteenth century, see Dennis C. Dickerson, *A Liberated Past: Explorations in A.M.E. Church History* (Nashville, TN: AMEC Sunday School Union Publisher, 2003). Dickerson, who teaches at Vanderbilt University and is editor of the *A.M.E. Church Review,* is a seminal scholar of African Methodist practices in black churches since the nineteenth century.

8. On the early founding of Lincoln University and Wilberforce University and the Christian social gospel theological discourse that influenced these universities, see Bond, *Education for Freedom.*

9. See John Aubrey Davis, *Regional Organization of the Social Security Administration: A Case Study* (New York: Columbia University Press, 1950). This book was originally Davis' doctoral dissertation (a field-research study), published as study 571 in Columbia University Press' revered series Studies in History, Economics, and Public Law. Davis' first book was a field-research study for the New York State War Council: *How Management Can Integrate Negroes in War Industries* (New York: New York State War Council, 1942). Davis was among a small group of African American professionals appointed as officials in the Roosevelt administration's Fair Employment Practices Committee (FEPC), whose task was to ensure fair employment for African Americans in industries associated with wartime production. Among that group of black professionals in the FEPC during World War II were Robert Weaver (economist), Elmer Henderson (lawyer), George Johnson (lawyer and dean of Howard University Law School), James Nabrit (lawyer), George Crocket (lawyer), and Clarence Mitchell (journalist and National Urban League staffer). For a study of Davis' years with the FEPC, see Martin Kilson, "Political Scientists and the Activist-Technocrat Dichotomy: The Case of John Aubrey Davis," in Wilbur Rich, ed., *African American Perspectives in Political Science* (Philadelphia: Temple University Press, 2007), 169–172.

1. The Rise and Fall of Color Elitism among African Americans

1. John Hope Franklin, *Reconstruction after the Civil War* (Chicago: University of Chicago Press, 1961).
2. See Monroe N. Work, *The Negro Year Book, 1931–1932: An Annual Encyclopedia of the Negro* (Tuskegee, AL: Negro Yearbook Publishing, 1932). On the early twentieth-century status of the Negro colleges founded by the Methodist Episcopal Church, see Jay S. Stowell, *Methodist Adventures in Negro Education* (New York: Methodist Book Concern, 1922), especially chaps. 4–6, 8–10.
3. See W. E. B. Du Bois, "The Talented Tenth," in Booker T. Washington, ed., *The Negro Problem* (New York: J. Pott, 1903), 33–75.
4. Seymour Martin Lipset, "American Intellectuals: Their Politics and Status," *Daedalus: Journal of the American Academy of Arts and Sciences* (Summer 1959): 460.
5. For a conceptually seminal probe of Marcus Garvey's leadership metamorphosis, see Lawrence W. Levine, "Marcus Garvey and the Politics of Revitalization," in John Hope Franklin and August Meier, eds., *Black Leaders of the Twentieth Century* (Urbana: University of Illinois Press, 1982), 105–138. See also Judith Stein, *The World of Marcus Garvey: Race and Class in Modern Society* (Baton Rouge: Louisiana State University Press, 1986).
6. Manning Marable, *Malcolm X: A Life of Reinvention* (New York: Viking, 2011). For a study of the first cohort of "self-made" African American intelligentsia-type personalities, see Richard J. M. Blackett's probe of pre–Civil War era black abolitionists, *Beating against the Barriers: Biographical Essays in Nineteenth-Century Afro-American History* (Baton Rouge: Louisiana State University Press, 1986). See also Benjamin Quarles, *Black Abolitionists* (New York: Oxford University Press, 1969). For a study of Malcolm X's radical legacy in African American intelligentsia circles, see Columbia University theologian James H. Cone's *Martin and Malcolm and America: A Dream or a Nightmare* (Maryknoll, NY: Orbis Books, 1991).
7. See Richard Bardolph, *The Negro Vanguard* (New York: Rinehart, 1959), and Willard Gatewood, *Aristocrats of Color: The Black Elite, 1880–1920* (Bloomington: Indiana University Press, 1991).
8. For Hylan Lewis' broad-based cultural understanding of "blackness," see his *Blackways of Kent* (Chapel Hill: University of North Carolina Press, 1955).
9. On the maternal side of my ancestors, my maternal grandmother's father—Luther Clayton—was a very light-skinned African American (best described by the old-fashioned term "octoroon") who rejected color-caste pretensions when he married my dark-skinned maternal great-grandmother, Bessie

Clayton. Their child, Cora Clayton, was my mother's mother. Luther Clayton was born to a Free Negro family in Westmoreland County, Virginia, which had a population of 50 percent Free Negroes by the start of the Civil War. See James H. Brewer, *The Confederate Negro: Virginia's Craftsmen and Military Laborers, 1861–1865* (Tuscaloosa: University of Alabama Press, 1969), 3. Brewer's book contains a map showing Westmoreland County's location on the northern Virginia side of the Chesapeake Bay.

10. See Gatewood, *Aristocrats of Color.*
11. Richard Bardolph, *The Negro Vanguard* (New York: Rinehart, 1959).
12. A. B. Caldwell, *History of the American Negro,* 8 vols. (Atlanta: A. B. Caldwell, 1923).
13. See C. Vann Woodward, ed., *Mary Chestnut's Civil War* (New Haven, CT: Yale University Press, 1981).
14. Bardolph, *Negro Vanguard,* 216.
15. Ibid.
16. Ibid., 217–218.
17. For Archibald Grimké's black leadership career, see Dickson D. Bruce's seminal study, *Archibald Grimké: Portrait of a Black Independent* (Baton Rouge: Louisiana State University Press, 1995).
18. Gatewood, *Aristocrats of Color,* 64.
19. For the early careers of Archibald and Francis Grimké, see Horace Mann Bond's history of Lincoln University, *Education for Freedom: A History of Lincoln University, Pennsylvania* (Princeton, NJ: Princeton University Press, 1976). The Grimké brothers, through their white South Carolina planter father, were the nephews of the prominent New England suffragette Angelina Grimké Weld, who supported them financially during their college and graduate school years. The Grimké brothers' decision in the early period of their careers to reject "passing" and join the progressive leadership ranks of the African American intelligentsia might have influenced the professional decisions of other light-skinned early twentieth-century intelligentsia personalities like John Hope (the first African American president of Atlanta University), James Weldon Johnson and Walter White (the first African American directors of the NAACP), Eugene Kinckle Jones (the first African American director of the National Urban League), and Mordecai Johnson (the first African American president of Howard University). On this issue, see Mordecai Johnson's biography by Richard McKinney, *Mordecai, the Man and His Message: The Story of Mordecai Wyatt Johnson* (Washington, DC: Howard University Press, 1997).
20. Gatewood, *Aristocrats of Color,* 64; emphasis added.
21. W. E. B. Du Bois, *The Souls of Black Folk* (Chicago: A. C. McClurg, 1903), 202.

22. Ibid., 203; emphasis added.

23. For an overview of the African American social context of the New Negro Movement as it was evolving, see Alain Locke, ed., *The New Negro: An Interpretation* (New York: Albert & Charles Boni, 1925).

24. See Ross Posnock, *Color and Culture: Black Writers and the Making of the Modern Intellectual* (Cambridge, MA: Harvard University Press, 1998).

25. For the overall dynamics of the New Negro Movement from the 1920s to the 1940s, see Nathan I. Huggins, *The Harlem Renaissance* (New York: Oxford University Press, 1971). See also David Levering Lewis, *When Harlem Was in Vogue* (New York: Alfred Knopf, 1981).

26. See Arthur Huff Fauset's *Black Gods of the Metropolis* (Philadelphia: University of Pennsylvania Press, 1944).

27. Bardolph, *Negro Vanguard,* 364.

28. See Robert Weisbrot, *Father Divine and the Struggle for Equality* (Urbana: University of Illinois Press, 1983).

29. For these black popular-society spheres where black populist figures gained leadership capabilities, see Fauset, *Black Gods of the Metropolis*, and Weisbrot, *Father Divine.*

30. Charles S. Johnson, *Growing Up in the Black Belt: Negro Youth in the Rural South* (Washington, DC: American Youth Commission, 1941), 135.

31. See Isabel Wilkerson, *The Warmth of Other Suns: The Epic Story of America's Great Migration* (New York: Random House, 2010).

32. See, for example, Robert Gregg, *Sparks from the Anvil of Oppression: Philadelphia's African Methodists and Southern Migrants, 1890–1940* (Philadelphia: Temple University Press, 1993).

33. St. Clair Drake and Horace R. Cayton, *Black Metropolis: A Study of Negro Life in a Northern City,* vol. 2 (New York: Harcourt Brace, 1945), 415.

34. George Osofsky, *Harlem: The Making of a Ghetto, 1890–1930* (New York: Oxford University Press, 1971), 144.

35. For the variety of populist-type leadership figures in type II churches during the interwar period, see Ira Reid, "Let Us Prey," *Opportunity: Journal of Negro Life* (September 1926); Miles Mark Fisher, "Negroes Get Religion," *Opportunity: Journal of Negro Life* (May 1930); Fauset, *Black Gods of the Metropolis*; Drake and Cayton, *Black Metropolis*; Robert Warner, *New Haven Negroes* (New Haven, CT: Yale University Press, 1940); Jon Michael Spencer, "The Black Church and the Harlem Renaissance," *African American Review* 30 (1996); and Randall Burkett, *Black Redemption: Churchmen Speak for the Garvey Movement* (Philadelphia: Temple University Press, 1978).

36. Osofsky, *Harlem*, 145–146.

37. Fisher, "Negroes Get Religion," 148.

38. For the Peace Mission Church's business endeavors, see Weisbrot, *Father Divine*.

39. See Burkett, *Black Redemption*.

40. For searching probes of the Garvey movement, see Levine, "Marcus Garvey and the Politics of Revitalization," and Stein, *World of Marcus Garvey*.

41. See Spencer, "Black Church and the Harlem Renaissance." See also Nick Salvatore, *Singing in a Strange Land: Rev. C. L. Franklin, the Black Church and the Transformation of America* (New York: Oxford University Press, 2005).

2. Black Intelligentsia Leadership Patterns

1. For data on the rise of the African American elected political class, see Carol M. Swain, *Black Faces, Black Interests: The Representation of African Americans in Congress* (Cambridge, MA: Harvard University Press, 1997).

2. W. E. B. Du Bois, *The Souls of Black Folk* (Chicago: A. C. McClurg, 1903), 105.

3. Adam Goodheart, *1861: The Civil War Awakening* (New York: Knopf, 2011), 65–66; emphasis added. Carl Sandburg, in his monumental and seminal six-volume history of Abraham Lincoln's life, reports the monetary value of Negro slaves at $3 billion: *Abraham Lincoln: The War Years*, vol. 4 (New York: Harcourt Brace, 1939), 114. These data on the monetary value of Negro slaves and their labor show the remarkable contribution of African Americans to fundamental wealth creation—core "capital accumulation"—in mid-nineteenth-century American civilization. Moreover, this wealth creation by African American labor was also significant in the post–Civil War era of the late nineteenth-century South.

4. In addition to W. E. B. Du Bois' progressive historiography perspective, *Black Reconstruction in America, 1860–1880* (New York: Harcourt Brace, 1935), see Eric Foner's *Reconstruction: America's Unfinished Revolution, 1863–1877* (New York: Harper & Row, 1988). See also John Hope Franklin, *Reconstruction after the Civil War* (Chicago: University of Chicago Press, 1961).

5. See Thomas Holt, *Black over White: Negro Political Leadership in South Carolina during Reconstruction* (Urbana: University of Illinois Press, 1977).

6. Eric Foner, *Forever Free: The Story of Emancipation and Reconstruction* (New York: Vintage Books, 2006), xxvi.

7. For an understanding of the roots of white vigilante violence and authoritarian state practices against Negroes in the post-Reconstruction South, see George C. Rable, *But There Was No Peace: The Role of Violence in the Politics of Reconstruction* (Athens: University of Georgia Press, 1984).

8. Lawrie Balfour, *Democracy's Reconstruction: Thinking Politically with W. E. B. Du Bois* (New York: Oxford University Press, 2011), 29.

9. Du Bois, *Souls of Black Folk,* 219.

10. W. E. B. Du Bois, *The Philadelphia Negro: A Study* (Philadelphia: University of Pennsylvania Press, 1899).

11. For a study of what I dub "white hegemonic maneuvers" and their impact on northern black communities, see Arnold B. Hirsch, *Making the Second Ghetto: Race and Housing in Chicago, 1940–1960* (Cambridge: Cambridge University Press, 1983). See also the role of such maneuvers in making the "first ghetto" in Nicholas Lemann, *The Promised Land: The Great Black Migration and How It Changed America* (New York: Knopf, 1991).

12. Victor Perlo, *The Negro in Southern Agriculture* (New York: International Publishers, 1953), 14–15.

13. See Douglas A. Blackmon, *Slavery by Another Name: The Re-enslavement of Black Americans from the Civil War to World War II* (New York: Doubleday, 2008), parts 2 and 3. Blackmon's main materials and data relate to the state of Alabama. For a study with a South-wide focus on the interplay of convict-labor practices and the South's wealthy agricultural capitalism from the 1880s into the twentieth century, see Alex Lichtenstein, *Twice the Work of Free Labor: The Political Economy of Convict Labor in the New South* (New York: Verso, 1995).

14. For the cruel and oppressive conditions of the white working class during the so-called robber baron phase of America's industrial growth, see Jacob Riis, *How the Other Half Lives* (New York: Charles Scribner, 1890). See also Upton Sinclair's novel based on the meat-packing industry in Chicago, *The Jungle* (New York: Doubleday, 1906). A review of *The Jungle* by the novelist Jack London characterized the book as "the *Uncle Tom's Cabin* of [modern] wage slavery" (see http://en.wikipedia.org/wiki/The_Jungle).

15. Gunnar Myrdal, *An American Dilemma: The Negro Problem and Modern Democracy,* vol. 1 (New York: Harper & Brothers, 1944), 558–559; emphasis added. The ultimate and most vicious assault against African American citizens in the South from the 1880s through the first half of the twentieth century was the widespread practice of lynching. See Stewart E. Tolnay and E. M. Beck, *A Festival of Violence: An Analysis of Southern Lynching, 1882–1930* (Urbana: University of Illinois Press, 1995); see also W. Fitzhugh Brundage, ed., *Under Sentence of Death: Essays on Lynching in the South* (Chapel Hill: University of North Carolina Press, 1997).

16. Horace Mann Bond, *The Education of the Negro in the American Social Order* (New York: Prentice Hall, 1934), 199–200. See also Isabel Wilkerson, *The Warmth of Other Suns: The Epic Story of America's Great Migration* (New York: Vintage Books, 2011).

17. See J. Morgan Kousser, *The Shaping of Southern Politics: Suffrage Restriction and the Establishment of the One-Party South, 1880–1910* (New Haven, CT: Yale University Press, 1974). Only in the North was electoral mobilization available to black folks. See also a study by NAACP official Henry Lee Moon, *Balance of Power: The Negro Vote* (Garden City, NY: Doubleday, 1948). Written by a journalist and a long-standing NAACP staff figure during the 1930s and 1940s, this was the first major book on the electoral dimension of African Americans' political development during the first half of the twentieth century.

18. Emphasis added. See Louis B. Harlan, *Booker T. Washington: The Making of a Black Leader, 1856–1901* (New York: Oxford University Press, 1972). For a searching account of Washington's accommodationist leadership that presents a shrewd critique of the operational dimensions of accommodationism in Alabama, see Horace Mann Bond, *Negro Education in Alabama: A Study in Cotton and Steel* (Washington, DC: Associated Publishers, 1939), chap. 14.

19. Booker T. Washington, *The Future of the American Negro* (New York: Small, Maynard, 1899), 132. See a recent appraisal of Booker T. Washington's leadership discourse—a sympathetic one, I think—in Holy Cross University historian Michael R. West's *The Education of Booker T. Washington: The Negro Problem, Democracy, and the Idea of Race Relations* (New York: Columbia University Press, 2006).

20. For the leadership dynamics of the Niagara Movement, see Francis L. Broderick, *W. E. B. Du Bois: Negro Leader in Time of Crisis* (Stanford, CA: Stanford University Press, 1959). See also Elliott Rudwick, *W. E. B. Du Bois: A Study in Minority Group Leadership* (Philadelphia: University of Pennsylvania Press, 1960).

21. Du Bois, *Souls of Black Folk,* 54–55; emphasis added.

22. Ibid., 55.

23. Ibid., 55–56; emphasis added.

24. Cornel West, *Democracy Matters: Winning the Fight against Imperialism* (Boston: Penguin Press, 2004), 74.

25. Ibid.

26. Texts of the 1905 Niagara Movement resolutions were reprinted in the NAACP's journal, the *Crisis* (October 1963).

27. Du Bois, *Souls of Black Folk,* 60–61, 63.

28. Ibid., 64–65, 67; emphasis added.

29. See David Levering Lewis, *W. E. B. Du Bois: The Fight for Equality and the American Century, 1919–1963,* vol. 2 (New York: Henry Holt, 2000), chap. 9.

30. Mamie Gavin Fields with Karen Fields, *Lemon Swamp and Other Stories: A Carolina Memoir* (New York: Free Press, 1983), 31.

31. Carter G. Woodson, *The Negro Professional Man and the Community* (Washington, DC: Associated Publishers, 1934), 124. Although numerous academic programs in the fields of African American studies and black studies exist today in American colleges and universities, to my knowledge none has produced a volume that updates Carter Woodson's pioneering book. It is hoped that this scholarship vacuum will be addressed in the years ahead.

32. Ibid., 115.

33. See ibid. for data on the education of professional-level African Americans during the first half of the twentieth century. On the training at mainly black hospitals and nursing institutions of over ten thousand African Americans in the nursing profession by the 1940s, see Darlene C. Hine, *Black Women in White: Racial Conflict and Cooperation in the Nursing Profession, 1890–1950* (Bloomington: Indiana University Press, 1989). It was in the fields of mathematics, biology, physics, chemistry, zoology, pathology, parasitology, and psychology, that professional-level education of African Americans during the first sixty years of the twentieth century depended on white universities.

34. See Horace Mann Bond, "Doctorate Degrees of Lincoln University Graduates," *Lincoln University Bulletin* (Spring 1957): 3, 14. The *Lincoln University Bulletin*—which had a century life span when it was discontinued in the 1980s and replaced by a photo-saturated popular college publication—is held in the Lincoln University Archives at the Langston Hughes Memorial Library. The *Bulletin* is a treasure trove of materials on the history of America's first institution for the higher education of African Americans and materials that relate the broad impact of Lincoln's graduates on African American life and society. In the 1960s, Bond completed a manuscript for the U.S. Department of Education that probed the demographic background of a sample of African American who had gained doctorate degrees by the 1950s. See Horace Mann Bond, *Black American Scholars: A Study of Their Beginnings* (Detroit: Balamp Publishing, 1969). This unique work contains fascinating material on the kinds of mainly small-town African American social backgrounds that were associated with African American achievers of doctorate degrees during the first half of the twentieth century. Independently published, Bond's *Black American Scholars* is an important work that has not received the recognition it warrants.

35. On the African American nursing profession and the arduous struggle to establish nursing education for African Americans owing to racist practices

by white hospitals and nurse-training institutions, see Hine, *Black Women in White*.

36. See Darlene Clark Hine, "Mabel K. Staupers and the Integration of Black Nurses into the Armed Forces," in John Hope Franklin and August Meier, eds., *Black Leaders of the Twentieth Century* (Urbana: University of Illinois Press, 1982), 241–258. A leading African American nurse in the Army Nurse Corps during World War II and later in the U.S. Women's Army Corps through the Vietnam War was Lt. Colonel Ruby Rose. It happens that Rose grew up in the eastern Pennsylvania factory town of Ambler—the same town I grew up in. It had a black population about three hundred in the 1930s among a total population of four thousand. From the 1920s into the 1960s, a good number of working-class African American youth in Ambler became schoolteachers, nurses, lawyers, academics, and businesspersons. See my forthcoming autobiography, *Between an African American Community and Harvard: A Black Intellectual Odyssey*.

37. See Mabel Keaton Staupers, *No Time for Prejudice: A Story of the Integration of Negroes in Nursing in the United States* (New York: Macmillan, 1961).

38. Martha Putney, *When the Nation Was in Need: Blacks in the Women's Army Corps during World War II* (Lanham, MD: Scarecrow Press, 1992).

39. Demographic data on Coatesville, Pennsylvania, are found in *Fourteenth Census of the United States Taken in the Year 1920: Population,* vol. 2 (Washington, DC: Government Printing Office, 1922), 869. For 1930 and 1940 Coatesville data, see *Sixteenth Census of the United States 1940: Population,* vol. 2, part 6, *Pennsylvania and Texas* (Washington, DC: Government Printing Office, 1943), 294, 158.

40. The following account of Atkinson's career in Coatesville, Pennsylvania from 1927 to the 1990s is based on interviews he gave to the *Philadelphia Inquirer* in the 1990s. See Andy Wallace's obituary on Atkinson, "Dr. W. C. Atkinson, 97: Physician Founded a Coatesville Hospital," *Philadelphia Inquirer,* January 5, 1991. Atkinson's parents were in the artisan segment of lower-middle-class African Americans (father was a carpenter, and his mother was a midwife), who struggled to send Whittier and his younger brother, Nolan, to Georgia's main public college for black youth, Georgia State College. The Atkinson brothers later attended the Howard University School of Medicine, which, along with the Meharry School of Medicine in Tennessee, educated the majority of African American medical doctors during the first half of the twentieth century.

41. See E. Franklin Frazier, *Black Bourgeoisie: Rise of a New Middle Class* (Glencoe, IL: Free Press, 1957). For a critique of what I consider Frazier's "caricature view" of the evolving twentieth-century black bourgeoisie, see

Martin Kilson, "E. Franklin Frazier's 'Black Bourgeoisie' Reconsidered," in James E. Teele, ed., *E. Franklin Frazier and "Black Bourgeoisie"* (Columbia: University of Missouri Press, 2002), 118–136.

42. Quoted in Wallace, "Dr. W. C. Atkinson, 97"; emphasis added.

43. Atkinson was widely honored during his professional career. In the 1950s, he was chosen president of the main professional association among African American physicians, the National Medical Association, founded in the 1921. In 1960, the Pennsylvania Medical Society named Atkinson General Practitioner of the Year, and in the late 1960s he was appointed president of the Chester County chapter of the Pennsylvania Academy of General Practice. In the early 1970s Atkinson was appointed president of the Philadelphia chapter of the Academy of General Practice.

44. Vincent P. Franklin, *The Education of Black Philadelphia* (Philadelphia: University of Pennsylvania Press, 1979), 95. Inasmuch as Franklin commences a discussion of the black-communitarian leadership social development pattern in Philadelphia with reference to activities of a leading African American women's sorority, that cutting-edge role of women's organizations in black-communitarian leadership patterns was keenly formulated by Darlene Hine in a 1999 essay. "Given the barriers of racial discrimination," Hine observed, "the reality of poverty, and formal powerlessness, Black women in the age of Jim Crow discrimination had to create and sustain . . . the twin engines of racial uplift and progress . . . wedded to an oppositional consciousness and culture of struggle." Hine elaborated this core proposition thus: "The church served as the initial organizational base for Black women's benevolent social welfare work. In numerable church clubs, such as Daughters of Ham, Eastern Star, and Sisters of Zion, Black women performed invaluable service. . . . When economic depression, bankruptcy, and disease struck the Black communities, the church women were there. They provided for the widows, and the orphans. They taught Sunday School, did missionary work, and participated in endless fund-raising drives. Most people would agree that the church rests most securely on the backs of Black women." See Darlene Clark Hine, "Introduction," in Kathleen Thompson, ed., *The Face of Our Past: Images of Black Women from Colonial America to the Present* (Bloomington: Indiana University Press, 1989). For a study of the black-communitarian leadership role of African American church women during the late nineteenth and early twentieth century, see Evelyn Brooks Higginbotham, *Righteous Discontent: The Women's Movement in the Black Baptist Church, 1880–1920* (Cambridge, MA: Harvard University Press, 1993). This seminal study relates the pioneering role of black women—led by Nannie Helen Burroughs—in facilitating a strong foundation for the black-communitarian leadership dynamic in the clergy sector of

the twentieth-century African American intelligentsia. The black Baptist church denomination has had the largest African American church membership since the start of the twentieth century. See the discussion in Chapter 1 of the early twentieth-century African American church types.

45. Dennis Dickerson, *Out of the Crucible: Black Steelworkers in Western Pennsylvania, 1875–1980* (Albany, NY: SUNY Press, 1986), 65.

46. Kenneth Kusmer, *A Ghetto Takes Shape: Black Cleveland, 1870–1930* (Urbana: University of Illinois Press, 1976), 94.

47. See St. Clair Drake and Horace Cayton, *Black Metropolis: A Study of Negro Life in a Northern City* vols. 1 and 2 (New York: Harcourt Brace, 1945).

48. Dickerson, *Out of the Crucible*, 57.

49. To mention just a few major studies: Robert Warner, *New Haven Negroes* (New Haven, CT: Yale University Press 1940); Drake and Cayton, *Black Metropolis;* Alan Spear, *Black Chicago: The Making of a Negro Ghetto, 1890–1920* (Chicago: University of Chicago Press, 1967); David L. Lewis, *When Harlem Was in Vogue* (New York: Oxford University Press, 1982); Kusmer, *A Ghetto Takes Shape;* Joe W. Trotter, *Black Milwaukee: The Making of an Industrial Proletariat, 1915–1945* (Urbana: University of Illinois Press, 1985); Harold McDougall, *Black Baltimore* (Philadelphia: Temple University Press, 1993); Nick Salvatore, *Singing in a Strange Land: Rev. C. L. Franklin, the Black Church and the Transformation of America* (New York: Oxford University Press, 2005); Robert Gregg, *Sparks from the Anvil of Oppression: Philadelphia's African Methodists and Southern Migrants, 1890–1940* (Philadelphia: Temple University Press, 1993); Henry Louis Taylor, *Race and the City: Work, Community, and Protest in Cincinnati, 1820–1970* (Urbana: University of Illinois Press, 1993); Megan Shockley, *We Too Are Americans: African American Women in Detroit and Richmond, 1940–1954* (Urbana: University of Illinois Press, 2004); Gretchen Eick, *Dissent in Wichita: The Civil Rights Movement in the Midwest, 1954–1972* (Urbana: University of Illinois Press, 2001).

50. See Cara L. Shelly, "Bradby's Baptists: Second Baptist Church of Detroit, 1910–1946," *Michigan Historical Review* 17, no. 1 (1991): 1–33.

51. Ibid., 16. To round out the foregoing discussion of the black church's black-communitarian leadership social development role, several broad-gauged studies in this area should be mentioned: University of South Carolina sociologist Andrew Billingsley's *Mighty like a River: The Black Church and Social Reform* (New York: Oxford University Press, 1999); Eric Lincoln and Lawrence H. Mamiya, *The Black Church in the African American Experience* (Durham, NC: Duke University Press, 1990); and Aldon Morris, *Origins of the Civil Rights Movement: Black Communities Organizing for*

Change (New York: Free Press, 1984). Morris' book is unique as a broad-ranging probe of the role of African American civil society agencies (civic organizations, churches, middle-class associations, and fraternal associations) in mobilizing social resources to facilitate what might be called "activist infrastructures" to sustain a viable Civil Rights movement against America's racist oligarchy from the 1950s to the 1970s.

52. Quoted in A'Lelia Bundles, *On Her Own Ground: The Life and Times of Madam C. J. Walker* (New York: Scribner, 2001), 242; emphasis added.

53. For Benjamin Davis' career, see Gerald Horne, *Black Liberation/Black Scare: Ben Davis and the Communist Party* (Newark, DE: Associated University Press, 1994). The first third of Horne's seminal probe of Benjamin Davis' career contains a history of the African American social class system in Atlanta, Georgia, during the late nineteenth and early twentieth century. That history is also probed in August Meier and David L. Lewis, "History of the Negro Upper Class in Atlanta, 1890–1958," *Journal of Negro Education* (Spring 1959): 128–139.

54. On William Hastie's role in the New Negro Alliance during the 1930s, see Martin Kilson, "Political Scientists and the Activist-Technocrat Dichotomy: Case of John Aubrey Davis," in Wilbur Rich, ed., *African American Perspectives in Political Science* (Philadelphia: Temple University Press, 2007), 169–172.

55. For Charles Houston Hamilton's career, see Genna Rae McNeil, *Groundwork: Charles Hamilton Houston and the Struggle for Civil Rights* (Philadelphia: University of Pennsylvania Press, 1983).

56. Sadie Mossell Alexander's grandfather, Bishop Benjamin Tanner, founded the African Methodist Episcopal Church's main journal, the *A.M.E. Church Review,* in 1884 in Philadelphia. The *Review* was one of the evolving twentieth-century black intelligentsia's major intellectual organs, articulating the Christian social gospel activism discourse in both its theological and practical dimensions. Its pages hold a wealth of information on the main intellectual currents among the activist strands of the twentieth-century African American intelligentsia. Presently edited by Vanderbilt University historian Dennis Dickerson, the *Review* is the black intelligentsia's oldest extant intellectual organ. Tanner was also the father of the first major African American painter, Henry Ossawa Tanner. Sadie Mossell Alexander's father, Dr. Nathan F. Mossell, was a late nineteenth-century graduate of Lincoln University—class of 1879—who became Philadelphia's most prominent African American medical doctor. In 1895, Mossell founded the earliest medical institutions for a major urban African American community: the Frederick Douglass Memorial Hospital and the Mercy-Douglass Nursing School.

57. See Franklin, *Education of Black Philadelphia*. See also David A. Canton, *Raymond Pace Alexander: A New Negro Lawyer Fights for Civil Rights in Philadelphia* (Jackson: University of Mississippi Press, 2010).

58. See John Hope Franklin and August Meier, eds., *Black Leaders of the Twentieth Century* (Urbana: University of Illinois Press, 1982), 167–190. See also Walter B. Weare, *Black Business in the New South: A Social History of the North Carolina Mutual Life Insurance Company* (Urbana: University of Illinois Press, 1973).

59. Carter G. Woodson, ed., *The Works of Francis J. Grimké*, vol. 3 (Washington, DC: Associated Publishers, 1942); emphasis added.

60. Richard Robbins used the term "sidelines activist" to characterize the leadership style of the prominent African American sociologist Charles S. Johnson, who founded the Institute of Race Relations at Fisk University in the 1930s. The institute produced major social science studies of racist dynamics in the South's social system, and those studies were employed to challenge racist constraints facing black people in the South during the 1930s and 1940s. See Robbins, *Sidelines Activist: Charles S. Johnson and the Struggle for Civil Rights* (Jackson: University of Mississippi Press, 1996). See also Patrick Gilpin and Marybeth Gasman, *Charles S. Johnson: Leadership beyond the Veil in the Age of Jim Crow* (Albany, NY: SUNY Press, 2003).

61. For a fulsome study of deindustrialization in urban areas from the 1960s onward and the kind of neighborhood devastation it produced, see Barry Bluestone and Bennett Harrison, *The Deindustrialization of America: Plant Closings, Community Abandonment, and the Dismantling of Basic Industry* (New York: Basic Books, 1982).

62. See Michelle Alexander, *The New Jim Crow: Mass Incarceration in the Age of Colorblindness* (New York: New Press, 2010). For a major study of the long-standing issue of the interplay between American racism and criminal justice practices, on the one hand, and the incarceration of African Americans on the other, see Khalil Gibran Muhammad, *The Condemnation of Blackness: Race, Crime, and the Making of Modern Urban America* (Cambridge, MA: Harvard University Press, 2010). Alexander claims that current incarceration data show that "today there are more African American adults under correctional control—in prison or jail, on probation or parole—than were enslaved in 1850, a decade before the Civil War began" (qtd. in Charles M. Blow, "Escaping Slavery," *New York Times*, January 5, 2013).

63. For a recent probe of incarceration practices related to the war on drugs vis-à-vis African Americans, see John Tierney, "For Lesser Crimes—Rethinking Life behind Bars," *New York Times*, December 12, 2012.

64. For another perspective toward the war on drugs that differs from Michelle Alexander's, see the Harvard Law School scholar Randall Kennedy's *Race, Crime, and the Law* (New York: Pantheon Books, 1997).

65. For an account of the history of the Wissahickon Boys' Club, see Erica M. Kitzmiller, "Memories of the Wissahickon Boys' Club," *Germantown Crier: Journal of the Germantown Historical Society* (Fall 2011): 60–65.

66. William Coleman Jr. presents an account of the Wissahickon Boys' Club and of life at Camp Emlen in his autobiography: *Counsel for the Situation: Shaping the Law to Realize America's Promise* (Washington, DC: Brookings Institution Press, 2010), chap. 3. Coleman was a unique figure among the evolving twentieth-century African American intelligentsia in several respects. He was a summa cum laude graduate of Harvard Law School in 1946—an achievement made by two other African American Harvard Law School graduates: Charles Hamilton Houston in 1923 and John R. Wilkins in 1947. (John R. Wilkins was the son of the first African American federal assistant secretary of labor, J. Ernest Wilkins—1954–1958—and uncle of David Wilkins, a current professor at Harvard Law School.) Coleman also participated in the NAACP's legal briefs for the U.S. Supreme Court's 1954 decision in *Brown v. Board of Education,* was the second African American corporation lawyer in the major law firm of Paul, Weiss, and was the second African American member of a federal cabinet (secretary of transportation under President Gerald Ford), the first being the economist Robert Weaver, who was secretary of housing and urban development in President Lyndon Johnson's administration.

   Strangely enough, to my knowledge, Coleman's 2010 book *Counsel for the Situation* received very little recognition by major African American news media. I have in mind newspapers like the *Amsterdam News,* the *Chicago Defender,* and the *Baltimore-Washington Afro-American,* and journals like *Ebony* magazine, *Essence* magazine, *Black Enterprise* magazine, the *Root* (the major African American online magazine), the *Crisis* (NAACP's journal), and the *Defenders* (the NAACP Legal Defense Fund's online magazine). There are about two hundred African American newspapers nationwide. One reason for this seeming neglect of Coleman's important autobiography might be his rather strange observation—at page 337 of his book—that he rejects the appellations "black" and "African American" so much that he refuses to use them in his book. As Coleman puts this issue: "Having fought to expunge all vestiges of racial segregation my entire life, I find the concept of black separatism unacceptable. I prefer not to use . . . the appellations 'Black' and 'African American,' which I consider inconsistent with my personal heritage." His "personal heritage" comment relates to some white ancestry in Coleman's background, which bequeathed him a light brown skin color—an interracial dynamic, by the way, that numerous African American families experienced in our American racially hypocritical history (I discuss this issue in Chapter 1), though Coleman views it as particularly special to him. Coleman prefers the term "colored people" as an appellation for African Americans. Politically, Coleman was an establishmentarian-type conservative and a Republican Party supporter during his career. Coleman has had a long life as he is in his nineties as of this writing.

67. See Charles L. Blockson, *Black America Series: Philadelphia, 1639–2000* (Charleston, SC: Arcadia Publishing, 2000), 95.

68. See Chapter 4 for a discussion of William Julius Wilson's analysis of the contemporary African American "have"/"have-not" class system.

3. Ideological Dynamics and the Making of the Intelligentsia

1. W. E. B. Du Bois, *The Souls of Black Folk* (Chicago: A. C. McClurg, 1903), 105.

2. Ibid.; emphasis added.

3. See W. E. B. Du Bois, "The Talented Tenth," in Booker T. Washington, ed., *The Negro Problem* (New York: J. Pott, 1903), 33–75.

4. Du Bois, *Souls of Black Folk*, 169–170; emphasis added.

5. Ibid., 172; emphasis added.

6. Ibid., 54.

7. Ibid., 54–55.

8. Ibid., 55–56; emphasis added.

9. See Douglas A. Blackmon, *Slavery by Another Name: The Re-enslavement of Black Americans from the Civil War to World War II* (New York: Doubleday, 2008). See also Alex Lichtenstein, *Twice the Work of Free Labor: The Political Economy of Convict Labor in the New South* (New York: Verso, 1995).

10. See, for example, William Banks, *Black Intellectuals: Race and Responsibility in American Life* (New York: William Morrow, 1996); James Blackwell and Morris Janowitz, eds., *Black Sociologists: Historical and Contemporary Perspectives* (Chicago: University of Chicago Press, 1974); John Bracey, August Meier, and Elliott Rudwick, eds., *The Black Sociologists: The First Half Century* (Belmont, CA: Wadsworth, 1971); Lawrence P. Jackson, *The Indignant Generation: A Narrative History of African American Writers and Critics, 1934–1960* (Princeton, NJ: Princeton University Press, 2011); James O. Young, *Black Writers of the Thirties* (Baton Rouge: Louisiana State University Press, 1973); John Hope Franklin and August Meier, eds., *Black Leaders of the Twentieth Century* (Urbana: University of Illinois

Press, 1982); Kevin Gaines, *Uplifting the Race: Black Leadership, Politics, and Culture in the Twentieth Century* (Chapel Hill: University of North Carolina Press, 1996); Harold Cruse, *The Crisis of the Negro Intellectual* (New York: William Morrow, 1967); Vincent P. Franklin, *The Education of Black Philadelphia* (Philadelphia: University of Pennsylvania Press, 1979); Dennis C. Dickerson, *African American Preachers and Politics: The Careys of Chicago* (Jackson: University of Mississippi Press, 2010); and Anetta Gomez-Jefferson, *The Sage of Tawawa: Reverdy Cassius Ransom, 1861–1959* (Kent, OH: Kent State University Press, 2002).

11. Richard Bardolph, *The Negro Vanguard* (New York: Rinehart, 1959), 153. See also Philip Butcher, ed., *The William Stanley Braithwaite Reader* (Ann Arbor: University of Michigan Press, 1972).

12. See Oscar Williams, *George Schuyler: Portrait of a Black Conservative* (Knoxville: University of Tennessee Press, 2007), and Jeffrey Ferguson, *The Sage of Sugar Hill: George S. Schuyler and the Harlem Renaissance* (New Haven, CT: Yale University Press, 2005).

13. Jonathan Holloway, "The Black Intellectual and the 'Crisis Canon' in the Twentieth Century," *Black Scholar* (Spring 2001): 11.

14. Ibid., 12.

15. Ibid., 3.

16. Ibid., 4; emphasis added.

17. See Alfred Moss, *The American Negro Academy: Voice of the Talented Tenth* (Baton Rouge: Louisiana State University Press, 1981).

18. See Banks, *Black Intellectuals*.

19. On this important issue, see Carter G. Woodson, *The Negro Professional Man and the Community* (Washington, DC: Associated Publishers, 1934); Joe M. Richardson, *A History of Fisk University, 1865–1965* (Tuscaloosa: University of Alabama Press, 1980); Lawrence E. Carter, ed., *Walking Integrity: Benjamin Elijah Mays, Mentor to Martin Luther King Jr.* (Macon, GA: Mercer University Press, 1998); Ross Posnock, *Color and Culture: Black Writers and the Making of the Modern Intellectual* (Cambridge, MA: Harvard University Press, 1998); Franklin and Meier, *Black Leaders of the Twentieth Century*; Zachary Williams, *In Search of the Talented Tenth: Howard University Public Intellectuals and the Dilemmas of Race, 1926–1970* (Columbus: University of Missouri Press, 2009); Wayne Urban, *Black Scholar: Horace Mann Bond, 1904–1972* (Athens: University of Georgia Press, 1992); and Raymond Gavin, *The Perils and Prospects of Southern Black Leadership: Gordon Blaine Hancock, 1884–1970* (Durham, NC: Duke University Press, 1977). Both Horace Mann Bond and Gordon Blaine Hancock were presidents of top-tier black colleges—Lincoln University (Pennsylvania) and Virginia Union University, respectively.

20. See Arthur Mann, *Yankee Reformers in the Urban Age: Social Reform in Boston, 1880–1900* (New York: Harper & Row, 1966); Robert S. Lynd and Helen Lynd, *Middletown: A Study in Modern American Culture* (New York: Harcourt Brace, 1929); C. Wright Mills, *The Power Elite* (New York: Oxford University Press, 1956); David Blight, *Race and Reunion: The Civil War in American Memory* (Cambridge, MA: Harvard University Press, 2001).

21. Holloway, "Black Intellectual and the 'Crisis Canon,' " 3; emphasis added.

22. Qtd. in Jonathan Holloway, *Confronting the Veil: Abram Harris Jr., E. Franklin Frazier, and Ralph J. Bunche, 1919–1941* (Princeton, NJ: Princeton University Press, 2002), 153. See also E. Franklin Frazier, "The Du Bois Program in the Present Crisis," *Race* (Winter 1935–1936).

23. Holloway, *Confronting the Veil*, 153.

24. Ibid., 153–154.

25. See William Darity Jr. and Julian Ellison, "Abram Harris Jr.: The Economics of Race and Social Reform," *History of Political Economy* (Winter 1990): 611–628. See also articles relating to Abram Harris in Thomas Boston, ed., *A Different Vision: African American Economic Thought* (New York: Routledge, 1997).

26. See Martin Kilson, "Political Scientists and the Activist-Technocrat Dichotomy: The Case of John Aubrey Davis," in Wilbur Rich, ed., *African American Perspectives on Political Science* (Philadelphia: Temple University Press, 2007), 169–172.

27. See Charles Henry, *Ralph Bunche: Model American or American Other?* (New York: New York University Press, 1999).

28. Kilson, "Political Scientists and the Technocrat-Activist Dichotomy," 172.

29. Holloway, *Confronting the Veil*, 52–53.

30. Ibid., 52.

31. Ibid., 53.

32. Ibid., 58.

33. Ibid., 196.

34. Ibid., 196–197.

35. Ibid., 197; emphasis added.

36. Jacqueline Jones, *American Work: Four Centuries of Black and White Labor* (New York: W.W. Norton, 1998), 15; emphasis added.

37. Holloway, *Confronting the Veil*, 197.

38. On the role of the black abolitionists J. W. C. Pennington and John Sella Martin in shaping Christian social gospel activism in the context of the antislavery movement, see R. J. M. Blackett, *Beating against the Barriers: Biographical Essays in Nineteenth-Century Afro-American History* (Baton Rouge: Louisiana State University Press, 1986). On the institutional role of

the African Methodist Episcopal Church denomination in the development and application of Christian social gospel activism leadership among
nineteenth-century African Americans, see Charles Wesley, *Richard Allen:
Apostle of Freedom* (Washington, DC: Associated Publishers, 1935); Dennis C. Dickerson, *A Liberated Past: Explorations in A.M.E. Church History*
(Nashville, TN: AMEC Sunday School Union Press, 2003). See also the biography of the prominent practitioner of Christian social gospel activism
among twentieth-century A.M.E. church leadership, Bishop Reverdy Ransom, in Gomez-Jefferson, *The Sage of Tawawa*.

39. Du Bois, *Souls of Black Folk*, 55–56.

40. Text reprinted in the NAACP journal, the *Crisis* (October 1963); emphasis
added.

41. See David Everett Swift, *Black Prophets of Justice: Activist Clergy before the
Civil War* (Baton Rouge: Louisiana State University Press, 1989), and Christopher L. Webber, *American to the Backbone: The Life of James W. C. Pennington, the Fugitive Slave Who Became One of the First Black Abolitionists*
(New York: Pegasus, 2011). On black abolitionist leaders who helped insti-
tutionalize Christian social activism ideas in pre–Civil War era African
American society, see Gary Nash, *Forging Freedom: The Formation of Philadelphia's Black Community, 1720–1840* (Cambridge, MA: Harvard University Press, 1988); Julie Winch, *A Gentleman of Color: The Life of James
Forten* (New York: Oxford University Press, 2002); William S. McFeely,
Frederick Douglass (New York: W. W. Norton, 1991); James O. Horton and
Lois E. Horton, *In Hope and Liberty: Culture, Community, and Protest
among Free Blacks, 1700–1860* (New York: Oxford University Press, 1996);
and John Stauffer, ed., *The Works of James McCune Smith: Black Intellectual and Abolitionist* (New York: Oxford University Press, 2006).

42. Holloway, *Confronting the Veil*, 197.

43. See, for example, Genna Rae McNeil, *Charles Hamilton Houston and the
Struggle for Civil Rights* (Philadelphia: University of Pennsylvania Press,
1983); Richard Robbins, *Sidelines Activist: Charles S. Johnson and the
Struggle for Civil Rights* (Jackson: University of Mississippi Press, 1996);
Francille Rusan Wilson, *Segregated Scholars: Black Social Scientists and the
Development of Black Labor Studies* (Charlottesville: University of Virginia
Press, 2005); and George Clement Bond, "A Social Portrait of John Gibbs
St. Clair Drake: An American Anthropologist," *American Ethnologist* 15
(1988): 762–781.

44. See Sidney Wilfred Mintz and Richard Price, *The Birth of African American
Culture: An Anthropological Perspective* (Boston: Beacon Press, 1992). See
also Sterling Stuckey, *Slave Culture: Nationalist Theory and the Foundation
of Black America* (New York: Oxford University Press, 1987); Lawrence W.

Levine, *Black Culture and Black Consciousness: Afro-American Folk Thought from Slavery to Freedom* (New York: Oxford University Press, 1977); and Barbara D. Savage, *Your Spirits Walk beside Us: The Politics of Black Religion* (Cambridge, MA: Harvard University Press, 2008), which probes the special role of female leaders as practitioners of Christian social gospel activism in black churches during the twentieth century.

45. See Barbara Ransby, *Ella Baker and the Black Freedom Movement: A Radical Democratic Vision* (Chapel Hill: University of North Carolina Press, 2003).

46. Thomas J. Sugrue, *Sweet Land of Liberty: The Forgotten Struggle for Civil Rights in the North* (New York: Random House, 2008), 280.

47. Du Bois, *Souls of Black Folk,* 55–56.

48. Frederick Douglass, "The Significance of Emancipation in the West Indies," in John W. Blassingame and John R. McKivigan, eds., *The Frederick Douglass Papers,* ser. 1, *Speeches, Debates, and Interviews,* vol. 3, 1855–1863 (New Haven, CT: Yale University Press, 1985); emphasis added.

49. For the argument that Booker T. Washington's accommodationist black leadership methodology might have produced superior systemic advancement for today's African American society, see K. A. Appiah, "Battling with Du Bois," *New York Review of Books,* December 22, 2011: 85. As Appiah puts this issue: "But suppose Washington had been correct. In that case, there was a question of nonideal theory to ask. Could it be right to act like Booker T. Washington, deferring a demand for justice for yourself if that would bring justice more swiftly for your descendants? Or is there something so discreditable, so slavish, in acceding to these [racist oligarchy] injustices that it is better [as Du Bois believed] to resist them whether or not your resistance brings forward the date when they will cease? In short, there remain interesting questions . . . to explore in the African-American debates over different visions of the black future."

4. Black Elite Patterns in the Twenty-First Century

1. See Henry Lee Moon, *Balance of Power: The Negro Vote* (Garden City, NY: Doubleday, 1948).

2. William E. Nelson Jr. and Philip J. Meranto, *Electing Black Mayors: Political Action in the Black Community* (Columbus: Ohio State University Press, 1977). See also David B. Colburn, "Running for Office: African-American Mayors from 1967 to 1996," in David B. Colburn and Jeffrey S. Adler, eds., *African-American Mayors: Race, Politics, and the American City* (Urbana: University of Illinois Press, 2001).

3. See Martin Kilson, "Analysis of Black American Voters in Barack Obama's Victory," in Charles P. Henry et al., *The Obama Phenomenon: Toward a Multiracial Democracy* (Urbana: University of Illinois Press, 2011), 34–59.

4. W. E. B. Du Bois, *The Souls of Black Folk* (Chicago: A. C. McClurg, 1903), 64–65, 67.

5. See John Michael Lee Jr. and Tafaya Ransom, *The Educational Experience of Young Men of Color: A Review of Research, Pathways and Progress* (Washington, DC: The College Board, 2011).

6. Lawrence D. Bobo, "Somewhere between Jim Crow and Post-racialism: Reflections on the Racial Divide in America Today," *Daedalus: Journal of the American Academy of Arts and Sciences* (Spring 2011): 19.

7. For an insightful analysis of the Tea Party movement and the rightist politics that define it, see Jill Lepore, *The Whites of Their Eyes: The Tea Party's Revolution and the Battle over American History* (Princeton, NJ: Princeton University Press, 2010).

8. For Gingrich's press conference remarks, see the *New York Times,* December 3 and 4, 2011.

9. Jennifer Aglesia and Sonya Ross, "Poll Finds Majority Holds Racist Views," *Boston Globe* (October 28, 2012); emphasis added.

10. See Andrew Billingsley, "Understanding African American Family Diversity," in Lee A. Daniels, ed., *State of Black America 1990* (New York: National Urban League, 1990). This annual survey series, produced during the 1990s by the National Urban League's publications director, Lee A. Daniels, is indispensable for up-to-date information on African America.

11. See *Black Enterprise* (June 2011): 64, 109–115.

12. It should be mentioned that evidence suggests that a related leadership feature of top-tier black females is a pattern of using their occupational achievement to assist other black females up the professional ladder. *Black Enterprise Magazine* (October 2013) carried a report on Daria Burke, director of Makeup Marketing at Estee Lauder Co., who, after gaining the MBA degree at New York University's Stern School of Business, organized "Black MBA Women," which facilitates career development for black females in the cosmetics industry.

13. William Julius Wilson, "The Declining Significance of Race: Revisited and Revised," *Daedalus: Journal of the American Academy of Arts and Sciences* (Spring 2011): 63–64; emphasis added.

14. Thomas M. Shapiro, *The Hidden Cost of Being African American: How Wealth Perpetuates Inequality* (New York: Oxford University Press, 2004), 7.

15. Ibid., x, 182.

16. Ross Eisenbrey, "Commentaries on the Kahlenberg-Marvit Article," *Poverty and Race: Poverty and Race Research Action Council* 23 (January/February 2013): 13.

17. Jacqueline Jones, *American Work: Four Centuries of Black and White Labor* (New York: W. W. Norton, 1998), 372.

18. For data on the negative impact of the Great Recession on African Americans, see Lawrence Mishel, *Sounding the Alarm: Update on the Economic Downturn* (Washington, DC: Economic Policy Institute, 2009).

19. Corydon Ireland, "Closing the 'Achievement Gap,'" *Harvard Gazette*, November 8, 2007.

20. Steven A. Holmes and Richard Morin, "Poll Reveals a Contradictory Portrait Shaded with Promise and Doubt," *Washington Post*, June 4, 2006.

21. See Marian Wright Edelman, "Weekly Column," *Philadelphia Tribune*, November 6, 2007; emphasis added. Edelman's no-holds-barred syndicated column appears in African American newspapers nationwide.

22. See Pew Research Center, *Optimism about Black Progress Declines: Blacks See Growing Values Gap between Poor and Middle Class*, Pew Research Sociographic and Demographic Trends Report (Washington, DC: Pew Research Center, 2007).

23. For an insightful probe of how Du Bois' intellectual and leadership discourse achieved a broad prominence among the evolving twentieth-century African American intelligentsia, see Thomas C. Holt, "The Political Uses of Alienation: W. E. B. Du Bois in Politics, Race and Culture, 1903–1940," *American Quarterly* (June 1990): 100–115.

24. Pew Research Center, *Optimism about Black Progress Declines*, 23.

25. See Derrick Bell, *Faces at the Bottom of the Well: The Permanence of Racism* (New York: Basic Books, 1992). A variant of Bell's argument was recently presented in Rochester University anthropologist Karen Fields and Columbia University historian Barbara Fields' book *Racecraft: The Soul of Inequality in American Life* (New York: Verso, 2012).

26. See Eduardo Porter, "At the Polls Choose Your Capitalism," *New York Times*, October 31, 2012.

27. Pew Research Center, *Optimism about Black Progress Declines*, 24.

28. Ibid., 25; emphasis added.

29. Ibid., 23.

30. See Michael Dawson, *Black Visions: The Roots of Contemporary African-American Political Ideologies* (Chicago: University of Chicago Press, 2001).

31. See Julia Preston, "Survey Points to Tensions among Chief Minorities," *New York Times*, December 13, 2007.

32. See Moon, *Balance of Power*, chaps. 2 and 3.

33. For Glenn C. Loury's independent liberal perspective following his exit from the ranks of mainstream conservative black intellectuals, see Loury, *Race, Incarceration and American Values* (Cambridge, MA: MIT Press, 2008). Mention should be made of a strand of independent conservative black intellectuals who contributed to conservative discourse during the 1980s and 1990s. A prominent such independent conservative black intellectual was the Harvard sociologist Orlando Patterson. For a critique of Patterson's variant of independent conservative discourse, see Martin Kilson, "Critique of Orlando Patterson's Blaming-the-Victim Rituals," *Souls: A Critical Journal of Black Politics, Culture and Society* (Winter 2001): 81–106.

34. I first probed the metamorphosis of conservative black intellectuals during the post–Civil Rights movement period in the first St. Clair Drake Memorial Lecture that I delivered at Stanford University in April 1992. The text of that lecture was published in *Transition* 59 (1993).

35. See Shelby Steele's discussion of affirmative action in his *The Content of Our Character* (New York: Harper Perennial, 1991), chap. 7.

36. For examples of this literature, see Steve P. Erie, *Rainbow's End: Irish-Americans and the Dilemmas of Urban Machine Politics, 1840–1985* (Berkeley: University of California Press, 1988). Erie's book provides references to affirmative action–type public benefits executed through city and state governments that have assisted a major white American group: Irish Americans. Erie's study argues that when the African American ethnic bloc gained political efficacy in American cities through the election of black mayoralties in the last two decades of the twentieth century (e.g., Cleveland, Detroit, Newark, New Jersey, Philadelphia, Baltimore, Chicago, New York), the financial capacity of city governments to execute affirmative action–type public benefits like those experienced by Irish Americans from the late nineteenth through most of the twentieth century had reached the "rainbow's end." Nowhere in Steele's *Content of Our Character* is there any evidence of his having knowledge of this historical process as related to white American groups. For another broad-gauged study of affirmative action–type public social mobility benefits that assisted white American groups during the twentieth century, see Ira Katznelson, *When Affirmative Action Was White: An Untold History of Racial Inequality in Twentieth Century America* (New York: Norton, 2005).

37. Charles P. Henry, "Introduction," in Henry et al., *Obama Phenomenon*, 8.

38. Steele, *Content of Our Character*, 151.

39. Aglesia and Ross, "Poll."

40. Steele, *Content of Our Character*, 174.

41. Douglas Massey and N. A. Denton, *American Apartheid: Segregation and the Making of the Underclass* (Cambridge, MA: Harvard University Press, 1993).

42. Steele, *Content of Our Character,* 119. In regard to Steele's cynical observation that "suffering cannot be repaid" through legislation and public policy, it seems that Steele would have opposed the crucial post–Civil War federal legislation that facilitated free citizenship rights and status for four million formerly enslaved Negroes. In contrast to Steele's perspective, I suggest a keen liberal analysis of the post–Civil War federal legislation: Garrett Epps, *Democracy Reborn: The Fourteenth Amendment and the Fight for Civil Rights in Post–Civil War America* (New York: Henry Holt, 2006).

43. On the early nineteenth-century American antislavery movement's role in advancing Christian humanitarian patterns that sought redemption vis-à-vis the sin associated with Negro slavery, see Horace Mann Bond's brilliant discussion of the founding of Lincoln University in Pennsylvania, the first American institution for the higher education of Negroes: *Education for Freedom: A History of Lincoln University, Pennsylvania* (Princeton, NJ: Princeton University Press, 1976).

44. See Stephen L. Carter, *Reflections of an Affirmative Action Baby* (New York: Basic Books, 1991), 103–107.

45. Ibid., 139–140.

46. See William Banks, *Black Intellectuals: Race and Responsibility in American Life* (New York: William Morrow, 1996). See also John Hope Franklin and August Meier, eds., *Black Leaders of the Twentieth Century* (Urbana: University of Illinois Press, 1982).

47. Jesse Washington, "Doctor Tries to Steer Blacks from Unwed Parenthood," *Boston Sunday Globe,* November 7, 2010.

48. Eugene Robinson, *Disintegration: The Splintering of Black America* (New York: Doubleday, 2010), 213.

49. In regard to the need for African American leadership organizations to persist in challenging racist patterns here in twenty-first-century American life, recent observations by the Harvard University sociologist Lawrence Bobo are noteworthy. He reported on a Harvard Department of Sociology survey that asked a sample of black and white Americans, "Do you think that blacks have achieved racial equality . . . ?" As Bobo observed: "Fielded after the 2008 election . . . , these results are instructive. Almost two out of three white Americans (61.3 percent) said that blacks have achieved racial equality. Another 21.5 percent of whites endorse the view that blacks will soon achieve racial equality. Thus, the overwhelming majority fraction of white Americans see the post-racial moment as effectively here (83.8 percent). Fewer than one in five blacks endorsed the idea that they have already

achieved racial equality. A more substantial fraction (36.2 percent) believe that they will soon achieve racial equality. African Americans, then, are divided almost evenly between those doubtful that racial equality will soon be achieved (with more than one in ten saying it will never be achieved) and those who see equality within reach, at 46.6 percent versus 53.6 percent." Bobo's summary concluding observation was, I think, on the realpolitik side of things racial: "The central tendencies of public opinion on these issues, despite real increasing overlaps, remain enormously far apart between black and white Americans. When such differences in perception and belief are grounded in . . . wide economic inequality, persistent residential segregation, largely racially homogeneous family units and close friendship networks, and a popular culture suffused with negative ideas and images about African Americans, then there should be little surprise that we still find it enormously difficult to have sustained civil discussions about race and racial matters. Despite growing much closer together in recent decades, the gaps in perspective between blacks and whites are still sizable." See Bobo, "Somewhere between Jim Crow and Post-racialism," 30.

50. Bob Herbert, "This Raging Fire," *New York Times*, November 15, 2010; emphasis added.
51. For quantitative data on the African American political class' growth, see the Joint Center for Political and Economic Studies' fact sheet "National Roster of Black Elected Officials" (November 2011). For studies of the developmental processes surrounding the African American political class' development during the 1980s and the 1990s, see, respectively Martin Kilson, "Problems of Black Politics," *Dissent* (Fall 1989); and Kilson, "The State of African American Politics," in Lee A. Daniels, *The State of Black America 1998* (New York: National Urban League, 1998).
52. For an account of Rob Nabors' policy-making activities, see Carol Lee and Janet Hook, "Budget Talks Marked by Slow Pace," *Wall Street Journal,* November 21, 2012.
53. For a study of the successful 2008 Obama campaign for the presidency of the United States, see Kilson, "Analysis of Black American Voters."
54. *New York Times*, October 28, 2012.
55. Frederick C. Harris, "The Price of a Black President," *New York Times,* October 28, 2012.
56. See Jackie Calmes and Megan Thee-Brenan, "Electorate Reverts to a Partisan Divide as Obama's Support Narrows," *New York Times*, November 7, 2012: sec. P5.
57. William Greider, "The Real Losers of 2012," *Nation*, December 3, 2012: 3–4; emphasis added.

ANALYTICAL BIBLIOGRAPHY

Antebellum Black Intelligentsia

Bell, Howard H. 1969. *A Survey of the Negro Convention Movement, 1830–1861.* New York: Arno Press.

Blackett, Richard J. M. 1986. *Beating against the Barriers: Biographical Essays in Nineteenth-Century Afro-American History.* Baton Rouge: Louisiana State University Press.

Blassingame, John W., and John R. McKivigan, eds. 1980. *The Frederick Douglass Papers.* Series 1, vols. 3 and 4, New Haven, CT: Yale University Press.

Foner, Philip S. 1950. *The Life and Writings of Frederick Douglass.* 4 vols. New York: International Publisher.

Foner, Philip S., and George Walker, eds. 1979. *Proceedings of the Black State Conventions, 1840–1865.* 2 vols. Philadelphia: Temple University Press.

Franklin, John Hope. 1943. *The Free Negro in North Carolina, 1790–1860.* Chapel Hill: University of North Carolina Press.

———. 1956. *The Militant South, 1800–1861.* Cambridge, MA: Harvard University Press.

Horton, James O., and Lois E. Horton. 1996. *In Hope and Liberty: Culture, Community, and Protest among Northern Free Blacks, 1700–1860.* New York: Oxford University Press.

Kilson, Marion. 2008. A Gathering Place for Freedom: Boston's African Meeting House. *A.M.E. Church Review* (April–June): 35–42.

McFeely, William S. 1991. *Frederick Douglass.* New York: W. W. Norton.

Nash, Gary. 1988. *Forging Freedom: The Formation of Philadelphia's Black Community, 1720–1840.* Cambridge, MA: Harvard University Press.

Quarles, Benjamin. 1969. *Black Abolitionists.* New York: Oxford University Press.

Robboy, Stanley, and Anita Robboy. 1973. Lewis Hayden: From Fugitive Slave to Statesman. *New England Quarterly* (December): 591–613.

Stauffer, John, ed. 2006. *The Works of James McCune Smith: Black Intellectual and Abolitionist*. New York: Oxford University Press.

Swift, David Everett. 1989. *Black Prophets of Justice: Activist Clergy before the Civil War*. Baton Rouge: Louisiana State University Press.

Webber, Christopher L. 2011. *American to the Backbone: The Life of James W. C. Pennington, the Fugitive Slave Who Became One of the First Black Abolitionists*. New York: Pegasus.

Wesley, Charles. 1935. *Richard Allen: Apostle of Freedom*. Washington, DC: Associated Publishers.

———. 1941. The Negro in the Organization of Abolition. *Phylon* (Third Quarter): 223–235.

Winch, Julie. 1988. *Philadelphia's Black Elite: Activism, Accommodationism, and the Struggle for Autonomy, 1787–1848*. Philadelphia: Temple University Press.

———. 2002. *A Gentleman of Color: The Life of James Forten*. New York: Oxford University Press.

Dynamics of Emancipation-Era African American Society

Bond, Horace Mann. 1939. *Negro Education in Alabama: A Study in Cotton and Steel*. Washington, DC: Associated Publishers.

Day, Caroline Bond. 1932. *A Study of Some Negro-White Families in the United States*. Cambridge, MA: Peabody Museum of Harvard University. Caroline Bond Day was the first African American to gain a graduate degree—the A.M. degree—from Harvard's anthropology department, which she did in 1930. Her book was the first major social science study of black-white American family phenotypes.

Du Bois, W. E. B. 1899. *The Philadelphia Negro: A Study*. Philadelphia: University of Pennsylvania Press.

———. 1910. Reconstruction and Its Benefits. *American Historical Review* (July): 781–799.

———. 1935. *Black Reconstruction in America, 1860–1880*. New York: Harcourt Brace. W. E. B. Du Bois was the first among the first generation of African American scholars to gain a doctorate degree in history, which he received from Harvard University in 1895. From the World War I era into the 1940s, Du Bois was followed by Carter G. Woodson (Harvard), Rayford Logan (Harvard), Charles Wesley (Harvard), John Hope Franklin (Harvard), Lorenzo Greene (Columbia University), and Benjamin Quarles (Columbia). From the late 1950s through the 1960s, the third generation to gain a doctorate in history included Nathan Huggins (Harvard), Otey Scruggs (Harvard), John Blassingame (University of Chicago), Sterling Stuckey (Northwestern University), and David Levering Lewis (University of London). The decades of the 1970s and 1980s saw a significant expansion of Ph.D.-trained black historians, such as Gerald Horne (Columbia), Barbara Fields (Columbia), Thomas Holt (Harvard), Dennis Dickerson (Washington University), Vincent P. Franklin (University of Chicago), Nell Irvin Painter (Harvard), Darlene Clark Hine (Kent State University), Evelyn Brooks Higginbotham (Rochester University), Adele Logan Alexander (Howard University), and Francille Rusan Wilson (University of Virginia), to name a prominent few.

Foner, Eric. 1988. *Reconstruction: America's Unfinished Revolution, 1863–1877*. New York: Harper & Row.

Graham, Leroy. 1971. *Baltimore: The Nineteenth Century Black Capital*. Lanham, MD: University Press of America.

Higginbotham, Evelyn Brooks. 1993. *Righteous Discontent: The Women's Movement in the Black Baptist Church, 1886–1920*. Cambridge, MA: Harvard University Press.

Holt, Thomas. 1977. *Black over White: Negro Political Leadership in South Carolina during Reconstruction*. Urbana: University of Illinois Press.

Jackson, Lawrence P. 2012. *My Father's Name: A Black Virginia Family after the Civil War*. Chicago: University of Chicago Press.

Johnson, Charles S. 1934. *Shadow of the Plantation*. Chicago: University of Chicago Press. Charles S. Johnson was among the first generation of African American scholars to gain a doctorate degree in sociology, which he received from the University of Chicago in 1920. Richard R. Wright, who went on to become a bishop in the African Methodist Episcopal Church, preceded Johnson in earning a Ph.D. in sociology from the University of Chicago just before World War I. From the 1920s through the 1940s, several others followed Johnson in gaining a doctorate degree in sociology, including E. Franklin Frazier (University of Chicago), Ira de Augustine Reid (Columbia University), Horace Mann Bond (University of Chicago), J. Max Bond (University of Southern California), and Hylan Lewis (University of Chicago). Adelaide Cromwell studied for a Ph.D. in sociology in the 1940s at Harvard, gaining her degree in 1952. Prominent among the group of African American Ph.D.-trained sociology scholars from the 1960s through the 1980s were William Julius Wilson (Washington University), Joyce Ladner (Washington University), Elijah Anderson (University of Chicago), and Lawrence Bobo (University of California, Los Angeles).

Johnson, Emory S., ed. 1913. *The Negro's Progress in Fifty Years*. Special issue, *The Annals: Journal of the American Academy of Political and Social Sciences* (September). This 237-page issue of *The Annals* was a major appraisal of black Americans' status fifty years after President Abraham Lincoln's 1863 Emancipation Proclamation. Contributors to the issue included prominent black intelligentsia figures such as W. E. B. Du Bois, Booker T. Washington, Kelly Miller (dean of Howard University), R. R. Wright Jr. (editor of the A.M.E. Church's *Christian Recorder*), George Edmund Haynes (director of the National Urban League), and Monroe N. Work (professor of sociology at Tuskegee Institute).

Johnston, Harry H. 1910. *The Negro in the New World*. London: Methuen.

Levine, Lawrence W. 1977. *Black Culture and Black Consciousness: Afro-American Folk Thought from Slavery to Freedom*. New York: Oxford University Press.

Litwack, Leon F. 1980. *Been in the Storm So Long: The Aftermath of Slavery*. New York: Vintage.

Litwack, Leon F., and August Meier, eds. 1988. *Black Leaders of the Nineteenth Century*. Urbana: University of Illinois Press.

Meier, August. 1963. *Negro Thought in America, 1880–1895*. Ann Arbor: University of Michigan Press.

Moses, Wilson J. 1989. *Alexander Crummell: A Study of Civilization and Discontent*. New York: Oxford University Press.

O'Donovan, Susan Eva. 2007. *Becoming Free in the Cotton South*. Cambridge, MA: Harvard University Press. O'Donovan's last chapter, "To Make a Laborer's State," brilliantly relates how the Reconstruction phase in Georgia during the Emancipation era was viciously truncated by the white planter class. The book focuses on the rich cotton-producing Dougherty County in southwest Georgia, whose Emancipation era W. E. B. Du Bois also probes in chapters 7 and 8 in *The Souls of Black Folk* (1903).

Painter, Nell Irvin. 1996. *Sojourner Truth: A Life, a Symbol*. New York: W. W. Norton.

Rabinowitz, Howard. 1980. *Southern Black Leaders of the Reconstruction Era, 1865–1890*. Urbana: University of Illinois Press.

Scarborough, William Sanders. 2005. *The Autobiography of William Sanders Scarborough: An American Journey from Slavery to Scholarship*. Ed. Michele Valerie Ronnick. Detroit: Wayne State University Press.

Silcox, Harry. 1977. Nineteenth Century Black Militant: Octavius V. Catto, 1839–1871. *Pennsylvania History* (January): 53–76.

Woodson, Carter G. 1921. *History of the Negro Church*. Washington, DC: Associated Publishers.

Developmental Dynamics of Twentieth-Century Black Intelligentsia

Alexander, Adele Logan. 1999. *Homelands and Waterways: The American Journey of the Bond Family, 1846–1926.* New York: Pantheon Books.

Angell, Stephen W. 1992. *Bishop Henry McNeal Turner and African American Religion in the South.* Knoxville: University of Tennessee Press.

Bacote, Clarence A. 1969. *The Story of Atlanta University: A Century of Service, 1865–1965.* Atlanta: Atlanta University Press.

Banks, William. 1996. *Black Intellectuals: Race and Responsibility in American Life.* New York: William Morrow.

Bell, Derrick. 1992. *Faces at the Bottom of the Well: The Permanence of Racism.* New York: Basic Books. Derrick Bell was a member of the faculty at Harvard Law School—the first African American full professor there, in fact—when he produced this pathbreaking book. Never before had a leading African American legal expert of Bell's standing (he was a counsel for the NAACP Legal Defense Fund) announced publicly the political perspective delineated in this book, namely, that American society's racist patterns had generic pathological roots, so to speak. Since the appearance of *Faces at the Bottom of the Well,* Bell joined the law faculty at New York University. Interestingly enough, a younger-generation African American faculty member at Harvard Law School, Randall Kennedy, published a seminal book in 2011 titled *The Persistence of the Color Line,* which delineates the tenacity of racial dynamics in American life as they relate to the politics surrounding the presidency of Barack Obama, the first African American president.

Blackwell, James, and Morris Janowitz, eds. 1974. *Black Sociologists: Historical and Contemporary Perspectives.* Chicago: University of Chicago Press.

Blight, David W. 2001. *Race and Reunion: The Civil War in American Memory.* Cambridge, MA: Harvard University Press.

Bond, Horace Mann. 1934. *The Education of the Negro in the American Social Order.* New York: Prentice Hall.

———. 1969. *Black American Scholars: A Study of Their Beginnings.* Detroit: Balamp Publishing.

———. 1976. *Education for Freedom: A History of Lincoln University, Pennsylvania.* Princeton, NJ: Princeton University Press.

Bone, Robert A. 1958. *The Negro Novel in America.* New Haven, CT: Yale University Press.

Brown, Sterling, Arthur P. Davis, and Ulysses Lee. 1941. *The Negro Caravan: Writings by American Negroes.* New York: Dryden Press. Sterling Brown was among the early cohort of African American intellectuals in the fields of literary studies and American studies. He attended the all-black Dunbar High School in Washington, D.C., and was among several graduates of Dunbar who attended Williams College in the 1920s and later gained an A.M. from Harvard in 1923. He taught at Howard University, and his book *Negro Poetry and Drama* (1938) was widely read among African American intellectuals. Another early black scholar in literary studies who, like Brown, taught at Howard University was Alain Locke (born 1885), who gained a Ph.D. in philosophy from Harvard in 1918. He edited an important collection of essays relating to the roots of the New Negro Movement titled *The New Negro* (1927) and published numerous additional essays. The combined writings by Brown and Locke in the field of literary studies helped lay the intellectual groundwork for African American scholarship in literary studies and American studies. Subsequently, a raft of first-class African American intellectuals, who stood on the shoulders of Brown and Locke, so to speak, emerged in the fields of literary and American studies.

I have in mind scholars like Melvin Tolson, who gained a B.A. at Lincoln University (Pennsylvania) in 1924, an A.M. at Columbia University, taught at two black colleges (Wiley College and Langston University), and published a major poetry collection, *Rendez-vous with America* (1944). Joseph Newton Hill was a major teacher of literary studies at Lincoln University during the 1930s–1950s, where he taught African American writers like the actor/poet Roscoe Lee Browne; Larry Neal, a founder of the 1960s Black Arts Movement; and biographer Donald Bogle. Arthur P. Davis (born 1905), who gained a Ph.D. in English at Columbia, taught at Howard University and coedited a collection of essays on African American social patterns titled *The Negro Caravan* (1941). J. Saunders Redding (born 1906), who gained a B.A. at Hampton Institute and his Ph.D. at Brown University, taught at Morehouse College and Hampton Institute most of his career, and his volume of essays, *To Make a Poet Black* (1939), had a broad influence among African American scholars in literary and American studies. Redding's book was required reading during my undergraduate years at Lincoln University (1949–1953). Nick Aaron Ford (born 1904), who gained a B.A. at Benedict College in South Carolina and a Ph.D. at the University of Iowa, taught literary studies at Morgan State College throughout his academic career. His book on African American literature, *The Contemporary Negro Novel: A Study in Race Relations,* had great influence among African American intellectuals in literary studies and American studies. Finally, among contemporary black scholars in literary and American studies, much of their work has been influenced by political and cultural patterns associated with the 1950s–1960s Civil Rights movement. The senior intellectual in this category is Ishmael Reed, who was educated at the University of Buffalo and taught for most of his academic career at University of California, Berkeley. Among his oeuvre are several novels, poems, and collections of essays, prominent among which are *Yellow Back Radio Broke Down* (1969); *New and Collected Poems, 1964–2007* (2007); and *Going Too Far: Essays about America's Nervous Breakdown* (2012). Following Reed, there has been a host of younger black scholars in literary and American studies. Robert O'Mealley, who gained a Ph.D. in literature at Harvard and taught literary studies and Afro-American studies at Wesleyan University before he became Zora Neale Hurston Professor of English at Columbia University, where he is also director of the Center of Jazz Studies. O'Mealley is coeditor of *Uptown Conversations: The New Jazz Studies* (2004). Farah Jasmine Griffin, who gained a B.A. at Harvard and a Ph.D. at Yale, teaches at Columbia University and has authored two seminal works in literary and American studies, *Who Set You Flowin': The African American Migration Narrative* (1995) and *If You Can't Be Free Be a Mystery: In Search of Billie Holliday* (2001). Perhaps the doyen intellectual among contemporary African American intellectuals in the fields of literary and American studies is Henry Louis Gates Jr. Born in 1950, Gates gained a B.A. at Yale and a Ph.D. at Cambridge University. After teaching at Duke University, he was appointed chair of Afro-American Studies at Harvard in 1991 and director of Harvard's W. E. B. Du Bois Institute. In these two academic roles, Gates qualitatively transformed the academic range in the department and the Du Bois Institute. Prominent among Gates' many publications are *Figures in Black: Words, Signs, and the "Racial Self"* (1987); *The Signifying Monkey* (1988); and *Loose Cannons: Notes on the Culture Wars* (1992).

Cromwell, Adelaide. 2007. *Unveiled Voices, Unvarnished Memories: The Cromwell Family in Slavery and Segregation, 1692–1972.* Columbia: University of Missouri Press.

Davis, Allison, Burleigh Gardner, and Mary Gardner. 1941. *Deep South: A Social Anthropological Study of Caste and Class.* Chicago: University of Chicago Press.

Detweiler, Frederick. 1922. *The Negro Press in the United States.* Chicago: University of Chicago Press.

Dickerson, Dennis C. 1986. *Out of the Crucible: Black Steelworkers in Western Pennsylvania, 1875–1980.* Albany, NY: SUNY Press.

———. 2010. *African American Preachers and Politics: The Careys of Chicago.* Jackson: University of Mississippi Press.

Drake, St. Clair, and Horace Cayton. 1945. *Black Metropolis: A Study of Negro Life in a Northern City.* Vols. 1 and 2. New York: Harcourt Brace.

Du Bois, W. E. B. 1903. *The Souls of Black Folk.* Chicago: A. C. McClurg.

———. 1903. The Talented Tenth. In Booker T. Washington, ed., *The Negro Problem*, 33–75. New York: J. Pott.

———. 1939. *Black Folk, Then and Now: An Essay in the History and Sociology of the Negro Race.* New York: Harcourt Brace.

Du Bois, W. E. B., and Augustus Granville Dill, eds. 1910. *The College-Bred Negro American*. Atlanta University Publications, no. 15. Atlanta: Atlanta University Press.

Dyson, Walter. 1941. *Howard University, the Capstone of Negro Education: A History, 1867–1940*. Washington, DC: Graduate School, Howard University.

Evans, Stephanie Y. 2007. *Black Women in the Ivory Tower: An Intellectual History*. Gainesville: University Press of Florida.

Franklin, John Hope. 1940. Courses Concerning the Negro in Negro Colleges. *Quarterly Review of Higher Education among Negroes* 8: 138–144.

———. 1956. *From Slavery to Freedom: A History of American Negroes*. 2nd ed. New York: Alfred Knopf.

Frazier, E. Franklin. 1939. *The Negro Family in the United States*. Chicago: University of Chicago Press.

———. 1957. *Black Bourgeoisie: The Rise of a New Middle Class*. Glencoe, IL: Free Press.

Gallagher, Buell. 1938. *American Caste and the Negro College*. New York: Harcourt Brace.

Gatewood, Willard B. 1991. *Aristocrats of Color: The Black Elite, 1880–1920*. Bloomington: Indiana University Press.

Gilpin, Patrick. 1980. Charles S. Johnson and the Race Relations Institutes at Fisk University. *Phylon* 41, no. 3: 300–311.

Gosnell, Harold Foote. 1935. *Negro Politicians: The Rise of Negro Politics in Chicago*. Chicago: University of Chicago Press.

Graham, Lawrence Otis. 1999. *Our Kind of People: Inside America's Black Upper Class*. New York: HarperCollins.

Gregg, Robert. 1993. *Sparks from the Anvil of Oppression: Philadelphia's African Methodists and Southern Migrants, 1890–1940*. Philadelphia: Temple University Press.

Harlan, Louis B. 1972. *Booker T. Washington: The Making of a Black Leader, 1856–1901*. New York: Oxford University Press.

Harris, Janette Hoston. 1998. Woodson and Wesley: A Partnership in Building the Association for the Study of Afro-American Life and History. *Journal of Negro History* (Spring): 109–119.

Higginbotham, Evelyn Brooks. 1996. Religion, Politics, and Gender: The Leadership of Nannie Helen Burroughs. In Judith Weisenfield and Richard Newman, eds., *This Far by Faith: Readings in African American Women's Religious Biography*, 140–157. New York: Routledge.

Hine, Darlene Clark, ed. 1993. *Black Women in America: An Historical Encyclopedia*. Brooklyn, NY: Carlson Publishing.

———. 1996. *Speak Truth to Power: Black Professional Class in United States History*. Brooklyn, NY: Carlson Publishing.

Holt, Thomas C. 2010. *Children of Fire: A History of African Americans*. New York: Hill & Wang.

Hughes, William H., and Frederick D. Patterson. 1956. *Robert Russa Moton of Hampton and Tuskegee*. Chapel Hill: University of North Carolina Press.

Johnson, Charles S. 1938. *The Negro College Graduate*. Chapel Hill: University of North Carolina Press.

Johnson, James Weldon. 1933. *Black Manhattan*. New York: Viking.

Jones, Maxine D., and Joe D. Richardson. 1990. *Talladega College: The First Century*. Tuscaloosa: University of Alabama Press.

Jones, Thomas Jesse. 1916. *Negro Education: A Study of the Private and Higher Schools for Colored People in the United States*. 2 vols. Department of the Interior, Bureau of Education Bulletin, no. 39. Washington, DC: Government Printing Office.

Kilson, Martin. 1971. Political Change in the Negro Ghetto, 1900–1940s. In Nathan I. Huggins et al., eds., *Key Issues in the Afro-American Experience*, 176–192. New York: Harcourt Brace Jovanovich.

———. 2001. Critique of Orlando Patterson's Blaming-the-Victim Rituals. *Souls: A Critical Journal of Black Politics, Culture and Society* (Winter): 81–106.

———. 2007. The Afro-Americanization of Lincoln University: Horace Mann Bond's Legacy. *A.M.E. Church Review* (April–June): 78–91.

Kilson, Martin, and Clement Cottingham. 1991. Thinking about Race Relations. *Dissent* (Fall): 520–530.

Kilson, Martin, and Robert Rotberg, eds. 1976. *The African Diaspora: Interpretive Essays*. Cambridge, MA: Harvard University Press.

Klein, Arthur, ed. 1929. *Survey of Negro Colleges and Universities*. Department of the Interior, Bureau of Education Bulletin, no. 7. Washington, DC: Government Printing Office.

Kusmer, Kenneth. 1976. *A Ghetto Takes Shape: Black Cleveland, 1870–1930*. Urbana: University of Illinois Press.

Landry, Bart. 1987. *The New Black Middle Class*. Berkeley: University of California Press.

Lane, Roger. 1991. *William Dorsey's Philadelphia and Ours: On the Past and Future of the Black City in America*. New York: Oxford University Press. This book by Haverford College historian Roger Lane relates the social history of Philadelphia's black elite sector from the 1880s through the first half of the twentieth century.

Lewis, Hylan. 1955. *Blackways of Kent*. Chapel Hill: University of North Carolina Press. "Kent" was a pseudonym for a mill town—York—in the Piedmont area of South Carolina, which Lewis had studied after World War II. His research was the basis for his University of Chicago Ph.D. dissertation.

Litwack, Leon F. 1998. *Trouble in Mind: Black Southerners in the Age of Jim Crow.* New York: Alfred Knopf.

Logan, Rayford W. 1954. *The Negro in American Life and Thought: The Nadir, 1877–1901.* New York: Dial Press.

———. 1969. *Howard University: The First Hundred Years, 1867–1967.* New York: New York University Press.

Manning, Kenneth R. 1983. *Black Apollo of Science: The Life of Ernest Everett Just.* New York: Oxford University Press.

Mays, Benjamin E. 1971. *Born to Rebel: An Autobiography.* Athens: University of Georgia Press.

Mays, Benjamin E., and Joseph Nicholson. 1933. *The Negro's Church.* New York: Institute of Social and Religious Research.

McKinney, Richard. 1997. *Mordecai, the Man and His Message: The Story of Mordecai Wyatt Johnson.* Washington, DC: Howard University Press.

Meier, August. 1960. The Racial and Educational Philosophy of Kelly Miller, 1895–1915. *Journal of Negro Education* 29: 121–127.

Meier, August, and David L. Lewis. 1959. History of the Negro Upper Class in Atlanta, 1890–1958. *Journal of Negro Education* (Spring): 128–139.

Moon, Henry Lee. 1948. *Balance of Power: The Negro Vote.* Garden City, NY: Doubleday.

Moses, Wilson J. 1987. The Lost World of the Negro, 1895–1919: Black History and Intellectual Life before the Renaissance. *Black American Literature Forum* 21: 61–84.

Moss, Alfred N. 1981. *The American Negro Academy: Voice of the Talented Tenth.* Baton Rouge: Louisiana State University Press.

Moton, Robert, 1929. *What the Negro Thinks.* Garden City, NY: Doubleday.

Ottley, Roi. 1955. *The Lonely Warrior: The Life and Times of Robert S. Abbott.* Chicago: University of Chicago Press. Robert Abbott founded the *Chicago Defender,* an African American daily newspaper.

Painter, Nell Irvin. 1976. *Exodusters: Black Migration Following Reconstruction.* New York: Alfred A. Knopf.

———. 2006. *Creating Black Americans.* New York: Oxford University Press.

Platt, Anthony M. 1991. *E. Franklin Frazier Reconsidered.* New Brunswick, NJ: Rutgers University Press.

Posnock, Ross. 1998. *Color and Culture: Black Writers and the Making of the Modern Intellectual.* Cambridge, MA: Harvard University Press.

Richardson, Joe M. 1980. *A History of Fisk University, 1865–1965.* Tuscaloosa: University of Alabama Press.

Rudwick, Elliott. 1964. *Race Riot at East St. Louis, July 2, 1917.* Carbondale: Southern Illinois University Press.

Shapiro, Herbert. 1988. *White Violence and Black Response*. Amherst: University of Massachusetts Press.

Spencer, Jon Michael. 1996. The Black Church and the Harlem Renaissance. *African American Review* 30: 453–460.

Stewart, Alison. 2013. *First Class: The Legacy of Dunbar, America's First Black Public High School*. Chicago: Chicago Review Press.

Terrell, Mary Church. 1917. History of the [Dunbar] High School for Negroes in Washington. *Journal of Negro History* (April): 253–256.

Thorpe, Earl. 1970. *The Mind of the Negro: An Intellectual History of Afro-Americans*. Westport, CT: Negro Universities Press.

Trotter, Joe W. 1985. *Black Milwaukee: The Making of an Industrial Proletariat, 1915–1945*. Urbana: University of Illinois Press. Trotter's study probes the interconnected development of the black working-class and middle-class sectors.

Tuttle, William M., Jr. 1970. *Race Riot: Chicago in the Red Summer of 1919*. New York: Atheneum. For the official study of the Chicago 1919 anti-Negro race riot, see Chicago Commission on Race Relations, *The Negro in Chicago: A Study of Race Relations and a Race Riot* (Chicago: Commission on Race Relations, 1922). As secretary to the Chicago Commission on Race Relations, the young sociologist Charles S. Johnson conducted much of the research on the riot and wrote the official report for the commission. Typical twentieth-century race riots devastated the modernization trajectory of both working-class and middle-class African Americans, which of course was precisely the purpose of the rioters.

Washington, Booker T. 1899. *The Future of the American Negro*. New York: Small, Maynard.

———, ed. 1903. *The Negro Problem*. New York: J. Pott.

Weare, Walter. 1973. *Black Business in the New South: A Social History of the North Carolina Mutual Life Insurance Company*. Urbana: University of Illinois Press.

Wesley, Charles. 1929. *The History of Alpha Phi Alpha: A Development in [Negro] College Life*. Washington, DC: Howard University Press. Reprint, Baltimore: Foundation Publishers, 2000.

Woodson, Carter G. 1934. *The Negro Professional Man and the Community*. Washington, DC: Associated Publishers.

Work, Monroe N. 1932. *The Negro Year Book: An Annual Encyclopedia of the Negro, 1931–1932*. Tuskegee, AL: Negro Yearbook Publishing.

Wright, Richard R., Jr. 1965. *Eighty-Seven Years behind the Black Curtain: An Autobiography*. Nashville, TN: A.M.E. School Union. Richard R. Wright Jr. was a bishop in the A.M.E. Church.

Leadership and Ideological Dynamics of Twentieth-Century Black Intelligentsia

Arsenault, Raymond. 2006. *Freedom Riders: 1961 and the Struggle for Racial Justice*. New York: Oxford University Press.

Baker, Houston. 2008. *Betrayal: How Black Intellectuals Have Abandoned the Ideals of the Civil Rights Era*. New York: Columbia University Press.

Baldwin, James. 1985. *Price of the Ticket: Collected Nonfiction, 1948–1965*. New York: St. Martin's Press/Marek.

Bardolph, Richard. 1959. *The Negro Vanguard*. New York: Rinehart.

Bond, George Clement. 1988. A Social Portrait of John Gibbs St. Clair Drake: An American Anthropologist. *American Ethnologist* 15: 762–781. St. Clair Drake was a member of the first two generations of African American anthropology scholars, which included Caroline Bond Day (Radcliffe College, M.A. in 1930), Laurence Foster (University of Pennsylvania, Ph.D. in 1931), Mark Hanna Watkins (University of Chicago, Ph.D. in 1933), Arthur Huff Fauset (University of Pennsylvania, Ph.D. in 1940), Allison Davis (University of Chicago, Ph.D. in 1942), Hugh Smythe (Northwestern University, Ph.D. in 1946), and Manet Fowler (Cornell University, Ph.D. in 1952), who was the first African American woman to gain a Ph.D. in anthropology. St. Clair Drake's first field-research project was a study of the Negro community in Chicago during the early 1940s, published with Horace Cayton in 1945 as *Black Metropolis: A Study of Negro Life in a Northern City*, 2 vols. [New York: Harcourt Brace]). His second project, for which Drake earned his Ph.D. in 1954 at the University of Chicago, was a study of immigrant West Indian workers in the port city of Cardiff, Wales. A third generation of African Americans to gain doctorates in anthropology emerged in the 1960s, which included George Clement Bond (University of London), Elliott Skinner (Columbia University), James Gibbs (Harvard University), Karen Fields (Brandeis University), and William Schack (University of London). The fourth generation included the first African American female scholar to gain a Ph.D. in anthropology from Harvard—Claudia Mitchell, who was also appointed an assistant professor and later gained full professorship at the University of California, Los Angeles. Also in the fourth generation was Lorand Matory, the first African American to gain full professorship in Harvard University's Department of Anthropology, who did his doctoral dissertation at the University of Chicago on Yoruba religion and subsequently pursued the study of Afro-Brazilian religious patterns.

Bracey, John, August Meier, and Elliott Rudwick, eds. 1971. *The Black Sociologists: The First Half Century*. Belmont, CA: Wadsworth.

Branch, Taylor. 1988. *Parting the Waters: America in the King Years, 1954–1963.* New York: Simon & Schuster/Touchstone.

Bruce, Dickson D. 1993. *Archibald Grimké: Portrait of a Black Independent.* Baton Rouge: Louisiana State University Press.

Bunche, Ralph J. 1973. *The Political Status of the Negro in the Age of F.D.R.* Chicago: University of Chicago Press.

Bundles, A'Lelia. 2001. *On Her Own Ground: The Life and Times of Madam C. J. Walker.* New York: Scribner.

Canton, David A. 2010. *Raymond Pace Alexander: A New Negro Lawyer Fights for Civil Rights in Philadelphia.* Jackson: University of Mississippi Press.

Carter, Lawrence E., ed. 1998. *Walking Integrity: Benjamin Elijah Mays, Mentor to Martin Luther King Jr.* Macon, GA: Mercer University Press.

Collier-Thomas, Bettye, and Vincent P. Franklin, eds. 2001. *Sisters in the Struggle: African American Women in the Civil Rights–Black Power Movement.* New York: New York University Press.

Cone, James H. 1991. *Martin and Malcolm and America: A Dream or a Nightmare.* Maryknoll, NY: Orbis Books.

Cromwell, Adelaide. 1994. *The Other Brahmins: Boston's Black Upper Class, 1750–1950.* Fayetteville: University of Arkansas Press.

Cromwell, Adelaide, and Martin Kilson, eds. 1969. *Apropos of Africa: Sentiments of Negro American Leaders on Africa from the 1880s to the 1950s.* London: Frank Cass.

Cruse, Harold. 1967. *The Crisis of the Negro Intellectual.* New York: William Morrow.

Dickerson, Dennis C. 2005. African American Religious Intellectuals and the Theological Origins of the Civil Rights Movement, 1930–1955. *Church History* (June).

Duberman, Martin B. 1988. *Paul Robeson: A Biography.* New York: Alfred Knopf.

Farmer, James. 1985. *Lay Bare the Heart: An Autobiography of the Civil Rights Movement.* New York: Arbor House.

Fauset, Arthur Huff. 1944. *Black Gods of the Metropolis.* Philadelphia: University of Pennsylvania Press.

Ferguson, Jeffrey. 2005. *The Sage of Sugar Hill: George S. Schuyler and the Harlem Renaissance.* New Haven, CT: Yale University Press.

Fox, Stephen R. 1971. *The Guardian of Boston: William Monroe Trotter.* New York: Atheneum.

Franklin, John Hope. 1989. Dilemma of the American Negro Scholar. In John Hope Franklin, *Race and History: Selected Essays, 1938–1988,* 295–308. Baton Rouge: Louisiana State University Press.

Franklin, John Hope, and August Meier, eds. 1982. *Black Leaders of the Twentieth Century.* Urbana: University of Illinois Press.

Franklin, Vincent P. 1979. *The Education of Black Philadelphia.* Philadelphia: University of Pennsylvania Press.

———. 1995. *Living Our Stories, Telling Our Truths: Autobiography and the Making of the African American Intellectual Tradition.* New York: Oxford University Press.

Gaines, Kevin K. 1996. *Uplifting the Race: Black Leadership, Politics, and Culture in the Twentieth Century.* Chapel Hill: University of North Carolina Press.

Garrow, David J. 1978. *Protest at Selma: Martin Luther King and the Voting Rights Act of 1965.* New Haven, CT: Yale University Press.

Gates, Henry Louis, Jr. 1994. *Colored People.* New York: Alfred Knopf.

Gates, Henry Louis, Jr., and Cornel West. 1996. *The Future of the Race.* New York: Alfred Knopf.

Gavin, Raymond. 1977. *The Perils and Prospects of Southern Black Leadership: Gordon Blaine Hancock, 1884–1970.* Durham, NC: Duke University Press.

Goggins, Jacqueline. 1993. *Carter G. Woodson: A Life in Black History.* Baton Rouge: Louisiana State University Press.

Gomez-Jefferson, Annetta. 2002. *The Sage of Tawawa: Reverdy Cassius Ransom, 1861–1959.* Kent, OH: Kent State University Press. Reverdy Ransom was an A.M.E. bishop from the 1930s through the 1950s. Tawawa was the name of Ransom's residence.

Hall, Robert. 2002. E. Franklin Frazier and the Chicago School of Sociology. In James E. Teele, ed., *E. Franklin Frazier and Black Bourgeoisie,* 47–67. Columbia: University of Missouri Press.

Hamilton, Charles V. 1991. *Adam Clayton Powell, Jr.: The Political Biography of an American Dilemma.* New York: Collier. Adam Clayton Powell Jr., a Baptist clergyman in New York City, in 1944 became the fourth African American elected to the U.S. Congress in the twentieth century. He was preceded in Congress by Oscar DePriest, Arthur Mitchell, and William O. Dawson, all of whom were elected from Chicago. Dawson served in Congress until 1973, the longest-serving black congressperson in the twentieth century. The 1950s saw two African Americans elected to Congress: Robert Nix from Philadelphia and Charles Diggs from Detroit.

Harlan, Louis R. 1983. *Booker T. Washington: The Wizard of Tuskegee, 1901–1915.* New York: Oxford University Press.

Harris, Abram L. 1936. *The Negro as Capitalist.* Philadelphia: American Academy of Political and Social Science.

Henry, Charles. 1995. Abram Harris, E. Franklin Frazier, and Ralph Bunche: The Howard School of Thought on the Problem of Race. In Matthew Holden Jr., ed., *The Changing Racial Regime*, 36–56. New Brunswick, NJ: Transaction Publishers.

———. 1999. *Ralph Bunche: Model Negro or American Other?* New York: New York University Press.

Hine, Darlene Clark. 1982. Mabel K. Staupers and the Integration of Black Nurses into the Armed Forces. In John Hope Franklin and August Meier, eds., *Black Leaders of the Twentieth Century*, 241–258. Urbana: University of Illinois Press.

Holloway, Jonathan. 2001. The Black Intellectual and the "Crisis Canon" in the Twentieth Century. *Black Scholar* (Spring): 2–13.

———. 2002. *Confronting the Veil: Abram Harris Jr., E. Franklin Frazier, and Ralph J. Bunche, 1919–1941*. Princeton, NJ: Princeton University Press.

Holt, Rackham. 1964. *Mary McLeod Bethune*. Garden City, NY: Doubleday.

Horne, Gerald. 1994. *Black Liberation/Black Scare: Ben Davis and the Communist Party*. Newark, DE: Associated University Press. A 1923 Harvard Law School graduate (along with William Hastie, Raymond Pace Alexander, and Charles Hamilton Houston), Benjamin Davis—son of a wealthy Atlanta black businessman—was the leading African American personality in the Communist Party during the 1920s–1940s. The professional career pattern of Davis' Harvard Law School African American classmates differed from his. Hastie was a co-leader of the first "Don't Buy Where You Can't Work" civil rights organization, which was founded in 1935 among activist middle-class African Americans in Washington, D.C. Hastie was later the first African American appointed to a federal court. Alexander practiced law in his hometown of Philadelphia, and starting in the late 1920s he provided legal counsel—free of charge—to the city's African American teachers' association in its struggle against Philadelphia's segregated public schools, a battle that lasted until the 1960s. Houston founded the NAACP Legal Defense Fund in Washington, D.C., and in the early 1930s was appointed the first African American dean of the Howard University Law School.

Huggins, Nathan I. 1971. *The Harlem Renaissance*. New York: Oxford University Press.

Hunter, Herbert, and Sameer Abraham, eds. 1987. *Race, Class, and the World System: The Sociology of Oliver Cromwell Cox*. New York: Monthly Review Press.

Jackson, Lawrence P. 2011. *The Indignant Generation: A Narrative History of African American Writers and Critics, 1934–1960*. Princeton, NJ: Princeton University Press.

James, Winston. 1998. *Holding Aloft the Banner of Ethiopia: Caribbean Radicalism in Early Twentieth-Century America*. New York: Verso. Winston James' book is the major study of the role of Caribbean immigrant intellectuals in early twentieth-century African American political activism.

Janken, Kenneth Robert. 1993. *Rayford W. Logan and the Dilemma of the African American Intellectual*. Amherst: University of Massachusetts Press.

——. 2003. *White: The Biography of Walter White, Mr. NAACP*. New York: New Press.

Johnson, James Weldon. 1933. *Along This Way: The Autobiography of James Weldon Johnson*. New York: Viking.

Kennedy, Randall. 2011. *The Persistence of the Color Line: Racial Politics and the Obama Presidency*. New York: Pantheon Books.

Kilson, Martin. 1982. Adam Clayton Powell: The Militant as Politician. In John Hope Franklin and August Meier, eds., *Black Leaders of the Twentieth Century*, 259–275. Urbana: University of Illinois Press.

——. 1992. Thoughts on Black Conservatism. *Trotter Institute Review* (Winter–Spring).

——. 1993. The Gang That Couldn't Shoot Straight. *Transition* no. 62: 217–225.

——. 1998. Styles of Black Public Intellectuals. *Black Renaissance/Renaissance Noire* 1: 1–17.

——. 2002. E. Franklin Frazier's "Black Bourgeoisie" Reconsidered. In James E. Teele, ed., *E. Franklin Frazier and "Black Bourgeoisie,"* 118–136. Columbia: University of Missouri Press.

——. 2004. Anatomy of Black Intellectuals and Nationalism: Harold Cruse Revisited. In Jerry G. Watts, ed., *Harold Cruse's "The Crisis of the Negro Intellectual" Reconsidered*, 43–74. New York: Routledge.

——. 2007. Political Scientists and the Activist-Technocrat Dichotomy: The Case of John Aubrey Davis. In Wilbur Rich, ed., *African American Perspectives on Political Science*, 169–172. Philadelphia: Temple University Press. John Aubrey Davis was among the first generation of African American scholars in political science. The first two African American political science scholars gained their doctorates in the 1930s: Ralph Bunche (Harvard University) and Emmett Dorsey (University of Chicago). The next group gained their doctorates in the 1940s: Merze Tate (Harvard), Robert Martin (University of Chicago), Robert Brisbane (Harvard), and John Aubrey Davis (Columbia University). The next group gained their doctorates in the late 1950s to early 1970s, which included Lawrence Howard (Harvard), Charles V. Hamilton (University of Chicago), Martin Kilson (Harvard), Matthew Holden (Northwestern University), Clement Cottingham (University of California,

Berkeley), Allen Ballard (Harvard), Charles Henry (University of California, Berkeley), Wilbur Rich (University of Illinois), Pearl Robinson (Columbia), Edmond Keller (University of California, Los Angeles,), Robert Smith (Howard University), and Hanes Walton (Howard University). The next-generation cohort saw a broad expansion of African American scholars trained at the doctoral level in political science from the 1970s through the 1990s. That cohort included Christopher Foreman (Harvard), Adolph Reed (Howard University), David Dickson (Harvard), James Jennings (Columbia), Jerry G. Watts (Yale University), Ernest J. Wilson (University of Michigan), Weldon Jackson (Harvard), Katherine Tate (University of Michigan), Germaine Hoston (Harvard), Frederick Harris (Rochester University), Michael Dawson (Harvard), Valerie Johnson (University of Maryland), Ollie Johnson (University of California, Berkeley), Marion Orr (Brown University), Cathy Cohen (University of Chicago), Claudia Gay (Harvard), and Melissa Harris-Perry (Duke University).

———. 2009. Thinking about Robert Putnam's "Analysis of Diversity." *Du Bois Review* (Fall): 293–308.

———. 2010. Ralph Bunche: African American Intellectual. In Robert A. Hall and Edmond J. Keller, eds., *Trustee for the Human Community: Ralph J. Bunche, the United Nations, and the Decolonization of Africa*, 3–18. Athens: Ohio University Press. This chapter was originally the keynote address for the University of California conference commemorating the hundredth anniversary of Ralph J. Bunche's birth, held at UCLA, June 3–4, 2004.

King, Martin Luther, Jr. 1950. *Stride toward Freedom: A Leader of His People Tells the Montgomery Story.* New York: Harper & Sons.

———. 1964. *Why We Can't Wait.* New York: New American Library.

Kirby, John B. 1980. *Black Americans in the Roosevelt Era.* Knoxville: University of Tennessee Press.

Lee, Chana Kai. 1999. *For Freedom's Sake: The Life of Fanny Lou Hamer.* Urbana: University of Illinois Press.

Levy, Eugene. 1973. *James Weldon Johnson: Black Leader, Black Voice.* Chicago: University of Chicago Press.

Lewis, David Levering. 1993. *W. E. B. Du Bois: Biography of a Race, 1868–1919.* New York: Henry Holt.

———. 2000. *W. E. B. Du Bois: The Fight for Equality and the American Century, 1919–1963.* New York: Henry Holt.

Lewis, John. 1998. *Walking with the Wind: A Memoir of the Movement.* With Michael D'Orso. New York: Simon & Schuster.

Locke, Alain, ed. 1925. *The New Negro: An Interpretation.* New York: Albert & Charles Boni.

Logan, Rayford W., and Michael Winston, eds. 1983. *Dictionary of American Negro Biography.* New York: W. W. Norton.

Marable, Manning. 1986. *W. E. B. Du Bois: Black Radical Democrat.* Boston: Twayne.

———. 2011. *Malcolm X: A Life of Reinvention.* New York: Viking.

May, Vivian. 2007. *Anna Julia Cooper: Visionary Black Feminist.* New York: Routledge.

McMurry, Linda O. 1999. *To Keep the Waters Troubled: The Life of Ida B. Wells.* New York: Oxford University Press.

McNeil, Genna Rae. 1983. *Groundwork: Charles Hamilton Houston and the Struggle for Civil Rights.* Philadelphia: University of Pennsylvania Press.

McPherson, James M. 1975. *The Abolitionist Legacy: From Reconstruction to the NAACP.* Princeton, NJ: Princeton University Press.

Meier, August. 1963. *Negro Thought in America, 1880–1915: Racial Ideologies in the Age of Booker T. Washington.* Ann Arbor: University of Michigan Press.

Moore, Jesse T. 1981. *A Search for Equality: The National Urban League, 1910–1961.* University Park: Pennsylvania State University Press.

Moses, Yolanda. 1999. Laurence Foster: Anthropologist, Scholar, and Social Advocate. In Ira Harrison and Faye Harrison, eds., *African American Pioneers in Anthropology,* 85–100. Urbana: University of Illinois Press.

Myrdal, Gunnar. 1944. *An American Dilemma: The Negro Problem and Modern Democracy.* 2 vols. New York: Harper & Brothers.

Ogletree, Charles J. 2004. *All Deliberate Speed: Reflections on the First Half-Century of "Brown v. Board of Education."* New York: W. W. Norton. Charles Ogletree was the third African American law scholar appointed to the Harvard Law School faculty. He was preceded by Derrick Bell and Clyde Ferguson. Four additional African American law scholars joined the Harvard Law faculty following Ogletree's appointment: Randall Kennedy, David Wilkins, Lani Guinier, and Annette Gordon-Reed.

Pew Research Center. 2007. *Optimism about Black Progress Declines: Blacks See Growing Values Gap between Poor and Middle Class.* Washington, DC: Pew Research Center.

Platt, Anthony M. 1991. *E. Franklin Frazier Reconsidered.* New Brunswick, NJ: Rutgers University Press.

Raines, Howell, ed. 1977. *My Soul Is Rested: Movement Days in the Deep South Remembered.* New York: G. P. Putnam's Sons.

Rampersad, Arnold. 1986. *The Life of Langston Hughes.* New York: Oxford University Press.

Ransby, Barbara. 2003. *Ella Baker and the Black Freedom Movement: A Radical Democratic Vision.* Chapel Hill: University of North Carolina Press.

Reddick, Lawrence. 1959. *Crusader without Violence: A Biography of Martin Luther King, Jr.* New York: Harper & Brothers.

Reed, Christopher R. 1977. *The Chicago NAACP and the Rise of Black Professional Leadership, 1900–1960.* Bloomington: Indiana University Press.

Reid, Ira. 1930. *Negro Membership in American Labor Unions.* New York: National Urban League.

Robbins, Richard. 1996. *Sidelines Activist: Charles S. Johnson and the Struggle for Civil Rights.* Jackson: University of Mississippi Press.

Rowan, Carl T. 1993. *Dream Makers, Dream Breakers: The World of Thurgood Marshall.* Boston: Little, Brown.

Rudwick, Elliott M. 1957. The Niagara Movement. *Journal of Negro History* (July): 177–200.

Rustin, Bayard. 1971. *Down the Line: The Collected Writings of Bayard Rustin.* Chicago: Quadrangle Books.

Schneider, Mark Robert. 2001. *"We Return Fighting": The Civil Rights Movement in the Jazz Age.* Boston: Northeastern University Press.

Solomon, Mark. 1998. *The Cry Was Unity: Communists and African Americans, 1917–1956.* Jackson: University of Mississippi Press.

Stein, Judith. 1986. *The World of Marcus Garvey: Race and Class in Modern Society.* Baton Rouge: Louisiana State University Press.

Sugrue, Thomas. 2008. *Sweet Land of Liberty: The Forgotten Struggle for Civil Rights in the North.* New York: Random House.

Tushnet, Mark V. 1987. *The NAACP's Legal Strategy against Segregated Education, 1925–1950.* Chapel Hill: University of North Carolina Press.

Urban, Wayne. 1992. *Black Scholar: Horace Mann Bond, 1904–1972.* Athens: University of Georgia Press.

Watts, Jerry G., ed. 2004. *Harold Cruse's "The Crisis of the Negro Intellectual" Reconsidered.* New York: Routledge.

Weiss, Nancy J. 1974. *The National Urban League, 1910–1940.* New York: Oxford University Press.

West, Cornel. 1993. *Keeping Faith: Philosophy and Race in America.* New York: Routledge.

———. 1994. *Race Matters.* Boston: Beacon Press.

———. 2004. *Democracy Matters: Winning the Fight against Imperialism.* New York: Penguin Press.

Wilkins, Carolyn Marie. 2010. *Damn Near White: An African American Family's Rise from Slavery to Bittersweet Success.* Columbia: University of Missouri Press.

Williams, Zachery R. 2009. *In Search of the Talented Tenth: Howard University Public Intellectuals and the Dilemmas of Race, 1926–1970.* Columbia: University of Missouri Press.

Wilson, Francille Rusan. 1996. Racial Consciousness and Black Scholarship: Charles H. Wesley and the Construction of Negro Labor in the United States. *Journal of Negro History* 81: 72–88.

———. 2005. *Segregated Scholars: Black Social Scientists and the Development of Black Labor Studies*. Charlottesville: University of Virginia Press.

Wilson, Sandra Kathryn, ed. 1999. *In Search of Democracy: The NAACP Writings of James Weldon Johnson, Walter White, and Roy Wilkins*. New York: Oxford University Press.

Wilson, William Julius. 2011. The Declining Significance of Race: Revisited and Revised. *Daedalus: Journal of the American Academy of Arts and Sciences* (Spring): 55–69.

Wolters, Raymond. 1975. *The New Negro on Campus: Black College Rebellions of the 1920s*. Princeton, NJ: Princeton University Press.

———. 2003. *Du Bois and His Rivals*. Columbia: University of Missouri Press.

Zangrando, Robert. 1980. *The NAACP Campaigns against Lynching, 1909–1950*. Philadelphia: Temple University Press.

Zinn, Howard. 1965. *SNCC: The New Black Abolitionists*. Boston: Beacon Press.

ACKNOWLEDGMENTS

In producing *Transformation of the African American Intelligentsia, 1880–2012,* I owe a special debt to the W. E. B. Du Bois Institute for African and African American Research at Harvard University and to its director, Professor Henry Louis Gates Jr. Professor Gates and the executive board of the W. E. B. Du Bois Institute gave me the honor of delivering the 2010 lectures in its W. E. B. Du Bois Lecture Series from March 30 to April 1, the texts of which were the test run, so to speak, for this book. I was among the several Harvard University faculty who were founding members of the W. E. B. Du Bois Institute in 1976 (along with professors William Bromley, Peter Gomes, John Kain, Preston Williams, and Stephen Williams), and I have much praise for Professor Gates' skillful shepherding of the Du Bois Institute into a first-class academic and research institution.

While writing this book, I received first-class intellectual and technical assistance from my wife, Marion Kilson. She listened to many discussions on reshaping the lectures into a book manuscript and read several versions of the manuscript. I owe her heartfelt thanks. I have had many hours of intellectually fertile conversations about processes related to the metamorphosis of the African American intelligentsia during the twentieth century with a number of my former Harvard College and Graduate School students. Among the students I wish to thank are Derrick Cephas (corporation lawyer), Leonard S. Coleman (former president of the National League in Major League Baseball), Lee A. Daniels (staff member at the NAACP Legal Defense Fund), David Dixon (professor at George Washington University), Michael Eastman (entertainment lawyer), Karen Fields (professor at Rochester University), Christopher Foreman (professor at the University of Maryland), Robert Hall (professor at Northeastern University), Charles Jordan Hamilton (corporation lawyer), Avarita Hanson (civil rights lawyer), Stefano Harney (professor at Queen Mary, University of London), James Hoyt (lawyer and Harvard administrator), Lowell Johnston (corporation lawyer),

Lewis Jones (finance investor), Eugene Matthews (finance investor), Tanya Jennerette (corporation lawyer), Fred Moten (professor at Duke University), Michael Robinson (corporation lawyer), Doug Schoen (election pollster), Jeffrey Tignor (civil rights lawyer), Jerry G. Watts (professor at City University of New York), Cornel West (professor at Princeton University), Mark Whitaker (former editor of *Newsweek* magazine), Ernest Wilson (professor at University of Southern California), and Robert Yarbrough (legal counsel at Pace University).

I must also thank a group of special individuals with whom I have had many hours of fruitful conversation—over many years—about the metamorphosis of the African American intelligentsia and professional class. They are Clement Cottingham, a childhood friend and political scientist who taught at Rutgers University and Pace University; George Clement Bond, a graduate school roommate and anthropologist who teaches at Columbia University; Thomas Kilson Queenan, my nephew, who is treasurer at Dickinson College in Pennsylvania; Jacqueline Goggins, a historian who wrote a major book on Carter G. Woodson, the scholar who launched core institutions in the field of African American history, such as the *Journal of Negro History* in 1916; Florence Ladd, a psychologist and novelist who grew up at Howard University and was a director of the Bunting Institute at Radcliffe College; Walter Carrington, who helped found the Harvard College NAACP chapter during my Harvard Graduate School years and was a civil rights lawyer and a U.S. foreign service official; Archie C. Epps, a deceased dear friend since my early teaching years at Harvard in the 1960s, who was dean of students at Harvard College and a brilliant nurturer of comity among students in our era of the multiethnic and multicultural university; Charles Blockson, curator emeritus of Temple University's Afro-American collection; Emery Wimbish, a retired director of the Langston Hughes Memorial Library at Lincoln University; and Adelaide Cromwell, a member of the third generation of twentieth-century African American scholars, now in her mid-nineties, who studied for a Harvard Ph.D. in sociology in the 1940s and was a professor of sociology and director of the African American Studies Program at Boston University. Her doctoral dissertation—which was published in 1994 as *The Other Brahmins: Boston's Black Upper Class, 1750–1950*—was a pioneering study of an ethnic group's elite features. Professor Cromwell, I should add, is a special figure among the twenty-first-century African American intelligentsia, insofar as she hails from an Emancipation-era black intelligentsia family. Her grandfather, John Wesley Cromwell, was in the first graduation class of Howard University Law School; published the leading Negro weekly newspaper in Washington, D.C., the *People's Advocate*; and, along with Alexander Crummell (theologian),William Sanders Scarborough (classics scholar), and Archibald Grimké (lawyer), was a founding member of the American Negro Academy in 1897. He also wrote an early history of African Americans, *The Negro in American History*, which was published by the academy in 1914. Furthermore, Adelaide Cromwell's father, John Wesley Cromwell Jr., was an early twentieth-century certified public accountant—the first African American CPA, in fact. Finally, Professor Cromwell's aunt, Otelia Cromwell, was an early African American woman to gain the Ph.D. degree, which she did in literature from Yale University in 1926.

As a graduate student at Harvard University in the fields of international affairs and comparative politics between 1953 and 1959, I was helped by several Harvard professors to sharpen my intellectual formation and academic skills through their enriching and inspiring courses: Ernest May (history of U.S. foreign policy), Samuel Beer (British politics), Gordon Allport (social psychology), Louis Hartz (American liberalism), Herbert Marcuse (Marxism), Robert McCloskey (American constitutional governance), and Rupert Emerson (international relations, international organization, nationalism, and decolonization in Africa and Asia). I owe a special debt to Rupert Emerson, who served as my graduate studies adviser, directed my Ph.D. dissertation on the United Nations trusteeship system in African colonies, and located research funds that allowed me to produce my first book, *Political Change in a West African State: A Study of the Modernization Process in Sierra Leone* (1966), as well as my second, *New States in the Modern World* (1975). Both were published by Harvard University Press.

I am dedicating this book to my immediate family. My wife has contributed intellectually and technically to the creation of this book. My three children—Jennifer (educator), Peter (accountant), and Hannah (lawyer)—are, like their paternal ancestors, witness to the long-standing viability of the African American intelligentsia ever since its formative phase in the post–Civil War Emancipation era. And I believe my six grandchildren—Jacob, Rhiana, Caila, Maya, Zuri, and Ciaran—will represent the wave of an expanding and fruitful African American intelligentsia in the twenty-first century.

Lastly, I owe a thank you to Julie Wolf. She spent several months doing superb copyediting on the manuscript for this book.

INDEX

African American academic scholars: anthropologists, 202; historians, 192–193; literary studies, 195–197; political scientists, 206–207; sociologists, 193

African American nurses: early dependence on black-run hospitals, 68–69, 173n33, 177n56; struggle to enter U.S. Women's Army Corps (WACS), 174nn36–38

African American professional workers: white-collar occupations held (1890–1930s), 61–63; white-collar occupations held (2006), 121–122

African Methodist Episcopal Church, 6–7

African Methodist Episcopal Zion Church, 6–7

African Union Methodist Protestant Church, 6–7

Alexander, Michelle, on the "war on drugs" and mass incarceration of black American males, 81, 178n62

Alexander, Raymond Pace, 78; on advancement of civil rights leadership in Philadelphia, 78–79

Alexander, Sadie Mossell, 78, 177n56

American Negro Academy, 94–96

Appiah, K. A., 184n49

Arnold, Anna, 91

Association for the Study of Negro Life and History, 61–63

Atkinson, Whittier, 69–71, 174–175nn40–43

Austin, Rev. J. C., on advancing black-communitarian leadership through black churches, 73–74

Baker, Ella, 111

Banks, William, on black intellectuals' ethnic-commitment leadership nexus with African American society, 91, 95

Bardolph, Richard, on social-class development of the African American elite sector, 13–27

Bell, Derrick, 131, 186n25; on pathological roots in American civilization of American racist practices, 195

Bethune, Mary McLeod, on civil rights leadership among twentieth-century African American women, 60, 91, 103

Billingsley, Andrew: on black American social stratification, 120–121; on black church communitarian leadership, 176n51

Black abolitionists, on leadership in antebellum African American society, 13, 183n41, 191–192

Black communitarian leadership, on its ideological origins and evolution, 86–91

Black conservative intellectuals: on denial of racism's injury to black American's lives, 141–142; evidence rebutting conservatives' "color blind society" discourse, 144–146; on their late twentieth-century evolution, 138–141, 187n34; on their manipulation of Reverend Martin Luther King Jr.'s social gospel discourse, 142–143

Black Enterprise Magazine, 121–123, 185n12

Black ethnic-commitment leadership orientation, on evolution among the twentieth-century black intelligentsia, 86–91

Black intelligentsia, development stages, 11–14

Black leadership, early twentieth-century classifications, 75–76

Blackmon, Douglas, on prison-based forced labor in southern agriculture, 48–49, 90, 171n13

Black populism, 35–42; on types of twentieth-century black populist leaders, 169nn35–36

Black Scholar Journal, 93–112

Blassingame, John, 191, 193

Blow, Charles, on comparisons between authoritarian slave patterns and twenty-first-century incarceration of African Americans, 178n62

Bobo, Lawrence D., 193; on black-white differences toward "post-racial" American society issue, 188–189n49; on twenty-first-century African American class system, 118

Bond, George Clement, 202; on academic career of St. Clair Drake, 202

Bond, Horace Mann, 193; on graduate degrees of Lincoln University graduates (1912–1953), 65–68, 173n34; on public education for black youth and production of black doctorates, 1, 22–24, 25–26, 31, 34, 165n1, 165n3; on social history of Lincoln University, 165n1, 165n3, 168n19, 188n43

Bond, J. Max, 26, 193

Bradby, Rev. Robert, 74–75

Braithwaite, William, 91–92, 136–137

Brown, Sterling, 195–196

Browne, Roscoe Lee, 31, 196

Bunche, Ralph J., 99, 206; as critic of black ethnic-bloc political mobilization, 100–106; as proponent of interracial class-based political mobilization, 102–104

Caldwell, A. B., 17–20

Carroll, Dr. Natalie, 148–149

Carter, Stephen, on black conservatives as "black dissenters," 146–148

Census Bureau: African American mulatto segment (1910), 27–29; African American regional population (1910–1930), 50–51

Chestnut, Mary, on mulatto slave children on southern plantations, 20–21

Civil Rights Act of 1964, 47

Coatesville, Pennsylvania, U.S. Census data and, 174n39

Coleman, William T., Jr., 83, 179–180n66

Color elitism: black populist role in democratization, 35–42; democratization of color elitism, 32–35; folk expressions of, 14–15; opposition to color elitism, 27–35; reactionary attributes, 15–16; social-class attributes, 22–29; social roots, 17–22

Cooper, Anna Julia, 30

Cromwell, John Wesley, 30, 94

Crummell, Alexander, 94–95

Daniels, Lee A., 185n10

Davis, Benjamin, 78; as prominent figure in the American Communist Party, 78, 177n53, 205

Davis, John Aubrey, 102–104, 166n9, 206

Dawson, Michael, 207; on African Americans' political attitudes, 135, 186n30

Day, Carol Bond, 192

Dickerson, Dennis C., 193; on communitarian leadership role of black churches in twentieth-century Pittsburgh, 71–74; on Negro Elks, 69

Douglass, Frederick, 3, 13, 113

Dowling, Monroe, 31

Drake, St. Clair, 202; on activism, 187n34; on Holiness and Spiritualist churches in Chicago, 38–40

Du Bois, W. E. B., 192; advanced progressive "mobilization-type" politics for the black intelligentsia, 51–56; classified the early twentieth-century black elite into reactionary and progressive sectors, 4–5, 32; favored Freedman's Bureau's black modernization role, 46–47, 147nn8–9; formulated "black-communitarian leadership orientation" for the intelligentsia, 54–57, 57–61; formulated "black ethnic-commitment ethos" for the intelligentsia, 86–91; organized Niagara Movement civil rights activism, 56–57; proposed a "Talented Tenth" to advance black modern development, 87–90

Edelman, Marian Wright, on negative influence on African American youth from hip-hop entertainment patterns and discourse, 129

Eisenbrey, Ross, on causes of wealth differentials between black and white families, 126

Erie, Steve, on history of affirmative action–type public benefits allocated to white citizens by late nineteenth-century and twentieth-century urban political machines, 187n36

Farmer, James, 111

Fauset, Arthur Huff, on the evolution of Holiness and Spiritualist black churches, 35

Fields, Barbara, 186n25, 193

Fields, Karen, 202; on communitarian leadership role of middle-class

African Americans in Charleston, S.C., 60–61, 186n25

Ford, Nick Aaron, 196

Foster, Laurence, 24

Franklin, John Hope, 192; on history courses about black Americans taught at Negro colleges before World War II, 198; on post–Civil War Reconstruction policy, 9; on White Anglo-Saxon Protestant (WASP) elite's radical "culture of militancy" in pre–Civil War South, 97–98

Franklin, Vincent P., 193; on autobiographical influences in shaping African American intelligentsia, 204; on black-communitarian leadership in early twentieth-century Philadelphia, 71

Frazier, E. Franklin, 193; antipathy to black ethnic-group political mobilization, 99–107; cynical perspective toward African American professional class, 69–70, 174–175n41; proponent of interracial class-based mobilization, 102–104

Freedman's Bureau, 46–47

Garvey, Marcus: and black populist movement, 41–42; Caribbean political origins, 12

Gates, Henry Louis, Jr., 197; role in African American Studies, 99

Gatewood, Willard: on an "aristocracy of color" in late nineteenth and early twentieth-century African American society, 29–31; on origins of "color elitism," 13

Goodheart, Adam, on core American capitalism wealth rooted in slavery, 45

Greider, William, on Obama's 2012 second-term election's significance, 153

Griffin, Farah Jasmine, 197

Grimke, Archibald: on biracial origins in South Carolina white planter class, 30; criticism of "color elitism," 29–31; role in African American leadership, 30–31

Grimke, Francis: on biracial origins in South Carolina white planter class, 30; criticism of Booker T. Washington's accommodationist leadership methodology, 79–80

Hamilton, Charles V., 206; on Adam Clayton Powell, 204
Harris, Abram, 182n25; antipathy to black ethnic-group political mobilization, 99–107
Harris, Frederick, on criticism of Barack Obama's election, 151–152
Hastie, William, 78; civil rights activist career, 177n54
Hayes, Rutherford B., and post–Civil War Reconstruction policy, 2
Henry, Charles, 207; on Bunche-Frazier-Harris, 205; on conservative black intellectuals' "color blind" discourse, 142; on Ralph Bunche's antipathy to black ethnic-group political mobilization, 102–103
Herbert, Bob, on tenacious social crises among the twenty-first-century black poor sector, 149–150
Higginbotham, Evelyn Brooks, 193; on black women's communitarian leadership role in black churches, 175–176n44
Hill, Joseph Newton, 22, 24, 196
Hine, Darlene C., 193; black women's communitarian leadership role in black churches, 175n44; on National Association of Colored Graduate Nurses, 68; struggle for professional training of African American nurses, 173n33
Holden, Matthew, Jr., 206; *The Changing Racial Regime*, 205
Holiness Churches: prominence in working-class black communities, 35–42; role in Chicago's black community, 38–40
Holloway, Jonathan: antipathy to black ethnic commitment among black intelligentsia, 96–99; generic view of twentieth-century black intellectuals,

93–94; opposition to the 1897 American Negro Academy, 94–96; proponent of intellectual discourse of Ralph Bunche, E. Franklin Frazier, and Abram Harris, 100–109
Holmes, Oliver Wendell, 96
Holt, Thomas, 193; intelligentsia mobilization inspired by W. E. B. Du Bois' intellectual leadership, 186n23; on political status of black citizens in Reconstruction South Carolina, 45–46
Horne, Gerald, 177n53, 193
Houston, Charles Hamilton, 78, 177n55, 193, 205
Huggins, Nathan, 193
Hughes, Langston, 31–35

James, Winston, on immigrant Caribbean intellectuals, 206
Johnson, Charles S., 150–151, 193; on social development of black churches, 37
Johnson, James Weldon, 31–35, 90
Johnson, Jeh, 150
Jones, Jacqueline: on origins of racist delineation of black Americans' social status, 105–106; on twenty-first-century crises of the black poor, 127

Katznelson, Ira, 187n36
Kennedy, Randall, on American racial dynamics vis-à-vis Obama presidency, 195
King, Martin Luther, Jr.: on creating organizational building blocks in the civil rights movement, 111–112; radicalization of the civil rights movement, 43

Lane, Roger, on history of black elite in late nineteenth-century and twentieth-century Philadelphia, 199
Lawson, James, 111
Lewis, David Levering, 193
Lewis, Hylan, 193; on oppressed black community in South Carolina's Piedmont region in the 1940s, 199
Lewis, John, 111–112

Lincoln University: as first institution for the higher education of African Americans, 10; graduated top-tier intelligentsia individuals, 22–24, 30–31, 63–68

Lipset, Seymour Martin, 11–12

Little, Malcolm (aka Malcolm X), example of "self-made" black intelligentsia personality, 12

Logan, Rayford, 192

Loury, Glenn, 139–140, 187n33

Marable, Manning, Malcolm X as a "self-made" intellectual, 12

Marshall, Thurgood, 31

Massey, Douglas, on racial segregation in housing during the twentieth century, 144–145

Methodist Episcopal Church, 9–11

Moon, Henry Lee, 115

Moses, Robert, 111

Moss, Alfred, on the 1897 American Negro Academy, 95–96

Mossell, Nathan, 68

Moton, Robert, 27

Muhammad, Khalil Gibran, on the long history of America's criminal justice system's racist practices against black citizens, 178n62

Myrdal, Gunnar, on state-sanctioned racist authoritarian practices toward black Americans in the twentieth-century South, 50, 171n15

Nabors, Rob, 150

Nabrit, James, 102

National Association for the Advancement of Colored People (NAACP), 30–31

Negro Baptist denomination, 39–40

Negro Elks, 69

New Negro Movement, on formative development, 13, 32–35

Niagara Movement, 56–58

Obama, Barack: *Nation magazine* and significance of Obama's 2012 second-term election, 189n57; *New York Times*' editorial support in 2012 presidential election, 151; stands at apex of African American political class, 150–151, 153; studies on rise of African American political class and, 185n3, 189nn51–53

O'Donovan, Susan Eva, on Georgian white planter class's reversal of Reconstruction gains, 194

Ogletree, Charles, 208

O'Meally, Thomas, 197

Oshinsky, David, on prison-based forced labor in southern agriculture in the first half of twentieth century, 49

Osofsky, George, on Holiness churches and Spiritualist churches in Harlem, 38

Painter, Nell Irvin, 193

Patterson, Orlando, 187n33

Perlo, Victor, on prominent role of African American labor in late nineteenth- and twentieth-century southern agriculture, 47–48

Pew 2007 Survey: attitudes on black social mobility problems, 132; on black ethnic attitudes among African Americans, 131, 134–135; on conservative trends among the black elite sector, 134–136

Porter, Eduardo, analysis of the OECD's data, 133

Powell, Adam Clayton, 204

Putney, Martha, 68–69, 174n38

Quarles, Benjamin, 191; on black abolitionists, 191

Rampersad, Arnold, 208

Randolph, A. Philip, 34, 71, 75

Ransom, Reverdy, 54–55, 90, 204

Reconstruction Policy, 1–4, 44–47

Redding, J. Saunders, 196

Reed, Ishmael, 196–197

Rich, Wilbur, 207; *African American Perspectives on Political Science,* 206

Robbins, Richard, 80, 178n60
Robinson, Eugene, 149
Roosevelt, Franklin Delano, 137

Sandburg, Carl, American capitalism's wealth rooted in slavery, 170n3
Scarborough, William Sanders, 94–95, 194
Schuyler, George, 91; antipathy to the post–World War II civil rights movement, 136–138; attack on awarding Nobel Peace Prize to Reverend Martin Luther King Jr., 92
Shapiro, Thomas, on deep income gap between blacks and whites in early twenty-first century, 125–126
Sowell, Thomas, 139–140
Spaulding, Charles Clifton, 79
Staupers, Mabel Keaton, 68
Steele, Shelby: on "blaming-the-victim" discourse, 143–144; on "color-blind" American society, 141–143
Stuckey, Sterling, 193; *Slave Culture: Nationalist Theory and the Foundations of Black America*, 183n44
Student Nonviolent Coordinating Committee, 111–112

Trotter, Monroe, 54

Walker, Madam C. J., 77–78
Washington, Booker T.: advised both the black masses and elite sector not to challenge America's racist oligarchy head-on, 53–55; advocate of conservative accommodationist-type black intelligentsia leadership, 51–53
Wells, Ida B., 146, 208
Wesley, Charles, 192; on black church, 182–183n38; on black workers, 210
West, Cornel, on Emerson, 56, 99
Whissahickon Boys' Club, 82–84
White, Walter, 30–31
Wilberforce University, 7, 9–11
Wilkerson, Isabel, on Great Black Migration, 50
Wilkins, John R., 209
Wilmington North Carolina Riot (1898), 2–3
Wilson, Francille Rusan, 193; on early research on black workers, 210
Wilson, William Julius, 193; on new black class patterns (e.g., females outdistancing males) in the twenty-first century, 124–126; on two-tier class system, 84–85
Woodson, Carter G., 61–63, 192, 204

Zangrando, Robert, on the NAACP's anti-lynching movement, 210